STANDING ALONE

by

Michael Loren Hastings

Published by Piscataqua Press
An imprint of RiverRun Bookstore, Inc.
142 Fleet Street | Portsmouth, NH | 03801
www.riverrunbookstore.com
www.piscataquapress.com
ISBN: 978-1-944393-09-0
Printed in the United States of America

TABLE OF CONTENTS

For Tanya

Lover of felines, hater of wars.

Preface

¤

Principle. As defined by Webster's dictionary, the word has several meanings. Often times it refers to a rule of conduct, especially of right conduct. Frequently when we encounter an individual who adheres to these right rules of conduct, collectively we will say of them that they are a man or a woman of principle. The word principle is also used to define the method of how something may operate, i.e., the principle upon which a gasoline engine operates is internal combustion. Whereas these definitions apply to different aspects of the world in which we live, the first being social, the second scientific, rarely if ever will these aspects overlap or come into competition. There may be however, certain instances throughout the course of human events where the principle or principles of an individual come into a state of convulsion or competition with certain principles of human behavior, those elements which tend to determine how societies composed of large populations tend to operate. There are and probably always will be social tendencies within mass societies which may tend toward instances of their undoing, phenomenon such as peer pressure or even the simple influence of fashion. These phenomenon, peer pressure and the influence of fashion can be powerful determinants in deciding the course or courses of action which a society or nation may take. Usually these forces are too powerful for an individual or even many individuals to resist or overcome.

It would probably be difficult for someone other than an individual such as a trained psychologist to understand completely all the nuances of the human mind that determine our exact behavior. However, I believe that all individuals understand the basic concepts of our behavior as we encounter them in our everyday lives. We are all familiar with the desire or need to be popular, even to the point where we will dress as the majority of our peers dress or adopt a certain vernacular so as to fit in with others. There is always a longing in our minds as well to want to be successful so as to be envied by those around us. Throughout recorded history many societies, including our own, have engaged in the use of slavery. No individual has ever worked as hard for as little compensation as the slave, which is why no one wants to be one. For centuries the heads of state, such as a king or queen, enjoyed all the luxuries of life with as little physical labor as possible, which explains why everyone wanted to be one. Much as water chooses the path of least resistance, so do humans, and we will always prefer leisure as opposed to hard physical labor. Hence, we arrive at what is referred to as the primrose path. Popularized after Shakespeare's Hamlet, the primrose path refers to the path of pleasure or self-indulgence, or a course of action that is deceptively easy or proper, but that can ultimately lead to disaster. As a norm, many will choose this path and whereas we as humans tend to be imbued with a certain fight or flight characteristic, when we as individuals come into a state of convulsion in the society or social group of which we are a part, we tend to fall into line, even if we know the chosen path or course of action to be wrong.

Fortunately for mankind, however, there are those few who are of principle who are willing to take a stand for what is right and against what is wrong, usually against great odds and at great personal sacrifice, even to the point of knowing that it may or will cost them their homes, their careers, or even their lives. They represent the best of mankind and are a credit to our communities, our countries and our species.

Some of these individuals are well known to history. All of us are familiar with the efforts of Abraham Lincoln to end slavery. No one can doubt his elevated levels of wisdom or intelligence or his great personal sacrifice. Yet he was not alone. There had been a strong abolitionist movement before him and he was only a part, though a very important part, of the new Republican political party. We tend also to idolize those who display great personal courage in defending a cause. Be it a fireman who rushes into a burning building to save a life, or the soldier who is so brave that he would march right up to the mouth of a cannon, we cherish those who tend to keep us out of harm's way, even though they must place themselves in harm's way to do so. No one can ever demean the sacrifices they make. They are not always alone either, as they have their fellow firefighters and soldiers with them as a means of support. They also have the assurance that they are just in their cause.

History affords us with many examples of individuals of principle who were either alone in their efforts or were part of a decided minority. They may have found themselves separated from the majority due to propinquity or circumstance, or they may have placed themselves in such position due to deep-seated beliefs, or an occasioned wisdom, or even just bad luck. But they stood, and because of that they will always stand the test of time. They knew they would fall victim to what Lincoln referred to as "positive enmity." No doubt many of them were familiar enough with human nature to have cause for alarm and to know in advance that their actions would cost them everything; yet they chose to follow the right path anyway.

This is their story.

Chapter I

¤

FOUR

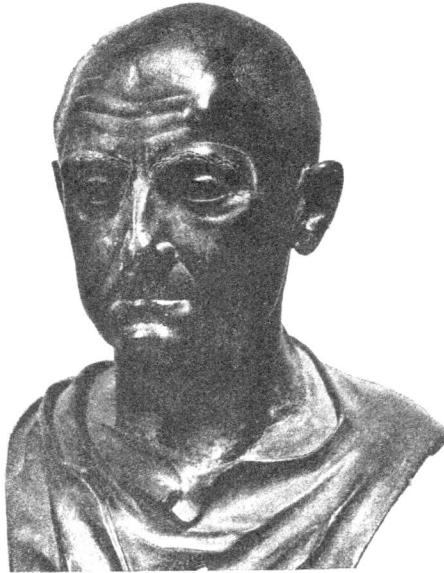

It is often times written or spoken of that there exist a tendency for history to repeat itself. Perhaps it might be more accurately stated that history precedes itself, as in many cases it tends to produce certain precedents. History is also filled with many cases of irony, and of tragedy. All too often the best and the brightest of our species are taken from us long before their time, before many of their blessings can be bestowed upon us, and all too often due to the folly of mankind and its petty prejudices. In this country, we are all familiar with the tragic loss of John F. Kennedy and how his death at the hands of an assassin's bullet put an end to a time pregnant with great possibilities for the future. But we forget about the loss of his very capable brother Robert F. Kennedy, and of his invaluable contributions to his country during the civil riots of the early 1960s and during the Cuban Missile Crisis. The loss becomes even more tragic when we contemplate the loss of his older brother Joseph P. Kennedy Jr. when his aircraft went down during a bombing mission during World War II, as well as the loss of his son when he too was lost in a plane crash as well.

There may, however, be a precedent in history to all of this, to be found during the years of crisis for the Roman Republic in their struggles against Carthage during the Punic Wars. Back during a time when it was fashionable to teach world and U.S. history in the public schools, which isn't the case anymore, many students became familiar with the name Scipio Africanus and how he saved Rome from its greatest enemy, Hannibal Barca. But what we were never taught was how Scipio would be forced, or would choose, to go into a self-imposed exile and retire from public life after false accusations of misappropriating booty from a campaign in Syria. But the story does not end with him, much the same as with the story of John F. Kennedy. It seems that Publius Cornelius Scipio Africanus and his family may have been born under the same unlucky star as the Kennedy family centuries later. Scipio Africanus' father and brother were soldiers of Rome as well, and both would perish by the sword fighting against Rome's ancient enemy Carthage in Spain. To further add to the tragedy, the architect of Rome's conclusive victory over Carthage in the

Third Punic War, Scipio Aemilianus, the adopted grandson of Scipio Africanus, would be persecuted for his upright beliefs and would die suspiciously in 129 A.D., possibly having been poisoned by his wife Sempronia.

However, for one to have a complete understanding of the Scipios, of the accomplishments they achieved and the sacrifices they made in serving the Roman Republic, it may be necessary to start with the life of the senior-most of this line of truly excellent soldiers.

Publius Cornelius Scipio was born in 260 B.C. to a mother who is unknown to history and to a father named Lucius Cornelius Scipio. Much of his early life is unknown to us and, as with many of history's great men, he would only become known to us due to his exploits in the field of battle. Of the facts that are known to history is that in the year 218 B.C., Scipio was serving as a consul of Rome when the Second Punic War, a contest between Rome and Carthage resumed. Carthage itself, located in North Africa, was largely a maritime power. Nevertheless, it did control much of modern day Spain, which placed their armies within striking distance of the Italian Peninsula. Carthaginian strategy in the war was to strike at Rome itself, and so its greatest general, Hannibal Barca, crossed the Alps and engaged the armies of Rome on their own soil. To have an understanding of the levels of destruction attained during the Punic Wars, it should be recognized that one in three Roman males of military age died during these wars, with enormous social consequences to follow.

Roman strategy in the war called for Roman armies to contain Hannibal and his forces on the Italian Peninsula, while other Roman forces would destroy Hannibal's base of operations in Spain. To this end, Scipio would depart Italy for

Spain with two legions of the Roman Army. (A legion was the major unit of the Roman Army consisting of 3,000 to 6,000 infantry troops and 100 to 200 cavalry troops.) However, upon reaching the River Rhine and finding that Hannibal had already crossed it in his march toward Italy, Scipio did an abrupt about face and pursued the Carthaginian force, catching up to it near the River Ticinus. Here he would engage the Hannibalic army, being himself severely wounded during a cavalry skirmish. This would be very unfortunate for Rome, as in his convalescence he would be replaced by the much less capable Tiberius Sempronius Longus. Against the advice of Scipio, Sempronius would lead two consular armies against Hannibal at Trebia in December of 218 B.C. Of the 40,000 Roman soldiers deployed for battle, only 10,000 survived. This would be but the first of three overwhelming defeats suffered by Rome in the initial phases of the war.

Having recovered sufficiently from his wounds, Scipio would return to the initial plan and would depart for Spain to join his brother Gnaeus, who had defeated a Carthaginian fleet at the mouth of the Ebro River and had won a notable victory over his Carthaginian foe at a place known as Cissa. Upon his arrival in Spain the war between the Roman Republic and Carthage would devolve into further tragedy for Rome. On the Roman side were the two Scipios, Gnaeus and Publius, on the Carthaginian side were Hannibal's two brothers, Hasdrubal and Mago Barca, as well as the brother in law of their father Hamilcar Barca, another man known as Hasdrubal.

Initially the two Scipios would succeed in their goal of preventing Hannibal from receiving much needed support from Spain, even destroying a Carthaginian army near the town of Thera in 216 or 215 B.C. However, treachery would lead to the ultimate defeat of the two Scipios. Whereas the Roman armies of the Scipios were essentially fighting on foreign soil, they could hope to receive little in the way of supplies from Italy. To make matters worse, corrupt contractors often made off with what could be sent. The Scipios were able to recruit some allies from the tribes of Spain, some 20,000 Celtiberians who were regarded as being some of the fiercest fighters of the war. However, the Carthaginians simply bribed the Celtiberians to withdraw from the contest, leaving the Scipios not only separated, but outnumbered. After years of campaigning in an attempt to relieve the pressure against Rome in Italy, the Scipio brothers would both be killed in action within a single month in 211 B.C. Publius Scipio would fall while attempting to fight his way through three Carthaginian armies to rejoin his brother. Shortly thereafter Gnaeus would fall with his entire army on a fortified hillside in an act that could be regarded as a precursor of Custer's Last Stand.

The redemption of the Scipio name would not be long in the offering. Publius Scipio's son was born in the year 236 B.C., so when the Second Punic War began he was of age to serve in the Roman Army. Popular legend has it that he was with his father at the Battle of Ticinus, even rescuing the senior Scipio from Hannibal's cavalry. We hear of his exploits again after the Battle of Cannae in 216 B.C., where, as a military tribune, he helped rally Roman survivors after that disastrous defeat. In 213 B.C. he became curule aedile, curule meaning of the highest rank, aedile, a position in ancient Rome wherein one was responsible for buildings, roads, civic games, etc. Two years later he would learn of the death of both his father and uncle, and at the age of 24 would become himself head of Rome's very powerful Cornelian family.

In the aftermath of three massive defeats in Italy at the hands of Hannibalic armies at Trebia, Lake Trasimene and Cannae, the Romans were finally able to stabilize the situation in Italy with the assistance of Quintus Fabius Maximus Verrucosus. In the aftermath of the Lake Trasimene disaster Fabius was elected dictator. Understanding that he probably could not defeat Hannibal in battle, he simply initiated a campaign of harassment and delay, thus hoping to weaken Hannibal's army by means of attrition and earning himself the sobriquet, Cunctator, or delayer.

Resuming its earlier strategy of attacking Carthage in Spain, Scipio Africanus departed Italy with two Legions of the Roman army (about 10,000 men), landing at modern day Ampurius, which would be used by the Romans as their base of operations for their Spanish campaigns.

Often regarded by history as being highly intelligent and humane, Scipio Africanus would be one of the first generals to use intelligence to his advantage. Upon landing in Spain one of his first tasks was gathering information about his enemies and about the terrain upon which he would be fighting. Realizing that the Carthaginian armies were too far away to render assistance, he immediately led an assault on Nova Carthago (Cartegena), which he was able to seize through good fortune and a knowledge of the local tides, which, when low, allowed his legionnaires the opportunity to assault the city by means of a shallow lagoon.

New Carthage would not be his only success and in the campaigns to come he would defeat two of the Barcid brothers who had been responsible for the death of his father and uncle. First he would defeat the army of Hasdrubal Barca at the Battle of Baccula. Hasdrubal would then flee Spain to join his brother

Hannibal in Italy. In this venture he would not succeed and ultimately he would be killed in battle, his head being thrown into the camp of his brother. Two years later, in 206 B.C., Scipio would defeat Mago Hasdrubal at Llipa near modern day Seville. For all intents and purposes, Spain now belonged to Rome. Also of importance, Scipio would convert the African King Masinissa from an enemy of Rome to an ally of the republic. King Masinissa would aid in the ultimate defeat of the Carthaginian state years later.

Having succeeded in his attempts to conquer Spain, Scipio returned to Rome and would run for consul in 205 B.C., while at the same time pledging to take the war against Carthage to the North African city itself. He would win the election, but the Roman Senate refused to grant him any troops. He therefore recruited volunteers himself, raising an army of about 30,000 superbly trained and equipped troops.

In 204 B.C., Scipio as proconsul, sailed fro Lilybaeum in Sicily and landed near the city of Utica, to the north and west of the city of Carthage itself. After initially investing the city, he was forced to end the seige in order to confront a relief force led by Hasdrubal Gisco and his ally Syphax. Signing a temporary armistice with the enemy army, Scipio and his army then settled into winter quarters in his fortified camp. With the coming of the year 203 B.C., Scipio suddenly ended the armistice and during a surprise night attack destroyed the enemy army and then immediately returned to his siege of Utica. When Hasdrubal and Syphax returned with a new army, Scipio simply defeated them at the Battle of Bagbrades.

In desperation, The Carthaginian Senate recalled Hannibal from Italy, while at the same time suing for peace. However, as soon as Hannibal arrived home, the Carthaginians regained their sense of overconfidence, raised a new army and broke off the peace negotiations. It was an ill-advised move, as by now they should have realized the mettle of their foe. The final confrontation of the Second Punic War would occur at Zama to the south and west of Carthage in 202 B.C. After an initial parley between the two generals, which proved unsuccessful, the battle began. Each army was drawn up in three lines of battle. However, Scipio aligned his maniples in straight lines instead of the usual checkerboard pattern. This created lanes through which the Carthaginian war elephants could be herded, which is just exactly what happened. Hannibal and his veterans who had returned from Italy fought well, but most of his troops were fresh recruits and his cavalry was few in number. In the end, the superior forces of Scipio and his more numerous cavalry were able to defeat the Carthaginians, who suffered 20,000 dead with another 15,000 taken as prisoners. Roman losses were about 15,000 dead with possibly 4,000 wounded.[1]

Tragedy would soon befall both the victor and the vanquished of Zama. In the years following the Second Punic War, Hannibal would prove so successful in rebuilding the Carthaginian state that the Romans would accuse him of planning to breech the peace. He would be forced to flee, joining his former ally Antiochus III. However, when Antiochus was himself defeated by the Romans, he would be forced to flee to Bithynia, where he would eventually take his own life

Scipio would fare better, at least for a time. In the aftermath of Zama he would assume the cognomen Africanus in recognition of his achievements and would return to Rome as the conquering hero who had freed the republic from any further fears of the Barcid armies. He continued to serve the Roman people, first as censor in 199, then as consul in 194. He would also take up arms defending the republic again, first campaigning against the Alpine tribes in northern Italy, and then serving as a legate with his brother Lucius in 190 B.C. during Rome's war against King Antiochus III of Syria.

It would be in the aftermath of this final campaign that Scipio would see the end of his military fortunes and public career. For years it seems that Scipio had enjoyed the adulation of the Roman people. However, due to a human characteristic, which Abraham Lincoln had referred to as "positive enmity," he had also earned the envy of his political peers. Chief amongst his political rivals was Marcus Porcius Cato, also know to history as "The Censor." Cato himself was from the city of Tusculum. He had started his career as a farmer and in true Roman fashion would serve the republic in the army. During the Second Punic War, he had befriended Quintus Fabius Maximus and was present for the recapture of Tarentum and for the defeat of Hasdrubal Barca at the Battle of the Metaurus in 207 B.C. In his capacities as a public servant, Cato is said to have been "frugal with state funds, utterly incorruptible, and totally impartial and pitiless in administering justice."[2] He was also known to have been prone to self-promotion as well as being very xenophobic, which would certainly cause him to be resentful of Scipio, who was one of the first Romans to appreciate Greek culture and to learn to speak its language. And then there was the issue of Scipio's military success. There has always existed a certain capacity within humans to be resentful of those who have achieved success, or maybe we tend just to be resentful of the wealth and privilege that seems to accompany good fortune. In Roman society from the beginning of the republic through to the end of The Principate, it seemed that the only thing that could prove more fatal to a Roman general than failure on the battlefield, was success upon it. Unfortunately for Scipio, he would be one of the first, although certainly not the last to find this out. In the aftermath of all that he had done for the republic, the traditionalists in Rome, with the assistance of Cato the Censor, accused him and his brother Lucius of misappropriating booty from the campaign in Syria. Though never actually condemned, as in all likelihood the charges were completely false, he chose to withdraw from public life altogether and exiled himself to Liternum in Campania. Within a year the man who had saved the republic from the dreaded Barcids was dead.

What happened to Scipio Africanus would be unfortunate enough, if the story ended with his tragic demise. It didn't. Much the same as the twentieth century gave evidence of the Kennedy curse, the Scipios of Rome would continue to endure a tough fate.

With the conclusion of the Second Punic War, Carthage was forced to accept a very humiliating peace, to include a huge indemnity payment of 10,000 talents, or roughly 300 million dollars over a period of fifty years. In addition, they were also forced to surrender all of their warships and war elephants and were not allowed to engage in any hostile actions against neighboring states without the prior approval of the Roman Senate.[3] Even still, there were many in Rome who still feared Carthage and were envious of its wealth and commercial success. Cato the Censor always concluded his speeches, no matter what the subject, with the words "Delenda est Carthago - Carthage must be destroyed." For many years it was the policy of Rome to use its ally in North Africa, King Massinissa of Numidia, as a counter to Carthage. It would be this rivalry between Numidia and Carthage as well as the final provision of the peace terms, "no war without permission from Rome," that would lead to the Third Punic War. After years of antagonism between Numidia and Carthage, Carthaginian patience finally snapped, and in 150 B.C. Carthage invaded the lands of Massinissa. Also expected, Rome immediately acted against Carthage. For having violated the terms of peace from the prior war, Rome demanded that Carthage cease operations against Numidia, as well as surrender most of its weapons and 300 hostages to Rome. Rome's final demand, and no doubt one which could never have been met, was to dismantle the battlements of the city and move the entire population to a new site no closer than 10 miles to the Mediterranean. With Carthage refusing to accept the final condition of these terms, hostilities were set to open between the two long-term antagonists, Carthage and Rome.

It would be upon this scene that another Scipio would step forward to win great acclaim. Scipio Aemilianus was born in 184 B.C. to a father named Aemilius Paullus who had served Rome as a praetor, consul, and censor. Aemilius Paullus had also served as a soldier of Rome, as a commander in further Spain, as well as in Liguria and Asia Minor. His final and greatest success would come in Rome's war against King Perseus of Macedon, during which he would be the victor at the Battle of Pydna in 168 B.C. During this battle, the troops of Aemilius destroyed the Macedonian phalanx and killed 20,000 Macedonians while losing less than 1,000 of their own men. Perseus himself would be captured and would finish out his life as a prisoner in Italy. Although regarded as being a very affectionate father, when Aemilius Paullus remarried, he gave the two sons from his first marriage away in adoption, the first being adopted by Fabius Maximus, with the second, Scipio Aemilianus, being adopted by Publius Cornelius Scipio.

Though not of Cornelian blood himself, Scipio Aemilianus most certainly had all of the necessary qualities to carry on the Scipionic tradition and would in time become perhaps the greatest man of his generation. While still a teenager, Scipio had fought under his father at Pydna where he was so aggressive in this contest that he became separated from the rest of the army while he and a group of fellow soldiers went off in hot pursuit of the retreating Macedonians. To add an exclamation point to his levels of personal courage, while serving in Spain under Licinius Lucullus, he would be awarded the corona muralis, which was an award given to those soldiers who were first atop the wall of an enemy fortification.

It would be during the Third Punic War, however, that Scipio Aemilianus would accomplish his greatest deeds. With the resumption of hostilities between Rome and Carthage in 149 B.C., Scipio found himself in North Africa fighting against the enemy that his adopted grandfather had defeated during the previous Punic war. During the first year of the war (148 B.C.) the initial assaults against Carthage were foiled by the surprisingly stoic resistance of the inhabitants of the hastily fortified city. In 147 B.C., Scipio returned to Rome so as to run for the office of aedile. However, public opinion of the young Scipio was so high that instead of becoming aedile, he would become consul, even though this was contrary to established procedure.

Returning to Africa later that year as Consul of Rome, he would assume command of the assault against the city, which had thus far nobly resisted each attempt to subdue it. After a determined land and sea blockade of the city, a final determined assault broke through the city's defenses and would be followed by house-to-house fighting until the entire city had been subdued. Nine tenths of the city's population would perish by disease, starvation or battle. The few survivors would be taken away and sold into slavery. As a final insult, and very much against the advice of Scipio, the city itself would be completely destroyed and salt would be sown into the soil so that it would no longer be fertile. For leading the assault, which had finally destroyed Rome's long time enemy and Mediterranean rival, Scipio was awarded the honor of a triumph.

For most, the destruction of Carthage would have been a lifetime achievement and the physical exertion of having accomplished this would probably cause many to seek an easy retirement. But Scipio had much more to give to the republic. Having destroyed Carthage, he returned to North Africa to oversee its new birth as a Roman province. Having completed this mission he then spent two years touring Asia Minor. Concluding his tour of Asia Minor, he returned to Rome in 142 B.C. to run for office as censor, an election easily won despite his Hellenistic tendencies. In consulting the works of Theodore Mommsen, we find it written that Scipio was "a man morally steadfast and trustworthy, his word held good with friend and foe. He avoided ostentatious building and speculation, and lived simply. In money matters, he acted not only honorably and disinterestedly, but also with a humanness and generosity that seemed the more singular alongside the mercenary spirit of his contemporaries. He was an able soldier and officer. He brought home from the African war the honorary wreath conferred on those who saved the lives of fellow citizens at peril of their own, and he terminated as a general the war he had begun as an officer."[4] These were to be the qualities that he would bring with him in his capacities as a civil servant.

As censor he displayed himself as being a stern Roman of the old school, while at the same time holding a position on the middle ground between the aristocrats and the more democratic factions. Perhaps his greatest contributions as censor came in his efforts to further promote the city of Rome as the focal point of the empire and the repair of the Aemilian budge, which had been built four decades before his censorship. His ability and desire to rise above the petty squabbles of his peers also was made evident in his stance on the Cassian law, brought forth by Lucius Cassius, which introduced vote by ballot for the popular tribunals, which comprised a very important part of the criminal justice system.

Having served Rome ably as an administrator, Scipio would be forced to return to active military service again during the Numantian War of 137 to 133 B.C. Numantia, which was a Celtiberian city on the Darius River in Upper Spain, had flown into open revolt and entrapped the Roman forces in the area who were under the command of C. Hostilius Mancinus. In order for his army to escape, Mancinus had been forced to accept terms of peace that were very humiliating for Rome. Scipio would urge the Romans to reject the conditions of this peace and to reject it as being dishonorable. Scipio himself was then appointed to take command in Spain and retrieve the situation. Much as had been the case when his adopted grandfather Scipio Africanus had been forced to recruit his own troops before he set out for Africa during the Second Punic War, now Scipio Aemilianus was forced to recruit his own army to take to Spain. Many of his troops were his own friends and relatives.

Upon his arrival in Spain, Scipio found that the forces which had existed there had not only been defeated, but were very disorganized and without the discipline for which the Roman armies were long noted. Nevertheless, Scipio was very much up to the task before him and according to Mommson, "when commanding before Carthage and Numantia, he drove the women and priest out of the camp, and once more subjected the soldiers to the iron yoke of the old military discipline."[5] What would follow would be a very brutal campaign with the concluding act coming as a siege of the city of Numantia itself where 4,000 diehard Celtiberians would hold out against superior Roman forces. It is interesting to note that during this siege, Scipio would build a wall of circumvallation around the city and simply starve the inhabitants into submission. This was a tactic to be seen again in the history of Rome, most notably with Caesar and his walls of circumvallation and contravallation at Alesia in 53 B.C. Scipio would succeed in his efforts and Numantia would fall, with Scipio then adding the cognomen "Numantinus" to his name.

Unfortunately, the man who had twice led the Roman army from despair and decline to victory would not meet his end on the field of honor, but as had been the case with Scipio Africanus, it would be the political arena that would cause his demise. As a young man, Scipio had married a woman named Sempronia, who was the sister of Tiberius Gracchus. Tiberius' father Sempronius Gracchus had come to the aid of Scipio Africanus when he was, falsely no doubt, accused of misappropriating booty from the Syrian campaign. Tiberius Gracchus himself had served with Scipio Aemilianus during the final defeat of Carthage, even winning the corona muralis for being one of the first soldiers to surmount the enemy's defensive wall. Scipio Aemelianus and Tiberious Gracchus' paths would cross again during the Numantian campaign in Spain from 137 to 133 B.C. When the army of Mancinus had become entrapped during an attempted night march while deep in enemy territory, it had been Tiberius Gracchus who had brokered an equitable peace which allowed the 20,000-man Roman army to escape with their lives, though they were required to leave most of their weapons behind. However, it was Scipio who urged the Roman Senate to reject the terms of the agreement as unacceptable and to resume war. This of course did much too diminish Tiberius' integrity, and to Tiberius, integrity was everything. But it would be Tiberius' attempts at land reform that would cause an eventual break between the two men. During the Punic Wars, much of the sturdy peasantry who had farmed the land had been siphoned off to fight in the armies. In their absence wealthy landowners had been able to acquire their lands, thus creating large estates known as latifundia. To make matters worse, as the soldiers were victorious they conquered large numbers of slaves, which the wealthy landowners could acquire to work their estates cheaply. In the end, for the peasant there could be but a career in the army, or poverty.

Of keen intellect, Tiberius Gracchus was quick to recognize this trend and understand the social and moral decay that would accompany this. Therefore, he set about a policy aimed at land reform. His policy was based upon the belief that by taking 30-acre parcels from the ager publicus, or public lands, and giving them to the poor and dispossessed, that this would strengthen Rome's agricultural base as well as guarantee a supply of the loyal peasant stock which had for years been the backbone of Rome's armies. In the end, his policies might have ensured that Rome would have survived as a republic. Such was not to be. As a tribune, Tiberius brought forth his proposals, only to have them vetoed by his co-tribune Marcus Octavius. But having already suffered the humiliation of having his peace treaty with Numantia abrogated by the Senate, his resolve only stiffened. In an attempt to overcome this impasse, Tiberius would use several ploys. He would initially remove the offer of compensation for confiscated lands from his proposed agrarian law. When this failed he decided to exert further pressure on his political rivals by using his own tribunican veto to shut down the affairs of government by vetoing every piece of legislation brought forward, thus affecting every section of government from the treasury to the courts of law. However, Octavius still refused to relent.

Having failed to overcome Octavius and his veto by constitutional means, Tiberius Gracchus then decided to remove the veto by electoral means. As a tribune, Marcus Octavius was supposed to support the interest of the plebs, the common people. Therefore, Gracchus simply issued Octavius an ultimatum: remove the veto or he would appeal to the people and have Octavius removed from office. Rome may have been a republic, but in a sense it was also an oligarchy, where much of the power rested in the hands of a wealthy upper class. To appeal to the common people and put them into a state of opposition to the government was almost an act of revolution and many, including Tiberius' own supporters, thought the act might possibly even be illegal. But having set his sights on a decided goal, Tiberius proceeded along this path, with Marcus Octavius being removed from the office of tribune. With Octiavius thus removed, Tiberius agrarian law would pass and go into effect, although this passage would nearly guarantee Tiberius' own downfall.

One of the provisions of Tiberius Gracchus' law called for a commission to oversee the implementation of its provisions, and while the law was passed, the Senate would not agree to finance the commission. Further inciting the situation itself, the three commissioners chosen were Tiberious himself, his twenty-year-old brother Gaius, and his father in law Appius Claudius. The task before them was not an easy one, and the very process of defining, reacquiring and redistributing the ager publicus brought strife and turmoil to every Roman community, often times setting neighbor against neighbor. When the Attalid kingdom of Pergamum in Asia Minor was bequeathed to the Roman people, Gracchus found in this act a source of revenue to fund the agrarian commission. He even went so far as proposing that the Pergamene treasure should be divided among the new landholders so as to purchase livestock and the necessary implements to farm the land. But while Tiberius may have been sincere in his attempts at land reform, his actions continued to incite the enmity of his political opponents, including one Scipio Nasica, who was himself a large holder of public lands which he had no desire to lose. There was even the announcement of Quintus Pomperus that "he would impeach Gracchus on the very day he resigned the tribunate."[6] Recognizing that his own future safety depended on the retention of his office as tribune, Gracchus continued his appeal to the plebs, proposing further measures such as shortening the period of military service, an extension of the rights of appeal and a law for admitting many of the Italian allies as full citizens of Rome.

Unfortunately, many of these attempts at reform would

place Scipio Aemilianus in a very compromised position in regard to his brother in law Tiberius Gracchus. Much of this may have had to do with the fact that many of Gracchus' supporters were freed men or new citizens of Rome. One must remember also that having spent much of his adult life as a soldier defending or expanding the republic, that his first allegiance would be to the state, and not to his brother in law. It is said that once when facing down a crowd of Gracchus' supporters in the streets of Rome, that Scipio told them "I, who have seen Rome's enemies in their full power in the field, am not going to be cowed by you, stepchildren of Rome."[7]

The concluding acts of the drama would take place while Scipio was away in Spain ending the Numantian War. Having entered upon a course toward social revolution, and having also promised more and more for the plebs of Rome, Tiberius was ensnared in his own trap. The only way to escape the prosecution he had been promised after leaving office as tribune, was to seek an unconstitutional re-election to that post. As for his personal safety, Tiberius had so aroused the enmity of his political opponents by this time that often he would traverse the streets of Rome with a retinue of three to four thousand supporters. Things would initially go well for Tiberius in the election, and when the assembly met to elect the tribunes for the following year, the first divisions would cast their votes in favor of him. However, the opposing party would cast a veto that would prevail in the end, throwing the election into a state of confusion. On the second day of the election, similar results would be achieved, with divisions for Tiberius and an opposition veto again throwing the election into doubt.

No doubt being intelligent enough to understand human nature to an extent as to realize there was by now virtually no chance of re-election, Tiberius would seek to garner the support of the plebs with a rally on the Capitoline. However, Scipio Nasica and several hundred of his followers armed with clubs would intervene. In the riot that followed, the man who had set a course toward social revolution was bludgeoned to death along with several hundred of his followers. As a final act of insult, their bodies were denied burial and simply thrown into the Tiber as would that of a common criminal. So as to legitimize what could best be described as an act of mass murder, the aristocracy gave sanction to the falsehood that Tiberius had sought for himself a higher power such as king or dictator and had formed a special investigative commission so as to prosecute many of Tiberius Gracchus supporters. Throughout the year 132 B.C. many lesser persons would find themselves falling victim to this political witch-hunt.

As for Scipio Aemilianus, when notified of the murder of his brother in law he would reveal his thoughts through the words of Homer, "So perish all who dare such deeds as he."[8] When repeatedly questioned about the circumstances of his brother in law's death, he simply could not, or perhaps would not, condemn the act. Shortly thereafter, the man who had led Roman armies from a state of despair to victory over two cities, which were extremely hostile to the republic, would die in his sleep. Conjecture would have it that he was probably poisoned by his wife, who was after all the sister of Tiberius Gracchus. Irregardless of the cause of death, everyone at the time, even Scipio's enemies, were forced to conclude that with his death Rome had lost an outstanding general and perhaps the greatest statesman of his time. Cicero would himself be inclined to regard Scipio Aemilianus as the greatest man of his age.

Although with his passing the Scipio name would not be

removed from the chronicles of Rome, we must conclude however, that his demise would mark the end of a line of great warriors and statesmen who had served Rome so well. As with the Kennedy family in the twentieth century, a void was left which could not be filled, with people of the time being left to ponder how history might have been altered for the better if those great men had escaped personal tragedy and remained on life's stage.

Chapter II

¤

Two

It always stirs the imagination of the historian when one contemplates the great people, places and societies of the past which are long since departed. Perhaps it is just the quality of not knowing for certain the facts of the past because none of us were there. We may know of names and dates and times, but the personal nuances of that time escape us, unlike the everyday experiences of our own lives, which become so familiar to us.

History is also filled with a lot of irony and tragedy, hence the constant pondering of, "what if?" In many instances great persons have made history, in other cases history has made them. And then there is the struggle: the competitions between man and his environment and the competition between man and man. Also, whereas men tend to be imperfect beings, there is always the struggle between good and evil. Unfortunately, good does not always prevail.

Given the very nature of the world in which we live and the fact that as individuals we are only very small components of a much larger machine called society, there are always conditions which tend to influence the events of history and how they are played out. When John F. Kennedy was president, he was considered as being a very liberal man. Yet, if he were alive today, we would probably find that he would be violently opposed to many of the policies that the Democratic Party has put forth and would probably be considered a diehard conservative.

Much as the experience of life leads us through certain stages with their accompanying transformations such as youth, maturity and old age, it should come as no surprise to us that the societies in which we exist experience these very same transformations. With the Scipio family of Rome we became acquainted with a group of citizen soldiers who helped transform a growing republic into a Mediterranean superpower. But just as they had served Rome in its period of late youth and early maturity, the task would be left to others to serve Rome during its period of old age. The transformations which would occur over the course of several centuries would be remarkable, the very characters themselves on this stage of life being dramatically changed as well.

With Rome having transformed its form of government several times, changing from a kingdom to a republic and then to a principate with the arrival of Octavian or Augustus Caesar, its chameleon-like characteristics would continue in the centuries after the birth of Christ. During the Julio Claudian years, Rome would exist as a virtual dictatorship, with a single head of state or emperor governing much of the states' machinery, although the Senate of the republican years still did exist. By the time of the emperor Diocletian in the late third century A.D., Rome had become a Tetrarchy, with an Augustus in the east and west as co-emperors, and a Caesar in the east and west as junior emperors who would become Augustus in the event of the death of the senior emperor. This system had become almost an absolute necessity after centuries of internecine warfare, with emperors rarely lasting more than a year or two. Whereas the empire had found itself on firm ground and in some instances even continued to grow during the years of the Antonine emperors in the late first and second centuries B.C., with the advent of civil war in 193 and the emperorship of Pertinax, Rome would from that point forward see its years of majesty and health fade away.

The Senate would suffer as well, with the emperors having become little more than despots who would rely almost entirely on the support of the army and the Praetorian guard for their right to govern; the Senate would become a virtual political non-entity. Then, in 212 B.C. during the reign of Caracalla, the rights of citizenship were extended to all and any persons living within the boundaries of the empire. However, in the words of Mommson, "this measure did not signify any improvement in the legal status of the masses, but the ruin of the Roman State – the Senate and people of Rome."[9] Though this act did not punctuate the end of Rome, it most certainly was a mistake that would contribute to the ultimate failure of the Roman State.

As the empire had grown during the years of the Julio Claudian and Antonine emperors, there had arisen a need to increase the size of the bureaucracy required to govern the empire. As with all things, when the size of the bureaucracy increased, the opportunity for graft and corruption increased as well. The once very pure Roman state, which was comprised of rural farmers and citizen soldiers, became something far less pure. It was a melting pot that began to boil over.

And then there were the external pressures, which would continue to influence the affairs of state. Since its inception, Rome had always been a very war-like state. There were the initial contests against the neighboring Italian city-states during the birth of Rome; there were the wars of survival and conquest, as with Carthage and Gaul; and there were the wars of expansion fought by emperors who sought popular support, such as Claudius' invasion of Britain and Trajan's invasions of Dacia (Romania), Arabea Nabatea (Jordan) and Parthia (Iraq). Nevertheless, by the end of the Antonine years, the wars of expansion had more or less ceased. From thence forward the wars of Rome would be defensive in nature, with the empire attempting to retain the territories it had captured in the previous centuries.

Not only had the nature of Rome's wars changed, Rome's war machine had changed as well. Whereas the Roman army had for years consisted of citizen soldiers who were fighting for their homes and were loyal to the land and the state, years of internecine warfare had seen a transformation of its armies. During the years of civil war during the late republic, the reforms of Gaius Marius had opened the ranks of the legions to all and any Roman citizens who wished to join. As the franchise and rights of citizenship had been extended to take in more and more of the subject peoples throughout the empire, this guaranteed that more and more non-true Romans would be allowed to serve in its armies. When Julius Caesar became dictator perpetuus, 49% of the Roman army was comprised of true Romans. By the time of the Antonine emperor Hadrian (117-138 A.D.), only one legionary out of 100 was a true Roman.

Not only had the composition of the army changed, but its quality and content had been affected as well. More often than not, the Roman army had held an organizational and technical advantage over its adversaries. As a fighting force, the 4,500-man legion of the late republic and early principate had no equal. However, for reasons largely political, the constitution of the legions had changed. Successive emperors had altered its composition to fit their needs. Also, as the empire had expanded and as the manpower needs to defend its borders had increased, more and more non-native troops had been allowed into the ranks of the legions. With assimilation being a natural byproduct of this infusion of foreign troops, the appearance of the troops themselves had changed. Whereas the legionary of the late republic was heavily armed and armored with his lorica segmentata and imperial Gallic helmet, by the later centuries of the principate he was largely without armor, especially in the eastern portion of the empire after the battle of Adrianople where most of the army had been destroyed and much of its armaments lost.[10] Often times a simple cloak was worn over a knee length sleeved tunic. Trousers were common apparel as well, having been adopted from years of contact with Germanic tribesmen. The imperial Gallic helmet, which had been of forged construction, was replaced by what is often referred to as the Spangenhelm helmet, which was of sectional construction with two halves being joined together by a ridge piece with neck and cheek guards added on.

The weapons of the soldiers of the late imperium had changed as well. The short stabbing sword or gladius had fallen into a state of disuse, replaced by the longer spatha, which was used by the cavalry and infantry alike. The throwing spear or pilum of the republican armies was still in use, although it was now referred to as the speculum. This type had a wide variety of spear points, which were now being used instead of the earlier type with its long point, which had been designed to bend on impact and render an enemy's shield useless.

But it was perhaps the nature of the wars which Rome was fighting that had changed the most. Caesar's war in Gaul and his invasion of Britain were clearly wars of conquest fought to further Caesar's personal ambitions and to extend the empire. During the early years of the imperium there were other wars of conquest, such as Claudius' invasion of Britain in 43 A.D. and Trajan's invasion of Cacia in 101 A.D. However, the problems of empire building were obvious from the start. As the first of Rome's emperors, Augustus had advised his adopted son and heir Tiberius against any further expansion of the empire. This advice may have come as result of the Varian disaster in A. D. 9, during which three Roman legions were lost in Germania. The emperor Hadrian, who reigned from 117-138 A.D., constructed a wall across northern Britain. Perhaps this was a tactic to keep Roman forces from going any further as well as to prevent invasions from the northern Celtic tribes of the island. Clearly, the size of the empire was causing a strain on the ability of the government to maintain and defend it.

It would be after years of internal and external wars that the empire would find itself in great peril. By the fifth century A.D., the Roman state was clearly very much weakened and in a state of decay. In the last century of its glorious existence, two men would step forward and attempt to arrest this decline and decay. Both would meet with some measure of success in their endeavors; both would suffer an untimely and unfortunate demise. The first would be a semi-barbarus, or semi-barbarbian. His father had been a vandal while his mother was a true Roman. Being of such extraction, the only logical career open to him would be a military one. Luck, an important aspect in the career of all truly great men, would also assist him during the early stages of his military career. As a young man he would begin his career in the protectores, an elite corps where only Romans of good birth or barbarian nobles were allowed to serve. His name was Flavius Stilicho, and in time he would become virtual regent of the Western Roman Empire.

Flavius' life would be relatively brief; his birth occurring in 365 A.D., and his death some 43 years later by means of execution. He would spend much of his adult life fighting for Rome, or what was left of it, and usually against great odds. He would for a number of years delay the fall of the Western Roman Empire, although ultimately he could not prevent it. His story, much like that of many of Rome's warriors, would entail both triumph and tragedy, leaving one to wonder if perhaps he himself had a keen understanding of what his ultimate fate would be.

Stilicho had been born into a very turbulent time, which had seen the empire divided into East and West. This had been occasioned by the Emperor Valentinian I, who had ruled from 360 to 375 A.D. and had graciously given the eastern portion of the empire to his younger brother Valens while he himself campaigned in the West against Germanic tribesmen who had crossed the Rhine and entered into the frontiers of Rome. During his early years, Gibbon writes that, "From his earliest youth he embraced the profession of arms; his prudence and valor were soon distinguished in the field; the horsemen and archers of the East admired his superior dexterity; and in each degree of his military promotions, the public judgment always prevented and approved the choice of the sovereign."[11] By line of promotion he would become a tribune of Rome, then tribune and notary, which would see him being attached to the imperial general staff.[12] It would be in this capacity wherein he would be sent in 383 and 384 A.D. as part of a diplomatic mission to the court of the Sassanid Persian Empire. With this mission being regarded as a success, Stilicho would be rewarded with a marriage to the adopted daughter of the emperor Theodosius, Serena. Naturally, this marriage into the royal family would assure a fine career for the young Stilicho, and after winning the favor of Theodosius, he would see a steady climb through the ranks of the army. Eventually he would become magister militatum, at that time one of the five highest-ranking officers in the Eastern Empire.

As usually happens during the lives of great men, it would be affairs beyond his control that would propel Stilicho towards greatness, and beyond to his unfortunate fate. In the Western Empire, civil war had flared up again as the usurper Magnus Maximus had gathered the support of the army in Britain and sought the imperial purple for himself. He would cross the English Channel and defeat the Western emperor Gratian at Paris in the year 383 A.D. For the next five years Maximus would control much of the Western Empire. However, the emperor of the East, Theodosius, had only reluctantly accepted the usurpation of Maximus. In 388 A.D., Theodosius would move west with a fast moving column of forces, which would corner Maximus at Aquileia. Maximus would be captured, stripped of his imperial robes and executed. His son Flavius Victor, who had been elevated to the position of co-Augustus, fought on for a while, though he would eventually be brought down himself in 388 by one of Theodosius commanders named Arbogast. In an attempt to stabilize the situation in the West, Theodosius would restore Valentinian II as ruler of the West. However, Valentinian II was in no way capable of accepting the responsibilities of ruling half an empire, and on May 15, 392 A.D. he was found hanged in his bedroom, though history cannot be sure if it was by suicide or intrigue. In the events to follow the same general Arbotgast who had helped put down the revolt of Maximus would eventually put forth a Christian educator and administrator named Flavius Eugenius as Augustus of the West. But the response by Theodosius was immediate and overwhelming. He first named his young son Honorius as Augustus of the West, then led his army west to Frigidus where he would defeat the army of Eugenius and Arbogast after a two-day battle. Eugenius would be captured and put to death. Arbogast would commit suicide rather than be captured.

In the aftermath of his victory, Theodosius would bring his ten-year-old son Honorius west and have him installed at emperor. However, given the boy's relative youth he placed him under the supervision of his daughter by adoption, Serena, and her husband Sticlicho, who by this time had attained the rank of general. To further secure the position of his son, "Theodosius conferred the rank of western magister peditum upon Stilicho, clearly hoping that the loyalty of Arbogast's successor would be secured by reason of his relationship by marriage to the imperial family."[13] That loyalty would soon be tested, as Theodosius would pass away barely four months after his victory.

The death of Theodosius in January of 395 A.D. left Stilicho in a rather unique position. As the empire had for years been divided into East and West, there had also been a division of the army. When Theodosius came to Frigidas to defeat Eugenius, he brought with him much of the eastern army. With his victory, he gained control of the western regiments as well. For a time then, much of the army was reunited. Because of his appointment by Theodosius as supreme military commander, and having been named as guardian of the young Honorius alongside Serena, Stilicho was left in a position few had known in centuries and none would ever know again. With control of much of the army he could easily have sought the imperial purple for himself. Yet he did not. Perhaps viewing the condition of the Eastern and Western empires as being weak due to the installation of the young Arcadius in the East and Honorius in the West, Hunnic and Gothic tribes would begin to exert pressure against both empires. In the East, predatory bands of Huns raided Rome's eastern provinces, as well as Sassanid Persia. Although the Huns were a definite threat to the security of the empire, perhaps the greater threat at that time were the Gothic tribes in the West. It should be remembered that at this time the Roman Empire was still recovering from the aftershocks of the Battle of Adrianople in 378 A.D. where the emperor Valens and the Roman legions had suffered a terrible and decisive defeat at the hands of Gothic cavalry.

The defeat at Adrianople did have consequences lasting well after the battle itself. The loss of much of the army deployed that day had left the Eastern Empire without the proper means to defend itself. As Valens himself had died in the battle, he was replaced as Eastern Augustus by Theodosius. Reacting to the situation at hand, Theodosius initiated a policy of firmness when practicable and conciliation when necessary when dealing with the empire's Gothic enemies. With the assistance of his able general Promotus, he was able to re-establish some measure of control over Thrace and Moesia. From the time of his becoming Augustus of the East in 379 A.D. until his death in 395, he had driven many of the Gothic invaders north across the Danube. On the other hand, he also allowed many of them to settle within the borders of the empire.

This was the condition of the empire, or what remained of it when Stilicho came to power after the death of Theodosius. As Theodosius had been forced to accept policies of conciliation and firmness, Stilicho would attempt similar policies. However, he would meet with resistance not only from Rome's Gothic enemies, but from factious elements within the empire as well. When the Gothic tribes began their rebellion in 395, they were led by the chieftain Alaric, who had served as a Roman officer and had fought for Theodosius at the River Frigidus. Initially the Goths began their campaigns of plunder in Thrace and Macedonia. With much of the combined army at his disposal, Stilicho moved east to meet this new threat. Moving through the Julian Alps, Stilicho would begin by conducting policing operations in Pannonia and Dalmatia. These actions were largely successful, for the fearful barbarians in the region ceased their raids. With the combined armies of the Western and Eastern Empires still at his disposal, Stilicho then moved into Thessaly, where he would eventually catch up to his Gothic foe and surround Alaric and his forces somewhere in the Peneus Valley. History has it that "If battle had been joined at that moment, Claudian says, Greece would have been saved from devastation and the calamities of the empire brought to an end."[14]

Such was not to be the case. When Theodosius had died, Stilicho had claimed that the dying emperor had appointed him as protector of the two young emperors, Honorius in the West and Arcadius in the East. That had been his pretense for moving east to deal with the rebellious Gothic tribes. However, at the very moment when he could have easily crushed the Gothic rebellion, he received word from the East that he was to desist in his operations, as his interference in Eastern affairs was not welcomed. He was further instructed to return those regiments in his army that belonged to the Eastern empire to Constantinople. Although these actions defy explanation and seem totally illogical, they do explain much of the illness of the time. For centuries Rome had frittered away its strength fighting amongst themselves, and no doubt Arcadius and his Master of Soldiers Rufinus were jealous of any success Stilicho had thus far attained. In addition, the Roman army of 395 A.D. was not the Roman army of the Scipios. Much of the army now consisted of regiments recruited from Rome's own enemies, who had been admitted into the empire as foederate. Their loyalty was always at question. Those regiments from the East, which Stilicho had to return to Constantinople, were under the command of an officer named Gainas, who was of barbarian extraction. Not only were the Romans guilty of being so uncautious as to allow their armies to be commanded by foreign mercenaries who owed little loyalty to the empire, but they were guilty of another vice as well. Gibben writes of how "the citizens and subjects had purchased an exemption from the indispensable duty of defending their country, which was supported by the arms of barbarian mercenaries."[15]

Given these flaws within the Roman military establishment, and no doubt fearful of causing a civil war between the Eastern and Western Empires, Stilicho declined further hostilities, returned the requested regiments to Constantinope, and marched west with the remainder of his army. It would prove to be one of the most unfortunate episodes of late Roman history, and in time the consequences would prove disastrous.

This would not be the last time that Stilicho and the Goths would encounter each other on the field of battle. In the aftermath of their first encounter, Alaric and his Gothic army had been left to plunder the provinces of Greece without interference. During this time Stilicho had spent his time bolstering his own army with recruits from the Germanic tribes along the Rhine. In 397 A.D. he felt secure enough to march east again, proving that he was more than willing to take unilateral action with neither permission nor assistance from Constantinople. As in the contest of 395, Stilicho would pursue his enemy, bringing him to bear on a hillside in Arcadia. True to Roman form, Stilicho's army would rely on their engineering prowess, and a wall of circumvallation would be built around Alaric's camp. The Roman forces would also endeavor to divert the water supply away from the Gothic camp by means of a ditch. Although, no doubt, some level of fighting took place between the two antagonists, what would follow would largely consist of an over-reliance on negotiation between the two parties. Surely Stilicho hoped to avert a battle in which he might lose much of his army, as it was by this time a very difficult commodity to replace. Stilicho would succeed in forcing Alaric to retire into Epirus, although Stilicho himself would retire back to the West without winning a conclusive victory.

As a reward for having forced the Gothic host to quit the region, the young emperor in the East, acting on advice of his court chamberlain Eurtropius, would declare Stilicho a public enemy. Clearly, Stilicho was regarded as being more of a threat than Alaric. It would prove in time to be a very severe mistake. Even worse, in their negotiations with the Gothic chief, the Eastern government in Constantinople had decided to make Alaric a Roman general, naming him as Master of Soldiers in Illyricum. This not only gave Alaric control of Roman troops, it also allowed him to control the Roman arsenals at Margus, Ratiaria, Naissus and Thessalonica. As Gibbon would have it, this allowed Alaric "to provide his troops with an extraordinary supply of shields, helmets, swords and spears; the unhappy provincials were compelled to forge the instruments of their own destruction; and the barbarians removed the only defect which had sometimes disappointed the efforts of their courage."[16] With the double advantage of his title of Master of Soldiers and his ability to provide arms to his troops, Alaric would now be raised on a shield and proclaimed King of the Visogoths by consent of the barbarian chieftains. All of these facts would provide Alaric with further leverage in his dealings with the divided empire and the young emperors Arcadius in the East and Honorius in the West.

During these years, things would not go quite as well for Stilicho. Late in the year 397 there would be a rebellion in North Africa when Gildo, who had been appointed commander of the provinces there by Theodosius, broke off relations with the West and formed a new liaison with the court of Arcadius in the East. As the North African provinces were a major source of cereal crops to feed the population of the West, this was a very serious situation. Stilicho was able to remedy the situation by sending Gildo's own brother and bitter enemy Mascezel to North Africa with a small expeditionary force, which quickly restored order to the region. The incident proved fortunate for Stilicho, as ample food supplies were again guaranteed for the City of Rome and the Italian provinces. It was far less fortunate for Mascezel, who shortly thereafter drowned under some very questionable circumstances.

Further pressure would be exerted against the Western empire when barbarian tribes began raiding in Raetia. Never at a loss to see a clear opportunity to further his own position, Alaric would decide to invade Italy while Stilicho was away dealing with this threat. Therefore, in 401 A.D. Alaric would lead his Gothic roman army from Thessalonica through Pannonia and across the Julian Alps. He would capture Aquileia and then move on to invest the City of Milan. In response, Stilicho would gather an army comprised of allies from Raetia and southern Germany, and roman garrisons from the Rhine and Gaul. Stilicho would then perform an exceptional logistical feat by crossing the Julian Alps in February of 402 and forcing Alaric to quit the siege of Milan. Stilicho would fight three battles against the Gothic army at Asta, Pollentia and Verona. Stilicho enjoyed some level of success during these campaigns, even capturing Alaric's wife and children. However, the decisive victory he sought all his life would still elude him. In 404 A.D. Alaric's first invasion of Italy would end in negotiation, with Alaric now being named Master of Soldiers in the West as well as being subsidized to hold Illyricum as a province for Rome, against both the barbarians and the Eastern

Empire.

Still, if Stilicho had hoped for a much needed respite, it was not forthcoming. In the year 405 a mass migration of mixed Germanic tribes numbering as many as a half million people moved into the Po Valley under a chieftain named Radagaisus. Without sufficient strength to do anything at that time, Stilicho would be reduced to the condition of a bystander. In 406 A.D. Radagaisus would move south into Italy proper with between one-third and one-half of his army, about 70,000 men. Stilicho would then move to check his advance with a much smaller army of about 30,000 legionaires, plus Hunic and Gothic allies numbering another 15,000 men. He would meet his foe at Florence, where in the fashion of Caesar he would encircle his enemy and starve them into submission. Radagaisus would be captured and executed, his troops sold into slavery. It is said that the market was so flooded with slaves at this time that there was a precipitous decline in the cost of slaves on the market.

If the old adage that there is no rest for the wicked is true, then one must infer that Stalicho was a very wicked man. The long chain of internal discord and attempted usurpation of Roman authority would continue in the year 407 A.D. when a new pretender to the throne would make his presence known. Having felt itself neglected as a part of the Empire, Britain would put forth not one but a series of three usurpers who would claim the right of emperorship. One would die within days, the second within a few months. The third however bore the name of Constantine, although he was of no relation to the great Christian emperor of the early fourth century. He would prove to be far more capable than his predecessors, both in terms of his organizational abilities and as a politician. Not content as a bystander in the backwaters of Britain, Constantine would cross the English Channel in 407 A.D. and gain control of most of Gaul. His actions would assist in setting into motion a series of events which would help lead to the end of the great general who had so often helped to deliver Rome from its enemies. With Constantine controlling large parts of Gaul and Spain, and with barbarian tribes launching fresh incursions into Roman territory from across the Rhine, Alaric decided that it may have been an opportune time to exert new pressures against the Western Empire. Assembling his army, he moved west in 407 A.D. and into negotiations with the regent of the West. He demanded four thousand pounds of gold as the price for not renewing war against the Empire. Viewing Constantine as the greater threat, and without the resources necessary to deal with not one, but two wars, Stilicho went before the Roman Senate to request the desired amount. Although necessity may have guided his decision, the Roman Senate was in bitter opposition to what they perceived as the bribing of the enemy. One of the more illustrious of the senators, Lampadius, proclaimed, "This is not a treaty of peace, but of servitude."[17] Undoubtedly already resentful of Stilicho's vandal heritage, and probably further resentful of his influence in the court of Honorius, the treaty writ and buying off of Alaric would be seized upon by Stilicho's enemies to portray him as being disloyal to the Empire.

To the east the young emperor Arcadius would pass away on the first of May in 408 A.D. at the very young age of thirty-one. Both Honorius and Stilicho would announce their intention of going to Constantinople to supervise the accession of the new emperor. This incident would be seized upon by one of stilicho's implacable foes to bring about his downfall and demise. Stilicho had long since been the trusted advisor to the Western emperor Honorius, who was at this time still only twenty-five years old. But now the artful and deceitful minister Olympius would introduce further intrigue against Stilicho, convincing the young Honorius that Stilicho had designs of placing his own son on the throne of the Eastern Empire. Although the accusation was undoubtedly false, as probably were many of the other accusations against the great general, it did work to undermine the loyalty and respect that Honorius had held for the guardian of his youth. The end for Stilicho would come swiftly. By this time the ill designs of Olympius had worked to remove Stilicho from the favor of Honorius, who decided to remove himself from Rome and to relocate his court to Ravenna. At Ticinum there would be a rebellion within the army that was being gathered to put down the revolt of the usurper Constantine in Gaul. During this revolt many of Stilicho's supporters and fellow officers would be massacred, probably because of very strong anti-German sentiments within the army. When word of the massacre reached Stilicho at his camp in Bologna, he called a council of those officers present with him so as to formulate a plan of action. Not surprisingly, many urged him to take up arms in revolt and to seek revenge against those who had massacred his supporters and who sought his demise. This he declined to do. Instead he went to Ravenna to seek council with his young emperor. Council would not be given. Instead he would find that a warrant had been issued for his arrest. Having sought sanctuary in a church, Stilicho would be enticed to reveal himself to his enemies when Count Heraclian and a body of troops arrived to execute his apprehension. However, after allowing himself to be taken into custody under the assurance that the warrant was for his arrest only, he was informed that the warrant called for his immediate execution as well. At this the faithful barbarians who guarded him urged his resistance and flight, but were informed by the faithful general to offer no resistance. The man who had saved Rome and had thrice defeated his enemies at Pollentia, Verona and Florence then willingly submitted his neck to the sword of his enemies.

For a hardened soldier who had spent his entire life in the defense of the Empire and who knew his motives to be without malice, to simply surrender without a fight defies explanation. Although the path of resistance and revolt was open to him, he declined to take it. Right up until the very end he remained true to himself. Adrian Goldsworthy may have said it best in describing the actions of Stilicho when he wrote, "It is hard not to want to believe that he put the good of the Empire before his own fate. It may even be true."[18] In the aftermath of his death, many falsehoods would be put forth by his enemies so as to explain the reason for his execution. All would be untrue. But perhaps the best epitaph for him would be written by his chief antagonist Alaric, who would return to Italy and sack the City of Rome in 410 A.D.

In some ways the story of Stilicho does not end with his death. In the aftermath of the initial sack of Rome in 410 A.D., the Western Empire would recover to some extent. Much of Gaul would be recovered, and for a time North Africa would remain as an essential part of the Empire. In 423 A.D. the emperor Honorius would die, leaving Rome essentially leaderless. And, in the spirit of Stilicho, another general would step forward to save the Empire from its barbarian enemies, only to be sacrificed by a jealous emperor who would rather risk ruin of the Empire than to be upstaged by a man of virtue.

This man would be the Danubian born soldier Aetius.

One must remember that with Stilicho and Aetius there existed a Roman Empire much different than the one built by Julius Caesar and Octavian. During the later years of the republic and the early years of the principate, it could be expected that Rome would win any war it chose to fight. It was a united empire, both wealthy and sound agriculturally and commercially. Although largely Roman, they were tolerant of other peoples within the empire. But by the fourth and fifth centuries A.D., there had been a precipitous decline in the fortunes of Rome. Largely, Romans did not want to fight their own wars; they would rather hire barbarians to fight barbarians. Agriculture was largely in decline. When the colonies in North Africa fell to the Vandal King Gaiseric, Rome was irreparably damaged. As a result, there was a lack of political stability with the Tetrarchy of Diocletian degenerating into a split empire with an East and a West. Although probably not recognized at the time, the task before Stilicho and Aetius was most likely far greater than that which confronted Julius Caesar. The price that Rome had to pay for its expansion during the later years of the republic and the early years of the principate was to come in the form of more and more enemies. Unfortunately, the resources needed to fight these enemies would continue to decline.

The world into which Aetius had been born was a world much different than the world of Julius Caesar. With the demise of Stilicho having taken place, the emperor Honorius had ensconced himself in Ravenna where it was relatively safe. However, he could do little more than preside over the beginning of the final break up of the Western Roman Empire. Alaric would sack Rome in 410 A.D. and Britain would be abandoned. Spain and much of Gaul would be lost to the Vandals, who would essentially control much of North Africa and separate the empire from much of its needed grain supplies. Even worse, when Honorius died in 423 A.D. he would do so without naming his successor as Augustus. The wife of Constantius III, who had been Honorius co-emperor, succeeded in having her son placed on the throne in Ravenna as Valentinian III. However, it would be Galla Placidia herself who would serve as virtual regent of the West.

As for Aetius, there would be many years of his younger life during which he would be a hostage of both the Visogoths and the Huns. During the time of Julius Caesar it had been customary for Rome to receive hostages from its enemies as a means of ensuring peace with its warlike neighbors. As an indication of how weakened the once terrible power of Rome had become, Rome was more inclined by this time to give concessions to its enemies than to receive them. This time spent as captive to the enemies of Rome, however, would prove to be of some benefit to Aetius, as it allowed him to learn of his future allies and enemies.

Born into a military family, it was only natural that Flavius Aetius would spend his adult life as a soldier and defender of the Empire. The first we hear of him in the pages of history is after the death of Honorius, when, as a supporter of the usurper John, he raised an army of Hunic warriors to serve as mercenaries in the contest for the vacant throne. Yet, he would arrive in Italy too late to play a definitive role in this contest, for by that time John had been executed, and Valentinian III had been proclaimed emperor with the assistance of an army from the Eastern Empire. One must surmise however, that Aetius' support of John against the six-year-old Valentinian must have placed him forever at odds with Galla Placidia, who seems never to have forgiven him for this act.

Although Galla Placidia had succeeded in placing her young son on the vacant throne, she would not succeed in uniting the generals of Rome and using them as a unified force to confront the enemies of the Empire. In Italy, the senior commander and Master of Soldiers was a general named Felix The provinces in North Africa were commanded by Count Boniface, an able soldier. He could have held the region for Rome but was a less capable politician who would fall victim to court intrigues. Aetius, who would use his military force of Huns as leverage against the new emperor, was to command in Gaul. Although Rome was in a definite state of decline by this time, one is left to ponder what might have been if the three warriors had been able to unite their forces under a unified command. Although it is unlikely that they could have arrested those forces which eventually brought down the empire, they may have been able to postpone them. Unfortunately, the Roman preoccupation with internal strife would prevent this, as Galla Placidia was more interested in playing the generals off against each other than in uniting them to secure the safety of the Empire. The results would prove disastrous.

As commander in Gaul, Aetius would prove both capable and successful. In 425 A.D. he would foil a Visogothic attempt to conquer Provence by defeating Theodoric, King of Toulouse, at Arles. After concluding terms of peace with Theodoric, he then fought a series of successful campaigns against the Franks and other Germanic invaders, re-establishing Roman control over most of Gaul with the exception of Aquitaine, which remained a stronghold of the Visogoths. Given the nature of the forces working against him, and the united number of resources available to him, one must conclude that his operations were a success. In Gaul, according to O'Flynn, "He made himself absolute master, disposing of people and making alliances as he saw fit, and acting more like a ruler than a genral."[19] When the Britons found themselves under repeated assaults from the Scots, Picts and Saxons, the appeal for help would be sent to Aetius. Likewise, most of the agreements between the Barbarian allies and Rome were concluded directly through Aetius, not with the court in Ravenna. Given the power struggles of the time, these acts could only have given his rivals further cause for enmity.

It would be a contest not with, but between his two rivals that would lead to Aetius increasing his influence and power in the West. In 427 A.D. Felix, as commander of the imperial army in Italy, would send an army to attack his colleague and rival Boniface in Africa. If Felix's intent was to rid himself of a potential rival, he would fail in his efforts, as Boniface would prove victorious over the force sent against him. Although his failure to defeat Boniface was not immediately fatal, his position was weakened, and by 430 A.D. Aetius had supplanted Felix as the power in Italy and ordered Felix's murder in that same year. Nevertheless, ridding himself of one rival only guaranteed that there would be further intrigue within the court by Galla Placidian and a renewed contest between Aetius and Boniface. If it was the hope of Galla Placidia to use one general as a means to destroy the other, she would get her wish. She would also further weaken what was left of the Empire.

By 432 A.D. Count Boniface had become not only Master of Soldiers but had been awarded the rank of patriciate as well. By that same year, Aetius was to become consul. He would serve in that position for three terms. Perhaps now fearing the success that Aetius had enjoyed in Gaul, or even possibly hoping the two generals would cancel each other out and leave her as virtual regent of the West, Galla Placidia summoned Boniface back to Italy in that same year of 432. He was accompanied no doubt with as large of a force of legionnaires as possible. Upon hearing of this, Aetius himself would, as Caesar had done five centuries earlier, march on Italy from Gaul. In a battle fought near Ariminum, the army of Boniface would prove victorious. However, Boniface himself was seriously wounded during the action, succumbing to his wounds a few months later. For a short period of time Placidia was rid of her two rivals, as Aetius, by marching against Boniface had placed himself outside of the law and was forced to flee after his defeat. He would first flee to his estates and eventually end up in Pannonia under the protection of the Huns and their king Rugila. With Count Boniface removed from the picture, there was no longer any protector for the colonies in North Africa and the way was clear for Gaiseric and his Vandal warriors to capture Hippo and the City of Carthage.

However, and very fortunately for Rome, Aetius would use his influence with the Huns to recruit a new force of mercenaries. In 433 A.D. he would return to Italy and force Placidia and the still young emperor to restore him to his position of Master of Soldiers and commander of what remained of the Western Empire's army. For the next two decades he would remain as the unchallenged power behind the throne. There would still exist three commanders or magistri within the army, yet none of them would ever step forward to challenge Aetius or aspire to the emperorship. There would be twenty years of needed respite from the endless chain of internal civil war which had for so long existed within the Empire.

Regrettably, there would be no respite from the external pressures of the barbarians. In 435 A.D. Aetius would take to the field of battle once again, first defeating a force of Burgundians, then defeating the Visogothic king Theodoric for a second time at Arles. A year later he would defeat the Visogoths again at Narbonne. There would be some further skirmishing with the Visogothic king, however by 442 A.D. Aetius was able to sign a treaty with his future ally Theodoric. With some level of freedom of action being guaranteed by his disentanglement from the Visogothic threat, Aetius was then able to engage the Salian Franks under their king Chlodio, defeating them on numerous occasions. By 446 A.D. Aetius would reach the pinnacle of his political power by being appointed consul for the third time.

However, if Aetius had by his actions managed to attain some level of strength, the policies of Rome betray to the world that the Empire was by this time dealing only from a position of weakness. Much as Stilicho had been forced to manage the Barbarians delicately by playing them off against each other, Aetius would be forced to do the same. But there were subtle differences. Whereas Stilicho had lived in a time when the Eastern and Western empires were still very much involved in each other's affairs, by the time of Aetius the two had become very much detached. All of Aetius efforts would then be spent in defending Gaul and the Western Empire and it would be in this theatre of operation where Aetius would achieve lasting fame. During the early decades of the fifth century the mass migration of barbarian tribes both around and within the borders of the Empire continued unabated. The Vandal occupation of North Africa was accompanied by Suevi domination in Spain and Visogothic unrest in Gaul. There was also an increase of power and prestige within the Hunic empire, which stretched from Germany in the west to the Volga River in the east. In 432 A.D. the emperor Theodosius had signed a treaty with the Hunic king Ruas, a treaty by which Theodosius agreed to pay tribute to the Huns as well as make Ruas a general in the Roman army. When Ruas died shortly thereafter, his nephews Attila and Bleda became co-rulers of the Hunic kingdom. Although the two-brother rulers initially agreed to renew the treaty with Constantinople, sometime in 441 A.D. Attila began marching on the Eastern Empire of Rome. This was probably due in large part to the fact that control over the Hunic tribes was dependent upon a ruler's ability to provide continued plunder to his supporters in exchange for the right to lead the Hunic empire.

In 445 A.D., Attila, who was a bold leader of light cavalry and possessed a level of strategic thinking, became sole ruler of the Huns when he murdered his brother Bleda. Two years later, Attila would invade the Eastern Empire for a second time. After being briefly halted by the imperial army at the Battle of Utus, Attila moved west toward Greece, although he would again be halted at Thermopylae where a small Greek army of Hoplites under Leonidas had repulsed the massive Persian army of Xerxes in 480 A.D. for three days. This time there would be no epic tale of resistance, for the end result would be another treaty between Theodosius and Attila with Constantinople's annual tribute to the Huns being tripled.

Shortly after Attila's second invasion of the Eastern Empire, the very weak emperor Theodosius would die. He would be replaced by one of his generals, Marcian, who took the deceased emperor's sister Pulceria in marriage. As a military man, Marcian was much tougher than Theodosius II had been and he favored policies that would make it far harder for Attila to extort money from the Empire. In fact, he was no sooner coronated as emperor before he began canceling payments of tribute that had flowed north to Attila for years. As a result of this change, Attila would decide that the time had arrived for him to attack and extort the much weaker Western Empire. For Aetius, the decision of Marcian in the East to draw a hard line with the Huns would mean immeasurable difficulties in his trying to hold together an already crumbling empire.

Unfortunately, just when Aetius would need a strong army the most, the tax policies of the Western empire would go far in trying to preclude him from having one. For years Rome had struggled to financially support itself. With the loss of North Africa to the Vandals and Spain to the Suevi, its revenues had been severely depleted. Added to this, "The Roman government suffered chronic financial difficulties owing partly to its failure to levy a fair share of taxes from the wealthiest landowners of Italy, who, thanks to a corrupt and inefficient bureaucracy, enjoyed great privileges and tax exemption."[20] Perhaps with a keen knowledge of how taxation policies were affecting the ability of the empire to defend itself, Aetius was more of the mind of Tiberius Gracchus when he initiated attempts to alleviate this problem during the years of the Roman republic.

Perhaps a sinful relationship would do as much harm to the Western empire as its tax policies. The sister of the emperor Valentinia III was named Honoria. In having a strong will she may have much resembled her mother Galla Placidia, who had for years been a rival of Aetius. Unmarried at the time, she had an affair with one of her stewards; an affair which left her pregnant. As punishment she was married off to an elderly senator and sent into a sort of exile. So as to extricate herself from this unpleasant situation, she sent a ring to Attila with a plea for help, a plea that provided Attila with an all too convenient excuse to invade the West, and one which he was very happy to exploit. Claiming one-half of the Western empire as his dowry, Attila called upon the emperor Valentinian III for Honoria's hand in marriage, a request which was obviously declined. From that point forward a clash between Aetius, Protector of the West, and Attila, scourge of the East, was inevitable.

Accordingly, in the spring of 451 A.D. Attila departed Pannonia with an army of perhaps 100 thousand warriors. He moved north and west, crossing the Rhine River somewhere north of Mainz in modern Germany. Along the way he was able to strengthen his army with contingents of Ostrogoths, Gepidae, Sciri, Rugi, Franks and other native tribes. He would move into Eastern Gaul along a front of more than 100 miles, laying waste to many of the towns before him. By June he had reached the city of Orleans, which somehow managed to resist capture. In response to this invasion of Roman Gaul, Aetius would raise an army of his own, consisting of what legions remained to the empire, as well as the Visogothic army of Theodoric, some Alan cavalry, some Franks and some Burgundians.

The two armies would meet in battle on the Catalaunian Plains somewhere between Troyes and Chalons. By all appearances, the battle could not have resembled the former contest of Imperial Rome, as the supremacy of the legions had been destroyed at Adrianople decades earlier and as most of the combatants that day in both armies were of barbarian descent. What followed was an all day battle, which was largely inconclusive and no doubt very bloody. While not a clear-cut victory for Aetius and his army, at day's end he did control the field of battle. There are even references in history that Attila, having failed to win the battle, considered suicide and even had a funeral pyre built for himself from the saddles of his warriors. However, what would happen in the aftermath of the Battle of Chalons is that both armies would break up and disperse. Attila would march east, though it would not be the last that history would hear of him. Aetius would largely find himself without an army, as the Visogoths returned to their homes to settle the question of succession, for their king Theodoric had been killed in battle. For the time being, Aetius was a hero and the savior of the Western Empire.

Lamentably, just as fortunes had changed so rapidly for Stilicho five decades earlier, they would now change rapidly for Aetius as well. Although Attila had returned to Pannonia for the winter, he did not desist in his request for a marriage to Honoria. Having been refused for a second time, he decided to attack the Western Empire again in the year 452 A.D. This time he did not attack the empire indirectly through Gaul, he attacked it directly by crossing the Julian Alps and attacking Italy itself. Aetius, with what remained of his army still in Gaul, was more or less powerless to resist the new onslaught. In addition, many of the allies he had been able to convince to fight with him at Chalons had no interest in fighting to save Italy, as their homes and interests were not in any direct danger. Thankfully, fate would intervene for Aetius. Throughout early history right up until modern times, famine, pestilence and disease have been as much of a threat to an army as any opposing army and such would be the case when Attila invaded Italy, making it very difficult for him to feed and maintain a standing army in enemy territory. In addition, the Romans sent Pope Leo I north as an emissary to persuade Attila to withdraw with his army. For whatever reason, fear for his army, or having been persuaded by the Pope, Attila did march his army north, thus saving Italy. The end would come for both Attila and Aetius shortly thereafter. As for Attila's death there is only speculation, as various sources attribute his death to a number of causes, ranging from possible assassination at the hand of a new bride, to a possible hemorrhage after a night of barbaric excesses. His empire would die with him, as would two of his sons while trying to hold together the remnants of the Hunic tribes. Within a few short years the Huns would disappear from European history.

Aetius would live long enough to see the downfall of his Hunnish antagonist, but not long enough to enjoy it. In 454 A.D. Aetius would die under circumstances very similar to those of Stilicho five decades earlier. However, in the case of Aetius, a jealous emperor would not send an assassin to kill off his most reliable generalissimo, he would do it himself. The very unwise emperor would then be informed that "he had cut off his right hand with his left."[21] Within a year, two of Aetius former lieutenants would return the favor and murder Valentinian. With this act, the path was now clear for the final dissolution of the Western Roman Empire. Historically, Stilicho and Aetius will never attain the status of a Julius Caesar or an emperor such as Trajan. But in some ways they need always to be remembered for their personal courage in the face of insurmountable odds. Most assuredly they must have understood that they could never prevent the fall of the Roman

Empire, yet they did all within their power to arrest the forces which caused that end. Until the very end they remained true to themselves, no matter what the odds. A man can do little more than that.

Chapter III

¤

ONE

There exist certain inconsistencies within history. As human history is interwoven with technological improvements, and as societies have become increasingly larger and more complicated, there is a mistaken belief that progress in the affairs of mankind is always forward. Yet we know that, with the fall of the Western Roman Empire in the fifth century, an illuminating light in the affairs of mankind was extinguished. In addition, from time to time, history must be re-examined with reference to both the importance of events, and the importance of individuals. In all likelihood, the sphere of history will only continue to grow as the historian and the archeologist continue to uncover and discover new references and artifacts which bring to light long forgotten facts from our collective past.

There are always those who are a part of history; those who are involved in it and those who courageously step forward to make it. And then there are those rare few who are such a dominant force in their time that they stand out as towers whose stature does not diminish with the passing of the centuries. With the passing of the very cultured societies of the Mediterranean world after the fifth century A.D., the world became a very dark place in which cold and filth, combined with hunger and disease, would cling to many of its inhabitants. There would be a few who would long for the more civilized past and try to restore its blessings to their own time. Most would fail, although a few like the Carolingian Charlemagne would succeed to a varying degree. In England, King Alfred the Great would succeed in re-uniting the south of England and preserving its Christian civilization against the onslaught of the Danes, who had ravaged the lost island for most of the ninth century. He is regarded as the father of the English navy, and fostered both the arts and education during his years as king. There is the definite possibility that Alfred was the impetus for the compiling of the Saxon Chronicle. Much the same as his near contemporary Charlemagne had sought to establish a code of laws in his Carolingian kingdom, Alfred would seek to do much the same through his Book of Dooms. Yet for all his greatness, he is often remembered to history as a refugee in his own kingdom, a man who was forced to seek refuge from his Danish enemies in the marshes of Athelney. After his death in 899 A.D., the Danish king Canute would invade the island once more and would establish himself as ruler of England, Denmark and Norway. Perhaps for this reason, his contributions to history are regarded in less of a light than they should be.

Whereas Alfred is regarded as being founder of the House of Wessex in the line of English monarchs, it would be another king in a later line of English kings whose actions would stand the test of time and attribute to his greatness. He would arise out of a time of chaos and civil war, in the aftermath of the Norman invasion of England in 1066. From these ruins he would establish a more united England in a form that would be much more recognizable to us today.

The future King Henry II was born to this world in the year 1133. His grandfather had been the Norman King Henry I. His mother Matilda had been married at age 26 to the young prince Geoffrey of Anjou, who was but 14 years old at the time. During the age when kingdoms were more often captured by marriage than by warfare, this union made perfect sense, as Anjou and Normandy had been enemies for some time. It was hoped by Matilda's father Henry I that the union formed by this marriage would provide an heir to Henry's throne, as his only son had been lost in the English Channel when the ship upon which he was sailing sank off the coast of Normandy. This unfortunate incident would leave England without a male heir to the throne, and perhaps guarantee that the day would arise when the young Henry of Anjou would have to fight for his right to rule the Anglo-Norman kingdom. As fate would have it, his mother and father would do much of the fighting while Henry was still in his youth.

As far as his youth, much of it would be spent in France and not in England. During a dark age when most were denied the benefit of an adequate education, we find that "at some time during this period, the young prince was put in the charge of Peter of Saintes, his first teacher, a man renowned for his knowledge of poetry and Henry and his brothers seem to have received a more than usually thorough education."[22] His time with Peter would be spent learning the basics of Latin, of reading, and of writing. Perhaps the more important aspect of his education would come while traveling with his father, as the count and his entourage conducted the necessary business of managing the affairs of Anjou. As events would unfold, whereas the young Henry was too young to champion his claim to the throne of England or his father's dominions in France, his parents would undertake these ventures on his behalf. When Henry I expired on December 1, 1135, he did so with the earnest hope that his daughter Matilda, or Maud as she was referred to by the English, would succeed him to the throne. However, Proximity and propinquity would now intervene. At that time, Matilda was in Anjou with her husband. The grandson of William the conqueror also had an interest in the crown of England. His name was Stephen of Blois, and by arriving in London before Matilda and using the influence of his brother Henry who was at that time the Bishop of Winchester, he would claim the crown of England. The thirty years of peace that had existed under Henry I would be followed by civil war and years of dissention. Matilda would challenge Stephen for the crown, and would for a time gain the upper hand over the usurper. She would be joined in her efforts by Robert of Gloucester, who was the bastard son of Henry I and half-brother of Matilda. However, in 1147, Robert would die and Matilda would be forced to leave England in 1148, spending the majority of her remaining years in France.

The young Henry of Anjou would make his first trip to England in September of 1142, while still under the age of nine. His uncle, the Earl of Gloucester, would campaign on his behalf, and the very young Henry would wet his teeth for the first time on the field of battle. But the campaign would be short-lived, as Stephen still held the upper hand in the island kingdom. Henry would retire to Bristol, which was the site of his uncle's court. Here he would resume his studies under a new instructor referred to as Master Matthew, who may have also acted as a chancellor for his mother Matilda. However, within two years he would return to Normandy, resuming his education there.

While the task of completing his education was essential, it could not curb his appetite for further action. In the early part of 1147, Henry would return to England with a small contingent of knights, in hope of resuming his quest for the crown of England. However, his small band of knights were neither trusted companions nor patriots to his cause. They were mercenaries. When success did not follow his campaign, the money soon ran out, and so did his knights. He would appeal to Matilda for help, but her position was every bit as precarious as his own. As the death of his uncle Robert of Gloucester soon followed, Henry's second attempt at the English crown would be unsuccessful as well. His deliverance would come from the most unlikely of all sources, Stephen. "Henry sent an envoy in secret to the very king whose throne he was attempting to claim, asking Stephen, as his kinsman, to relieve his plight."[23] This unfortunate episode seemed only to stiffen the young Henry's resolve.

In 1149, Henry would seek to strengthen his position within the realm by means of knighthood. In the spring of that year

Henry landed in the south of England and then gradually made his way north to Carlisle where he was greeted by his great uncle, King David of Scotland. He then immediately renewed his attempt for the crown. If it holds true that fortune has her favorites, then at this time Henry was not one of them. Although David had brought with him a sizeable force of Scots hoping to gain some advantage from the continued discord over the English crown, when Stephen appeared before York with a well organized and sizable force of his own, the Scots abandoned their efforts. During this attempt to seize the crown, Henry would experience his first personal military success, when with the assistance of the earls of Gloucester and Hereford, he was able to seize both the town and castle of Bridgeport. However, as in his previous attempts, there just was not enough support for his cause or material resources to allow him to overcome the advantages held by Stephen. He would, as before, return to his father's lands in Western France.

His return to the continent would not be without incident. In 1150 Henry would be invested by his parents as the Duke of Normandy. With his father's passing a year later, he became the inheritor of more lands, becoming the Count of Anjou, Touraine, and Maine. In an age of feudal ties, this would require him to render homage to King Louis VII of France, who, by the accepted practices and laws of the age, was his lord and master. It would be during this trip to Paris that he would present himself before the King of France, which would probably lead to one of the more convulsive acts of the medieval age. It would also be one of the more fortuitous for Henry.

In July of 1137, King Louis VII had married the fifteen-year-old heiress of Aquitaine. It was a marriage that had been arranged by Louis' father, with the intended end of securing her future estates in central and southern France for the royal house of France. Unfortunately, like so many of the politically motivated marriages of the time, no consideration was given for differences of either age or temperament. Louis VII is regarded by history as being a very pious man. According to Churchill, "All his days were spent in devotion, and his nights in vigil or penance. When he left his own chapel he would delay the whole court by waiting until the humblest person present had preceded him."[24] In contrast, his young wife was of a much more fiery disposition, and had even traveled to Palestine during the Second Crusade. After fifteen years of marriage, the union had produced two daughters, but no son to act as a legitimate heir. This failure to produce an heir, as well as other failures within the relationship, would lead to a permanent rift within the marriage and an eventual divorce in 1152, "on the nominal grounds of consanguinity."[25]

This was a period in time when divorce was seen as a scandalous act. What was to follow would shock the feudal world even more. Having been granted her divorce from Louis Vii, Eleanor then returned to her inherited lands in Aquitaine. Within two months, in May of 1152, Eleanor would become the new bride of the young Henry, who was ten years her junior. When the lands of the two newlyweds were combined, it comprised an empire that would span from Scotland in the north, to Spain in the south. These dominions would become known to history as the Angevin Empire. As an emblem of his royal house, Henry would adopt the broom, or planta genesta, a sprig of which was usually worn in the helmets of the knights of Henry's lands that he had inherited from his father. Hence, Henry would become known to history as Henry Plantagenet.

The line of kings which would follow him after his ascension to the throne of England would then become known as the House of Plantagenet.

If the marriage of Henry Plantagenet to Eleanor of Aquitaine had proven to be a successful coup for its time, and had provided for a concentration of power in western Europe not seen since the time of Charlemagne, it would also prove to be a very convulsive act whose effects could not go unchallenged by either Stephen of England or Louis VII of France. Within months, Henry and Eleanor would find themselves at war with not only the two kings, but also with the Count of Champagne and Henry's own brother Geoffrey. Fortunately for Henry, not only had he inherited a very sizeable kingdom, but he was privileged enough to inherit a very efficient Norman army to go with it. With these Norman knights he was able to overcome his adversaries in the field and further secure his power and prestige.

Within months, Henry had obtained his position on the continent, and having done so , his gaze turned quickly to that arena where he had known little success in the past. In an act reminiscent of Julius Caesar and his great grandfather William the Conqueror, Henry departed Barfleur in a fleet of thirty-six ships with somewhere between 1,500 and 3,000 men, landing on the English coast on January 6, 1153. In an age when kings ruled according to claims of divine right, the first act that Henry took upon landing in the island kingdom was to enter the nearest chapel where he would "pray for a space, in the manner of soldiers."[26] As an answer to his prayers, the priest would proclaim, "Behold there cometh the Lord, the Ruler, and the kingdom is in his hand."[27]

Since the death of his grandfather Henry I eighteen years

earlier, England had known few years of peace, as the struggle for the throne had ebbed to and fro between the forces of Stephen and the Angevin party. With the arrival of Henry, more of the same would follow. There would be more battles, the first occurring at Malmesbury. And in a time when the landscape of England was dominated by no less than several hundred castles, there would be innumerable sieges as well. However, as had happened when Matilda and Stephen had fought for the right to rule as supreme monarch, neither side was able to gain the upper hand. Much of this failure by either side to triumph may have had to do with the baronage of that time, as a weak king generally meant that they themselves would hold a greater share of the available power. Perhaps recognizing this and realizing that neither would gain the advantage over the other, in November of 1153, Stephen and Henry agreed to the Treaty of Winchester. According to the terms of this treaty, of which there is no surviving text, Henry became the adopted son and heir of Stephen. In return, Henry agreed to pay homage to Stephen as King of England. Further possible provisions within the treaty called for the destruction of many illegal castles that had been built in the years of turmoil since the death of Henry I and for the expulsion of many of the mercenaries who had been hired to fight for both parties, as well as the universal enforcement of the existing laws. As with any treaty, there were provisions intended to mollify but not completely satisfy all parties involved. Nevertheless, this would prove to be largely irrelevant, as Stephen would expire within a year of the treaty signing and Henry Plantagenet would assume the throne of England as King Henry II.

As Churchill would write, "The accession of Henry II began one of the most pregnant and decisive reigns in English history."[28] But it would not be without its problems. Even though she was older than Henry by several years, Eleanor would provide him with eight children, who in turn would provide the king with no end of difficulties. It is possible that Henry II of England may have also had twelve illegitimate children, no doubt much to the frustration of his queen.[29] The very nature of his extensive empire, which extended from the Arctic Ocean in the north to the Pyrenees in the south and consisted of several cultures and languages, would also provide for some level of difficulty, as would the very nature of the feudal society in which he would live. Henry himself spoke French and could largely have been considered as an invader, although this seems to have not mattered to an island nation that had experienced the invasions of the Romans, the Saxons, the Danes and the Normans. Ultimately, by a combination of both skill and determination he would break the eighteen-year-old spell that had gripped England and bring stability to a largely divided land.

It was said of King Stephen that he was "the mildest of men upon earth, the slowest to take offense, the readiest to pardon, - in fact, the most suitable man to be king of an unruly feudal state."[30] Henry would share none of these attributes. Immediately upon becoming king, he would issue a coronation charter as his grandfather Henry I had done. However, whereas his grandfather's charter had consisted largely of promises to win the support of the baronage and the Church, Henry's charter was an attempt to establish a new legal basis for the reforms he intended to enact. He would also begin efforts to surround himself with a group of reliable officials to assist him in his efforts. One of his first appointments was that of Thomas Becket as Chancellor.

Other actions were to follow. Whereas the Treaty of Winchester had required the destruction of all the illegal castles that had been built since the death of Henry I in 1135, and for the expulsion of all mercenaries from the island, Stephen had proven unequal to this task in the last year of his reign. Therefore, Henry II would issue new decrees to these ends. Within a few short years, the number of baronial castles was reduced to 217, as opposed to 52 that were garrisoned by soldiers loyal to the king, and the vast majority of the mercenaries were removed from the country within three months.[31]

As an administrator, Henry proved both innovatory and wise. If the situation required him to do so, he could take ancient customs and reapply them to fit current circumstances. During a dispute with the Count of Toulouse in 1159, Henry returned to using a form of taxation known as scutage to pay for the necessary expenses in raising an army. By this system, if a knight wished to excuse himself from a military campaign in a foreign land, he could instead pay the sum of five shillings to the king as compensation for his lack of service. Barons could be taxed at a higher rate. If they were required to provide twenty knights in lieu of the amount of lands they held, then they were required to pay compensation for each knight. By invoking this former form of taxation, Henry was able to raise an army for the necessary invasion.

Perhaps Henry Plantagenet's greatest contribution to English society came with his judicial reforms. For years there had existed within England a system of baronial courts and verdicts could vary from shire to shire according to the whim or political views of the barons who controlled these courts. Within these courts, innocence or guilt could be determined according to oath, an ordeal, or a duel. Recognizing the faults within the system while also attempting to further strengthen his own position, Henry would resort to a Frankish custom, which had been instituted during the time of the Carolingian kings. This custom was trial by jury. One must remember that at this point in time the memory of William the Conqueror still lived within the hearts and minds of many of the English people. Henry Plantagenet was considerably more French than English, and he controlled far more of the lands of France than did the French king. No doubt realizing these facts and recognizing as well that treading upon English customs could return his northern realm to the days of anarchy and civil war which had been so prevalent during the years of King Stephen, when Henry II sought to introduce innovations into the legal system of England, he did so without any forms of obvious legislation and as unobtrusively as possible. Much as he had brought back scutage so as to assist in raising an army for war on the continent, he would now rely on the ancient Saxon custom of the King's Peace so as to employ custom vs. custom in his campaign toward judicial reform. Essentially, according to this custom every man in England had his own Peace, of which it was a crime to break; the greater the social status of the individual, the greater the crime in breaking this Peace. Therefore, as the king was the most important person in the land, breaking the King's Peace was therefore the offense that could carry the greatest penalty. It would also mean that this offense would be tried in the King's court, as opposed to the lesser manorial or baronial courts. This use of the King's Peace as well as the King's courts would be the back door through which Henry II would bring his innovations into the English legal system. It has been written that "English law and its modes of procedure were neither invented under, nor by, Henry II; instead, the law became articulate – developing after some years – into a habit of legal practice, with its writs and its forms of action, its juries and its assizes."[32] Henry Plantagenet would gain much by use of his new legal procedures, and he would do so by means of evolution and not by revolution.

One of the first steps of replacing the old baronial courts would be to lure more and more cases into the King's courts. One method of doing this was by simply offering a better form of justice than could be hoped for in the older, lesser courts. There was also the employment of new royal writs. By definition, a writ is simply a formal legal document either ordering or prohibiting some action. If an English subject could establish a relationship between one of these royal writs and his case, then he was entitled to have his case brought before one of the King's courts. As more and more of Henry's subjects sought justice in his courts, it just brought about conditions whereby the old courts and their archaic forms of justice fell into greater levels of disuse.

For most sovereigns of the time, the achievements that Henry II had accomplished by this period in his life would have satisfied them for a lifetime. But for Henry Plantagenet, there seemed to be more to accomplish. Having unified the island in the aftermath of the years of Stephen, and having used the ancient customs of scutage and the King's Peace to further consolidate his power within his Angevin Empire, Henry now sought to gain some level of control over that other most powerful of institutions, the Church.

The Church had played an increasingly important role in Western Europe ever since Constantine the Great had Christianized the Roman Empire in the fourth century A.D. For a very long time it had even existed as a near co-equal of the other powers of state. In Saxon England, it was generally regarded that the monarch was appointed by God with not only the intention of ruling the state but to protect and guide the Church in England as well. However, by the time of Pope Gregory VII in 1073, this view was beginning to change. The new Gregorian view was that the Church was now separate from the state and that the government of the Church should be exclusively in the hands of the clergy under direct supervision from the Pope in Rome. The king was to be but a layman whose sole purpose was obedience to the Church hierarchy. Bishops by this time were fully as powerful as barons, as they were great landowners who could, if need be, field armies of their own. Bishops held one other great authority as well; in that they had the authority to excommunicate those they might view as being enemies of the Church. To a man such as Henry Plantagenet, such challenges to his authority could not have gone unnoticed.

In 1162, eight years into his reign, the opportunity to impose his will over that of the Church seemed to appear before him. In that year, Theobold, the Archbishop of Canterbury passed away. As could be expected, Henry viewed this as a clear opportunity and asked his chancellor Thomas Becket to fill the vacant post. For years Becket had acted as the King's loyal council and it was said that, "Never in Christian times were two men more of a mind."[33] It had been Becket who had assisted the king with scutage and with the razing of the illegal castles that had become so common during the years of Stephen. In 1158, Becket had acted as a royal diplomat, traveling to Paris at the head of an entourage said to number in excess of 200. Initially, Becket would decline the offer to become archbishop, claiming that it would be nearly impossible for one man to serve both the king and the Church at the same time. To the King whom he had served so ably for years he is said to have remarked, "You will soon hate me as much as you love me now, for you assume an authority in the affairs of the Church to which I shall never assent."[34] Having served Henry Plantagenet for so many years as Chancellor, Thomas A. Becket must surely have known the mind of the man he would be dealing with.

Events would prove his prophecy true. During the reign of Henry I, the local courts of the feudal baronage had been shorn of much of their power, and Henry Plantagenet had for years continued these policies. The one exception had been the Church courts, who were regarded as having a right of justice over the whole body of educated men throughout England. With the appointment of Becket as archbishop, Henry at once proposed to the bishops that a clerk, convicted of a crime, should be removed from the jurisdiction of the Church and handed over to the King's tribunals. The actions of Henry II should have come as no surprise, as his grandfather Henry I had years earlier introduced edicts that the monarch should be supreme in all civil matters. However, having assumed the post as Archbishop of Canterbury, Becket dedicated himself in his entirety to the job at hand. He would, without the support of either the Pope or the monks, set about to defend church rights in opposition to the king.

A year after becoming archbishop, Becket traveled to the continent with his bishops to meet with Pope Alexander III. This meeting served to stiffen his resolve, and he returned to England more determined than ever to defend the rights of the Church from interference from his monarch. In response, Henry drew up his Constitution of Clarendon. "Many of its clauses were simply a re-enactment of the system established by the Conqueror."[35] There were many provisions binding the bishops and abbots to the King. However, there was new legislation contained within this document regarding ecclesiastical jurisdiction, as Henry once again attempted to assert the authority of the King's courts over the Church courts in civil matters. As could be expected, the king's former chancellor and confidant put forth a passionate refusal. Eventually Becket would place his seal of approval on these constitutions. However, at a council held in Northampton a short time later, Becket would be heard reasserting the authority of the Church, much to the further dismay of Henry II. By this point the rift between the determined monarch and the stubborn clergyman had reached a point of no return. Undoubtedly fearful of an enraged king, Becket retired to France, where he would remain for the next six years.

It is perhaps at this point that one might regard the power and influence of Henry Plantagenet as having reached its high water mark. There would be further successes, and many challenges to his authority would be put down. However, the winds of change were beginning to blow, and not in a direction favorable to Henry. Green once wrote that "There is throughout a tragic grandeur in the irony of Henry's position, that of a Sforza of the fifteenth century set in the midst of the twelfth, building up by patience and policy and craft a composite dominion, alien to the deepest sympathies of his age, and swept away in the end by popular forces to whose existence his very cleverness and activity blinded him."[36] Perhaps the greatest tragedy would be that most of the reasons for his demise would come from those who had always been closest to him.

The rift between the King and his principal antagonist,

Becket, would in time subside. For six years the King and the Prelate would hold firm in their respective positions, with Henry having his oldest son coronated by the Archbishop of York in defiance of Becket, and with Becket resorting to the use of excommunication as his weapon of choice. In 1170 a reconciliation would occur between Henry and Becket at Fretheval with the Archbishop being allowed to return to England. Upon nearing the English coast the ever-prescient Becket is reported to have remarked to his entourage, "You will wish yourself elsewhere before fifty days are gone."[37] Upon his return to Canterbury he is reported to have said to his congregation, "the more potent and fierce the prince is, the stronger stick and harder chain is needed to bind him."[38] To the further dismay of Henry, Becket even went so far as to excommunicate those members of the clergy who had supported Henry during Becket's six-year absence from England.

By December of 1170, the breach between the former friends had reached the point that there could be but one inevitable conclusion. During a fit of rage, Henry cried out while in the presence of others, "What miserable drones and traitors have I nurtured within my household, that they let their lord be treated with such shameful contempt by a low-born cleric?"[39] Whether or not the King was speaking literally or figuratively would be hard to ascertain. As events would transpire on the twenty-ninth of December of that year, four knights would descend upon Becket while he was at prayers in Canterbury and he would be struck down in front of the altar much as Julius Caesar had been stricken down in the Senate of Rome.

Although Henry played no actual part in the death of his former friend and chancellor, because of the violent words he had blurted out during his fit of rage months earlier, the death of Becket was attributed to him. All Europe was shocked by the murderous act, the consequences of which would plague Henry for years to come. They would in a way also signal a change in his fortunes, which had until this time always been good. In addition, other unfavorable conditions in his life would combine to sap him of his will and strength.

In an attempt to placate the Church and absolve himself of any responsibility in the death of Becket, Henry would agree to make concessions with the Church and even allow himself to be scourged in public as a means to expiate him of his sins. Becket would be canonized and become the most popular of English saints.

For Henry there would be further clouds on the horizon. His marriage to Eleanor of Aquitaine had proven to be the coup of the century and had added much to his Angevin Empire. However, Henry was a conqueror of women as much as he was a conqueror of kingdoms. It is rumored that in addition to his children from Eleanor, that there may have been several illegitimate children as well, perhaps as many as a dozen. The most notorious of his mistresses was a damsel known to history as Fair Rosamund. Learning of the mistress would cause an irrevocable break between Henry and Eleanor, as the queen chose to return to the Angevin capital of Poitiers, from which she would spend much of her later years conspiring with her children to bring about the fall of the King and just generally giving him no end of grief. In England the queen would incite a rebellion by the English earls Robert of Leicester and Bigod of Norfolk. On the continent, Louis of France viewed the rift between Henry and Eleanor as an opportunity, and in the years to come would be all too happy to assist her in her efforts to undermine the authority of Henry II in France. Perhaps most hurtful for the King would be the fact that Eleanor and Louis of France would be assisted in their attempts to undermine the king by the King's own sons. Of the eight children which Eleanor had born for Henry, there would be several daughters who would be married off to kings of Sicily, Castile and Saxony. For the three eldest sons there would be titles and lands, as young Henry would be given Normandy, Richard would receive Aquitaine, and Geoffrey would receive Brittany. The problem was, however, that there was much of the father in the sons. Having been given power, the sons could only aspire to more power. For whatever reason the younger son, John, would become the King's favorite. In 1183, grief would come to Henry Plantagenet when his eldest son died in Aquitaine. The next in line of succession would be Richard, who would become known to history as Coeur DeLion, or Richard the Lionheart. Richard would spend much of his life as a soldier, and at that time he possessed a fervent desire to travel to the Middle East so as to participate in the Third Crusade. However, he was reluctant to depart until Henry had settled the issue of succession by naming him as heir to the throne. This, Henry was reluctant to do. Perhaps offended and perhaps as a means of retaliation, Richard would join his mother and the French king in an assault on his father's dukedom of Anjou. In fact, in the latter years of his life, Henry would be forced to put down no less than four assaults from his own wife and sons.

In the midst of these many crises Henry II continued about his work toward legal reform in England. Although he had been forced to back away from some of the provisions in his Constitution of Clarendon with the Compromise of Avranches in 1172, he was able to settle his dispute with the Papacy on terms which were comparatively easy. During his many struggles with his own sons, in the years to come even the Papacy was very supportive of him. Henry would also continue in his efforts to expand the Angevin Empire, settling disputes in Wales and gaining some measure of control over Ireland with the Council of Cashel in February of 1172. With the following constitutions resulting from this council, Henry agreed to grant certain privileges to the clergy of Ireland. In exchange they swore an oath of fealty to him and agreed to his over-lordship of the island. As for the barons of Ireland, Henry was able to gain some measure of control over these lands as well by accepting their lands from them in a form of formal surrender and then re-granting them to them in exchange for their loyalty. His actions proved to be a valiant and shrewd effort to gain control over a region that seemed to know only perpetual warfare.

For nearly his entire life, Henry had either been fighting to gain control over a kingdom or fighting to keep it from breaking apart. In his early years he was known to have had great reserves of physical strength and a very determined will which had allowed him to overcome his many adversaries. In 1180, France received a new king known to history as Philip Augustus. He would rule France for four decades and prove to be an able antagonist for the aged Angevin king.

Yet it would be troubles within his own family that would cause Henry Plantagenet the greatest harm and provide an opportunity for Philip Augustus to break Angevin power in France. In 1183, civil war broke out between Henry's sons in regard to a castle built by Richard at Clairvaux, which the young Henry regarded as being on lands which were given him by his father. As a result of the dispute, the young Henry, assisted by his brother Geoffrey, would attack Poitiou and those castles held by Richard. In an attempt to settle the dispute, Henry Plantagenet gathered an army that he used to blockade Limoges, which was the center of operations for the two rebellious sons Henry and Geoffrey. As fate would have it, the young Henry would become ill during the rebellion and would die on June 11 of that year. Henry would soon take Limoges and Geoffrey would be forced to quit the rebellion and ask for his father's forgiveness.

Unfortunately, although the death of the young Henry had brought about the end of the civil war and had erased one problem, it only led to a set of conditions that would cause a worse problem. As the young Henry had been named as a successor to the Angevin Empire, with his passing there was the need to put forth a new successor. At a meeting with his remaining sons in Normandy in September of 1183, Henry proposed that as next in line, Richard would receive Normandy, Anjou and England and hold suzerainty of Brittany, Aquitaine, Scotland, Wales and Ireland. Geoffrey would hold Brittany under Richard and John would receive Aquitaine with Richard as overlord. However, in his attempts to placate his wayward sons, he may have unintentionally inflamed the situation. As Henry had just been forced to deal with rebellion at the hands of one heir, he was not inclined to naming another so soon. This would bring about a rift between the father and the son he had just assisted in the recent rebellion.

For a time Henry remained in control of the situation and there would be the usual moves and countermoves between Henry, Philip Augustus of France and Henry's troublesome sons. On August 19, 1186, Henry would lose another son when

Geoffrey was killed during a tournament. It was an unpleasant death as he died from internal injuries after being trampled to death by a horse. As Geoffrey had already displayed signs of loyalty to the French king as opposed to his own father, there could be but little remorse on the part of the father. Perhaps there was even some measure of relief.

However, it would be a combination of the third rebellious son, Richard, along with the continued intrigues of Philip Augustus that would lead to the end of the greatest man of his age. In May of 1187 war broke out between Henry and the French king, although perhaps fortunately for both the crises was averted when a two-year truce was signed on June 23 of that year. But two years passes quickly when dealing with two very strong personalities who have been thrown into conflict. The two-year truce would hold, but by the summer of 1189, war would break out again. This time Henry would face two determined antagonists, as Richard was demanding concessions from his father so as to guarantee that he would inherit his fathers' realm, and Philip simply sought the destruction of Angevin power on the Continent. When the combined forces of Richard and Philip struck in 1189, Henry found himself without the Angevin luck that had sustained him for so many years. City after city fell to the French army. In June of 1189, LeMans, which was the birthplace of Henry Plantagenet, fell to the French as well. It was a cruel blow to a man who had never tasted the bitter cup of defeat. By July, the situation had worsened to the point that Henry was forced to seek terms. Deathly ill and possibly suffering from blood poisoning from a wound in his foot, the fifty-six-year-old king would be forced to submit to humiliating terms. He was to pay homage to Philip, to make all of his barons swear allegiance to

Richard, to pay an indemnity of 20,000 marks, and surrender castles to Richard and Philip Augustus.[40] It appears to be the worst setback of his illustrious career. With the terms of peace settled upon, Henry returned to Chinon in Normandy.

Henry was not to suffer from the agony of defeat long. Still extremely ill, the final straw that would end the career of this lion of his age would come on July 5 when he learned that his longtime favorite son John had joined forces with his brother Richard and the French king. Upon hearing the news of this latest act of treachery from his sons Henry simply stated, "Now let things go as they will – I care no more for myself or for the world."[41] The following day, July 6, 1189, would be his last. Perhaps recognizing his end was at hand, he had himself carried into the chapel and placed before the altar. It is recorded that his last words were "Shame, shame on a conquered king."[42] Such sentiments could most likely be expected from a man who had accomplished so much in a mere fifty-six years of living during such a turbulent age.

As with the Carolingian dynasty of Charlemagne, the Angevin dynasty would not last long without the force that Henry II had always been. With his father's passing, Richard would visit his father's body as he lay in state. He would stay but just minutes, apparently with little remorse at the death of his own father. Soon he would depart for the Third Crusade, but would prove himself no Godfrey of Boullion and most certainly no equal to his father. He would be captured and held for ransom, only adding to the weight of taxation incurred by his people who were already being taxed to pay for the Third Crusade. With his death from a crossbow wound in April of 1199, he would be forced to name his brother John as heir to the throne. The disaster that had been the reign of Richard was followed upon by the worse disaster of the reign of John, who would manage to lose nearly all of his father's possessions in France to the man of the hour, Philip Augustus.

But while his sons may have unwisely lost most of what their father had gained, they could never lose the legacy of his contributions to English society in the sphere of his legal reforms. English Common Law as initiated by Henry remains today, and its benefits have over the years been transferred from the old world to the new. It is said that Henry Plantagenet died as a lion savaged by jackals. He was no doubt far from perfect. Yet he was certainly the greatest statesman of his era, as well as a capable soldier. During his years as king the English people would know security and peace, as well as prosperity. It is a great irony that popular history has made Richard the Lionheart and John far more famous. But the failures of the sons have never been able to erase the successes of the father, and that is the importance of Henry Plantagenet, greatest of his age.

Chapter IV

¤

GREATNESS UNKNOWN

It has often been said that fortune has her favorites, those who seem to have an unexplainable streak of good luck that propels them to fame and fortune. History seems to have its favorites as well; those who may be entirely without luck but for some unexplained reason become the stuff of legend or lore. Incongruous as it may seem, sometimes the best intentioned men of their time may be swept away into a condition of complete obscurity while the most ill intentioned of men are carried along to become forever renowned. This happenstance can occur within any society, to include our own. In examining our own history, one need not look long before we encounter an individual who was the equal of his peers in intellect, ability and accomplishment, yet is a virtual unknown among the giants of his day.

Many if not all Americans are aware of the circumstances of the founding of this nation. The names of George Washington, Benjamin Franklin and Thomas Jefferson will forever be recognized with the Spirit of '76 and our War of Independence from Great Britain. Many of the same names will always be associated with this nation's formative years when the issue of this new nation's survival was still very much in doubt. George Washington will always be regarded as the father of our country, while James Madison is said to be the father of the Constitution. Rarely in history does one find a collection of individuals as intellectually gifted as our founding fathers, or as judicious and wise. Perhaps all of them are deserving of an equal share in the credit for the birth of our country, yet issues of popularity and personality seem to have elevated a few to a position above the rest, while others equally as deserving or perhaps politically less astute have either become obscure to us or have simply achieved a less favorable status.

Much of this may simply be conditional. George Washington will always be thought of as one of our greatest presidents. Yet John Adams, who did much to secure the blessings of constitutional government for this nation and sacrificed many years of his life to that end, is far less popular and perhaps even unknown to many. Much of this may be due to his very intractable nature. He is not unique in this very unfortunate situation.

Unknown to many there was another man of limitless energy and unlimited ability who served his state and his country admirably during the very uncertain years when this country first fought to become independent, and then struggled to retain that same independence. Born as a subject of Great Britain in December of 1745, he would become one of the greatest statesmen of his time, and then somehow become obscure to the citizens of a country that owed him a substantial debt of gratitude. He would serve at all levels of government, both state and federal, though some of the greatest prizes, such as the presidency, would elude him. Like many of his peers, after many years of active and important service to his nation, he would retire peacefully to a life of farming in his native state.

Like so many of the men who would participate in the events of 1776 through our nation's formative years, John Jay would be born into a wealthy colonial family when he was born in New York City in December of 1745. Members of his family were not only part of the mercantile class in colonial America, but many also served at various levels of government in the fledgling colonies. This providential set of circumstances would afford him the opportunity to receive a high level of education during a time when the majority of the inhabitants of colonial America were engaged in agriculture, literally hacking their existence out of the wilderness. The family of John Jay was descended from the Huguenots who had come to New York to escape religious persecution in France. John's paternal grandfather, Augustus Jay, was the first of the Jay family to arrive in colonial America, where he set about to establish his own mercantile empire. His son Peter Jay, who was to become John Jay's father, was born in New York City in 1704. He would follow in the footsteps of his father, becoming a wealthy trader of furs, wheat, timber and other commodities, prevalent to the early British colonies. In 1728, Peter Jay married Mary Van Cortlandt, whose father had twice served as mayor of New York City, and held a number of other judicial and military offices. The couple would have a total of ten children together, seven of whom would survive until adulthood during an age when infant deaths were frequent, if not expected. Three months after the birth of John Jay, the family relocated from New York City to Rye, New York.

As for his early life and education, as was true for most of the young men of his generation, he would begin by being educated at home for a time before being sent away to continue his education under the tutelage of someone from the church. In the case of John Jay, he would be sent by his parents to New Rochelle where he would be instructed by an Anglican Priest named Pierre Stoupe. He would remain there for a period of three years until returning home again to receive further instruction from his mother and one George Murray. At age fifteen, John Jay was admitted to Kings College, an institution which would at some point become Columbia University. While at Kings College, he would make several influential friends, friends who would one day share in the trials and triumphs of founding a new nation. In 1764, Jay would graduate Kings College.

Within weeks of his graduation from Kings College, Jay would become a law clerk for the prominent New York lawyer, Benjamin Kissam. His initial salary was 200 pounds for five years of service. However, as with all men of ability and ambition, he would eventually move on, establishing his own law firm in 1771. Under normal circumstances, Jay might have spent his whole life in anonymity, his abilities going unnoticed by history. However, the prevailing winds of political change and the differences between the mother country of England and her North American colony would force Jay to become a participant in the formation of a new, democratic country. When the New York Committee of Correspondence was formed in 1774, Jay would become an active member and serve as its secretary. It would be the first time, but by no means the last, that his countrymen would hear his name. As relations between the mother country and her colony worsened, Jay attempted to maintain a course of moderation, though he did tend to distance himself from the loyalists, of which there were plenty in New York City. He would represent his colony during both Continental Congresses, though he was opposed to immediate separation from the mother country and continued to urge reconciliation.

As the storm clouds continued to gather, Jay would unsheathe his pen and draft the first of many important writings on continental and governmental policies. He would write his "Address to the People of Great Britain" in an attempt to clarify the position of the British colonies in their opposition to British rule. Even after hostilities had begun, he helped draft the Oliver Branch Petition, which was sent directly to King George III. But a defiant King was by this time unwilling to deal with his unruly stepchildren in the colonies. In the aftermath of the Battles of Lexington and Concord in the spring of 1775, and with the siege of Boston having begun when nearly 15,000 colonial militia surrounded the city and its British garrison shortly thereafter, any path toward reconciliation seemed unlikely. On June 15, 1775, the Second Continental Congress would adopt the militia surrounding Boston as a new Continental Army and appoint Colonel George Washington of

Virginia as its general. On July 3 of that year Washington would assume command of the provincial force on Cambridge Common, and Jay, along with his fellow colonists, would find themselves at war with the mother country.

Having already served in the Continental Congress for some time, Jay would decide to resign in May of 1776 so as to attend New York's new provincial legislature, where he served from 1776 until 1777. The decision to resign at this time cost him the ability to be a participant in the signing of the Declaration of Independence in July of that year. However, even at that late date "His ambivalence about independence is a matter of record."[43]

British actions in the spring and summer of 1776 would alter Jay's perception of the rebellion when, in the aftermath of the British evacuation of Boston, they would move an army of 30,000 men to Staten Island. Although always more of a scholar than a soldier, Jay would begin to actively participate in the war by employing a number of spies in a counterintelligence operation. He would also help to uncover a Tory plot to capture George Washington, an act which if successful may have altered the course of history. As a member of the provincial legislature, he assisted in the framing of the New York State Constitution and, possibly due to his previous legal experience and education, was appointed first chief justice of his state's supreme court. It would be a capacity in which he would not serve long, as he would be re-elected to the Continental Congress in 1778.

No sooner would Jay return to Congress, than affairs in Europe and a factional split in Congress would propel him into another position of importance. Once the war against the mother country had begun it became of paramount importance for the newly independent nation to acquire military provisions. The most likely source of these provisions would be England's natural enemy, France. To that end, in 1776, Silas Deane had been dispatched to France to acquire the needed aid, a task in which he succeeded admirably. However, Arthur Lee of Virginia would later join Deane and Benjamin Franklin in Paris. Within a very short time span the ever suspicious and combative Lee would begin making accusations that Deane was more concerned with adding to his own fortunes by means of personal profits gained from the aid being sent to America from France. The situation became serious enough that Deane would be recalled from France to answer before Congress. The Silas Deane-Arthur Lee rivalry then split the Congress into factions, those who were supportive of Deane and those who were supportive of Lee. The acting president of Congress, Henry Laurens of South Carolina, who was a supporter of Lee, felt compelled to resign over the issue. Within three days of his arrival as a delegate from New York, John Jay found himself as the new president of Congress, perhaps because he was regarded as being pro-French. But by this time Jay was regarded as being a man of consummate ability as well. On the day of Jay's election to the new post, Gouverneur Morris was to write to George Clinton "the weight of his personal character contributed as much to his election as the respect for the state which hath done and suffered so much or the regard for its delegates which is not inconsiderable."[44]

Jay served as president of Congress from December 10, 1778 until September 29, 1779. In his capacities as president of the Congress, he would be confronted with innumerable obstacles. As a result of the Deane-Lee rivalry, the Secretary to the Committee for Foreign Affairs, Thomas Paine, became entangled in an imbroglio of his own when he sided with Lee and was so indiscreet as to disclose secret information in regard to France and to America prior to the alliance which had been signed between the Continental Congress and France in 1778. As a result of his indiscretions, Paine was called before Congress but would resolve the issue himself when he chose instead to resign his post before any disciplinary action could be taken against him.

Other issues of far greater importance were to arise during the nine-month presidency of Jay. As the fortunes of war alternated between victory and defeat for the Continental Army and its commander, there would be many who would be critical of General Washington and, in the aftermath of the Conway Cabal, would still seek his dismissal as commander of the army. Realizing that there existed no other person in the colonies with the ability to hold together an army of raw recruits and volunteers under the worst of conditions, Jay was quick to offer his support to Washington by writing to Washington personally of his "unshaken confidence, respect, and affection for the Commander in Chief."[45]

As President of the Continental Congress, Jay was also involved in attempts to get the thirteen separate colonies to accept the Articles of Confederation as a new form of federal government. Most of the states were in favor of accepting the Articles as a new form of government. However, tiny Maryland was in opposition to this measure unless the other states which had claims to western lands agreed to place control over these areas under the authority of the Congress. In response to this crisis, Jay would pen his letter "From Congress to their Constituents." He would invoke many arguments in favor of passage of the Articles of Confederation in this letter, to include that all thirteen states had agreed to the Declaration of Independence, and that twelve of the thirteen had agreed to the Articles. However, unanimity was required for passage, and Maryland would hold up passage until March 1, 1781; well after Jay had left his position as President of Congress.

Perhaps as a result of the continued fallout from the Silas Deane affair, by 1779 the Congress had decided that what was now needed were single emissaries to each of the European powers from which the new nation sought support in its efforts to become free and independent from Great Britain. Benjamin Franklin was the obvious choice for representative to France, while John Adams became the emissary to Great Britain. As a representative to the United Provinces or Holland, Henry Laurens was chosen. While the supporters of Arthur Lee argued in his favor to have him appointed as minister to Spain, John Jay would ultimately receive this important post. It was hoped that he could convince Spain to recognize American independence as well as secure new loans to help fund the continuing war against the British. This mission would consume the next four years of his life. Unfortunately, Spain still held possessions in North America, and no doubt because of this the Spanish were not at all pleased by the thought that the United States might arise from the war supreme and gain control of the continent. Ultimately, Jay would be less than successful in his mission, although this would prove to be no fault of his own.

In the summer of 1782, John Jay found himself in a new role, one which suited his abilities admirably, that of peacemaker. Before stepping down as President of Congress, Jay had predicted that "the independence of America is now fixed as fate, and the petulant efforts of Britain to break it down are as vain and fruitless as the raging of the waves which beat against her cliffs."[46] His prediction had proven true. In the aftermath of Cornwallis' defeat at Yorktown, Virginia in October of 1781, it became increasingly obvious that in all likelihood England would not subdue her rebellious colonies. When the ministry of Lord North collapsed on the twentieth of March 1782, Britain initiated peace talks. To that end, on June 23, 1782, John Jay and his wife Sally arrived in Paris from Madrid and joined Benjamin Franklin and John Adams as a negotiator for the American cause. The task before these very capable statesmen could not have been more difficult, as the European powers and their longstanding rivalries slowed negotiations considerably. Also restrictive to the three American emissaries were the instructions from Congress from June 15, 1781, which instructed them to "govern themselves by the advice and opinion of the King of France."[47] They were further advised that independence by peace or truce and the maintenance of the country's alliance with France were the two most important objectives of their mission. This of course put Jay and his contemporaries in a most difficult position, as instead of having to arrive at a peace treaty between two nations with sizeable differences, they found themselves in a position of having to conclude a treaty between multiple nations with a long history of animosity between them.

Finding themselves in a most difficult position, the three very able American ambassadors found a solution. And in that solution Jay may have taken the lead. When it was learned that France was delaying negotiations intentionally so as to find out the fate of Gibraltar, Jay, in response to a question from Franklin about their instructions remarked, "We can depend on the French only to see that we are separated from England, but it is not in their interest that we should become a great and formidable people, and therefore they will not help us become so."[48] He would further add that, "Unless we violate these instructions the dignity of Congress will be in the dust," and when further pressed by Franklin on the issue, offered as his final response, "If the instructions conflict with America's honor and dignity, I would break them – Like this!"[49] It is reputed that his comment was accompanied by the throwing of his clay pipe into the fireplace. Eventually, his fellow commissioners were to join him in his view, and a separate treaty of peace would be achieved between the newly formed United States of America and Great Britain. By November of 1782, a preliminary agreement was reached between the two nations. In September of 1783 the Treaty of Paris was signed, which formally ended the Revolutionary War. Its provisions recognized American independence; ceded territory east of the Mississippi River to the United States with the exception of Spanish Florida; provided for fishing rights off the coast of Newfoundland and; provided for the British evacuation of some of its forts along America's new frontier. Though far from perfect, it can be said that Franklin, Jay and Adams had accomplished fully as much as could be expected, given the circumstances.

With the end of his mission resulting in peace between the two nations, Jay could possibly have been expected to return to a life of peace himself in his former practice of law. However, when he returned to Congress in 1784, he found that he had already been appointed as the secretary of foreign affairs as provided for under the Articles of Confederation. Much of the task before him would involve ironing out the terms of the newly signed peace treaty. However, under the Articles of

Confederation, very little power was afforded to the Congress and the federal government. Within months it became apparent that the infant nation would need to draft a new form of government if it chose to survive and thrive in the future. To that end, in the spring of 1785, a new Federal Convention was formed when a dispute arose between the states of Maryland and Virginia in regard to navigational rights on the Potomac River. Initially, all of the states with the exception of Rhode Island would send delegates to the convention with the intended purpose of revising the Articles of Confederation. In fact, after the Annapolis Commission had recommended the convention to Congress, it appointed seventy-four delegates to meet in Philadelphia with "the sole and express purpose of revising the Articles of Confederation." What was to follow was no revision at all, but the drafting of a new constitutional form of government, which was to serve as an experiment in self-government.

John Jay did not participate in the Constitutional Convention, as it came to be known. Also conspicuous by their absence were Thomas Jefferson, who was in France, John Adams, who was in England and some of the firebrands of 1776, such as Samuel Adams and Patrick Henry. However, even after the new Constitution had been drafted, it still had to be accepted by Congress and ratified by the states. It would be during the struggle for ratification when John Jay would again lend his abilities to his new nation. In favor of a strong national government, Jay assisted Alexander Hamilton and James Madison in writing a series of arguments in favor of ratification. Written under the pseudonym Publius, the arguments became collectively known as the Federalist Papers.

As Jay had just spent four years in Spain as an emissary

during the latter years of the Revolutionary war, had served as a member of the peace commission during the negotiating of the Treaty of Paris which ended the war, and had been appointed to serve as secretary of foreign affairs under the Articles of Confederation, it should come as no surprise that in the Federalist Papers much of Jay's writings would concern dangers to the new nation from foreign force and influence.

Unfortunately for Jay, due to illness, his contribution to the Federalist Papers would constitute only five of the eighty-five articles written. Therefore, history has consigned his role in the effort as being only a "part time" contribution. But his arguments were clear and concise and, thanks to the efforts of Jay and his fellow nationalists, the United States Constitution would be ratified by the requisite number of states and become the law of the land.

When the Constitution took effect as the nation's new form of government and George Washington was elected president, Jay would be remembered for both his abilities and his past contributions to the cause of the new nation. As the new Constitution called for not only a Chief Executive but also a Vice President and numerous Secretaries as well, there were many positions which needed to be filled. Also, as George Washington was to be the first of his kind in his capacity as president, it was necessary to set a precedents. Washington himself would write, "The eyes of Argus are upon me and no slip will pass unnoticed that can be improved into a supposed partiality for friends or relatives."[50] There was the possibility of John Jay as first Vice President, however, "The vice presidential candidates Madison and Washington had spoken of most highly in their private conversations, John Jay and General Henry Knox, were unwilling."[51] As the Judiciary Act of

September 24, 1789 allowed for the creation of a Supreme Court consisting of a Chief Justice with five associate justices, there existed the need for someone with a legal mind and noticeable abilities to fill the position of first Chief Justice. Washington himself had written, "Impressed with a conviction that the due administration of justice is the firmest pillar of government, I have considered the first arrangement of the Judicial department as essential to the happiness of our country and the stability of its political system."[52] Therefore, Washington appointed John Jay to fill the vacant position, with his advisor James Madison concurring readily.

The choice of Jay as Chief Justice would prove a wise one. When the court held its first session in New York on February 2, 1790, they would immediately begin setting precedent simply by discarding the famous white wig which had become the custom of English judges in English courts. Jay and his contemporaries would begin to establish other precedents as well. Judicial review, which is the ability of the court to declare state and federal laws as being either constitutional or unconstitutional, was established while Jay served as Chief Justice during a number of cases. In the case of Chisholm v. George, the first court ruled that an ordinary citizen had the constitutional right to sue any state or corporation. Furthermore, in 1791, in a case brought before the court in regard to British debts from the Revolutionary War, the court struck down a Connecticut law as having infringed upon Article VI of the Treaty of Paris. In 1792, the court found a Rhode Island state law unconstitutional as it violated the obligation of contracts.

In addition to judicial review, Jay may have also done his country a great favor by establishing the principle of judicial impartiality. This would happen when his co-writer of the Federalist Papers, Alexander Hamilton, asked the court to rule against opponents of a bill that would allow the federal government to assume state debts. It was, in the opinion of Jay, the court's responsibility to rule on the constitutionality of bills, not to act as a legislative agent to lobby for or against them. And in this, he was right.

Yet for John Jay, as with many other great men, his intelligence and probity would thrust him into a situation of much animosity and unpopularity. In the aftermath of the Revolutionary War, the commercial ties between Great Britain and the United States remained strong. Yet in defiance of the Treaty of Paris, the British did not relinquish many of their forts along the American frontier, and with a preponderance in naval might they engaged in the impressments of American sailors and in an unfair balance of trade with heavy tariffs being placed on American goods. When these conditions both continued and escalated, George Washington asked John Jay go to England to resolve these issues. It would require Jay to take a leave of absence from the court and would place him in a less than advantageous position, much the same as when he was emissary to Spain and peace commissioner in Paris. It must be remembered that in 1794 the United States had an enormous debt from the previous war. It had a diminutive army and virtually no navy, and with an untried new form of government America was probably not secure enough to enter into a new war. Therefore, Jay found himself with little leverage at the bargaining table. Perhaps recognizing this and realizing that Jay would be wise enough to understand much of the same, Washington sent forth his able agent, secure in his hopes that Jay would arrive at a bargain that could be as good as expected under such disadvantageous conditions, while at the same time avoiding a war America could not expect to win and certainly could not afford.

Unfortunately for Jay, the timing of his mission coincided with the birth of the two-party political system in this country and there were many who hoped he would not succeed. As a Federalist, his views put him at odds with those in the Jeffersonian Republican party. There were many who felt him to be too much of an anglophile and feared he would be soft in his negotiations. This is a curious viewpoint, for all of his grandparents had moved to the New World from either France or Holland. Therefore, he had no real ties to England. To make matters worse, "Hamilton had secretly assured the British Minister that the United States would not under any circumstances enter into agreements of armed neutrality hostile of Great Britain, and that, learning this, the British negotiators of the treaty were emboldened to resist every American claim."[53] Any leverage that Jay might have had going into the negotiations was removed before he even left for England.

Also troubling for Jay was the fact that many of the issues he was sent to negotiate involved matters purely financial. There were many in America who sought compensation from England for slaves who had been confiscated during the war, while English creditors sought compensation for debts owed to them by Americans who had borrowed extensively from English merchants and banks prior to the war. The planters of Virginia were most notable as having incurred large amounts of debt, and as could be expected, they were not at all eager to repay debts that they hoped independence from Great Britain had freed them from.

There was much speculation as to what the results of the

treaty would be and, as it was such a contentious issue, both the Federalist and Democratic Republicans were quick to put a political spin on the results. Even before the results of the treaty were known, the Federalists began to defend it while the friends of Thomas Jefferson viewed it as an issue that could be divisive and possibly act as a brake on Federalist gains in the governance of the new nation. As to the situation, Jay was confronted with such conjectures as, "Republicans sought to prepare the people to be indignant should Jay return with a treaty in the least subservient to England, while Federalist spared no industry to prepare the public mind to echo the praises of Jay should he return with an agreement assuring peace with Great Britain."[54]

During an age when seagoing vessels were powered by the wind and there existed no telegraph or telephone, the results of the 1794 Treaty of Amity, or Jay's Treaty as it became known, were not received for some time. When they finally became known, the reaction was not favorable toward Jay. His Federalist friend and co-author of the Federalist Papers, Hamilton, referred to it as "an old woman's treaty." Even though Jay was able to get the British to evacuate the western forts which were on American territory, many of the other issues were either unresolved or the terms favored the British. In commerce, Great Britain was granted a most favored nation status, which guaranteed that America would remain dependent on British trade. This caused great consternation to the Republican party, which sought better trade with France and an end to American dependence on British markets. The slave issue went unresolved as did the issue of impressments of American sailors by the Royal Navy. There was a provision in the treaty for commissioners to examine pre-Revolutionary debts, boundary claims and the seizure of American vessels, but without guarantees that American grievances would be resolved. The treaty that Jay had entered the United States into "was a repudiation of the Franco-American Alliance of 1778, which had been so instrumental in gaining French military assistance for the winning of the American Revolution."[55]

The terms of the treaty were so unpopular on this side of the Atlantic that Washington attempted to keep its provisions secret until after it had been ratified by the Senate. John Jay himself concluded that in the summer of 1795 he could travel from Boston to New York at night by the light of his effigies that were burned. Washington's house in Philadelphia was surrounded daily by angry mobs demanding war with England. Thomas Paine, who had always been a supporter of Washington told the President that he was "treacherous in private friendship and a hypocrite in public... The world will be puzzled to decided whether you are an apostate or imposter; whether you have abandoned good principles, or whether you ever had any."[56] Much worse would be said of Jay. The treaty would even cause the country's first constitutional crises as there was debate as to whether the authority to enter into treaties with foreign governments was a power granted to the executive or legislative branches of the new government. From his retirement at Monticello, Thomas Jefferson would write of the issue of treaty-making powers and Jay's treaty in particular, "I trust the popular branch of our legislature will disapprove of it and thus rid us of this infamous act, which is really nothing more than a treaty of alliance between England and the Anglomen of this country against the legislatures and people of the United States."[57]

As with so many of the unpopular acts in history, time

would prove that in his efforts and beliefs Jay may have made the best bargain that was possible at that time. Even though reluctant to enter into the treaty, and needing much time to contemplate its consequences, Washington predicted that with the passage of time "when passion shall have yielded to sober reason, the current may possibly return."[53] John Jay was probably correct in his assessment that a war with England was not advisable at the time. The nation had incurred a massive national debt during the Revolution, and it would need time for the economic policies of Alexander Hamilton to put the United States on firm financial ground. In the aftermath of the Revolution, the attempt to pay off the war debt would cause the incomes of Americans to decline forty-six percent, so the cost of another war was totally beyond reason.

Other advantages to the treaty could be found as well. In the nineteenth century, England became the world's most important nation commercially, so close economic ties to that nation could only guarantee that our own economy would flourish in time, as it did. France, however, would never see a similar economic growth. It was in essence a very prophetic treaty. When the British garrisons maintaining the western forts were removed, so too was removed a barrier to the inward movement of American settlers; in time the thirteen original states would grow to become forty-eight states, spanning all the way to the Pacific Ocean.

The Jay Treaty would not be the end of John Jay's career. Even before he returned home, his name was submitted by Alexander Hamilton as a candidate for governor of New York, an office to which he would be elected. This would cause him to resign his position of first Chief Justice of the Supreme Court. He would serve his state well and during his tenure would abolish the practice of flogging, enact judicial reforms and eliminate corruption in state government. The Constitution had provided for an end to the slave trade by 1808. As governor of New York John Jay worked to abolish the practice of slavery in his state, but it would require numerous attempts. Nevertheless, he succeeded in his efforts and slavery would cease to exist in the State of New York during his lifetime. In 1801 John Jay retired from public life after nearly three decades of service to his state and country. As with so many of his co-founding fathers, he would retire to a life of quiet solitude away from the public eye. He continued to campaign against slavery and stay informed of agricultural reform. He was, perhaps, one of the most accomplished men of his time. Yet because he chose to put the needs of the new nation first without regard to the needs of party or popularity, his reputation was for a long time tarnished.

In the end, however, history would prove him right in his actions, although many of his contemporaries may have been blind to his attempts to act in their best interests. Eventually, 600,000 British pounds would be paid by the United States to satisfy pre-Revolutionary war debts. However, England would pay more than twice that amount, 1,317,000 pounds, as compensation for the seizure of American vessels.[59]

As an example of Jay's scruples, he, as a young man had found himself in a compromised position when some of his fellow students at Kings College destroyed a dining table in an act of mischief. When the president of the college questioned the young Jay as to who committed the act he simply replied "I do not choose to tell you, sir." It was not that Jay was in favor of the act committed, it was simply that he was a man of integrity. He would be temporarily suspended, but would retain the respect of his peers until his death. It would be his integrity and wisdom that would make him one of the unsung giants in an age where other famous names take the spotlight. Largely forgotten himself, his actions will forever stand out as an example of what a true statesman should be.

Chapter V

¤

THE WORST HARD TIME

The history of the United States has been punctuated with periods when its rise from infant nation to world superpower has been arrested by periods of severe economic distress, political and social divide and even civil war. To those alive today who lived through it, The Great Depression may seem as the country's most difficult time, as it is familiar to them through personal experience. A more recent generation may regard the years of Watergate and Vietnam in a similar light.

To the historian and the reader of American history, there may be other periods that occupy a similar niche. They might view the years 1776 to 1783 as the hardest years, as we had to fight the strongest nation on earth for our independence, which under no circumstances was assured. However, to most people, the time of greatest peril in our nation's existence must have been during the years after the culmination of our American Civil War and the assassination of perhaps our greatest chief executive.

Though at peace after the Civil War, the newly re-united nation was still very much divided, and would remain so for decades. There was the defeated South, vanquished and impoverished, yet defiant and proud. There was the issue of slavery, which as of yet was not entirely resolved, for the Emancipation Proclamation had freed only those slaves in the rebellious states. Of greater importance there remained the issue of how to integrate the former slaves both socially and economically. Aside from the shattered bodies and broken homes, the wounds of war needed to be resolved, as well as the natural resentments left behind in the aftermath of four years of the worst bloodshed known in the nation's long and celebrated history.

Fortunately for our nation, some wounds heal faster than others. The soldier must make the greatest sacrifice during times of war, and because of that he shares a special bond with his comrades that is rarely broken. There is also the respect for his enemies in defeat, as soldiering tends to be a very sobering and honorable profession. When Grant met General Robert E. Lee at Appomattox Court House in April of 1865, the terms of peace offered to the South were magnanimous and the atmosphere cordial. During the actual surrender ceremony on the 12th of April 1865, General Joshua Lawrence Chamberlain began the process of healing when he had the victorious Union soldiers show respect to a defeated foe by a salute of arms. Though much criticized for his actions, he would write of the occasion:

> *Well aware of the responsibility assumed, and of the criticisms that would follow, as the sequel proved, nothing of that kind could move me in the least. The act could be defended, if needful, by the suggestion that such a salute was not the cause for which the flag of the Confederacy stood, but its going down before the flag of the Union. My main reason, however, was one for which I sought no authority nor asked forgiveness. Before us in proud humiliation stood the embodiment of manhood: men whom neither toils and sufferings, nor the fact of death, nor disaster, nor hopelessness could bend from their resolve: standing before us now then, worn, and famished, but erect, and with eyes looking into ours, waking memories that bound us together as no other bond; was not such manhood to be welcomed back into a Union so tested and assured?*

Unfortunately, whereas those who had born the brunt of the fighting and suffering were willing to work towards a quick and peaceful restoration of the national fabric, those who had born little of the fighting and perhaps less of the sacrifice, those in the political arena, were not nearly so peaceful in their desires nor so anxious for a return to national unity. For them there would exist a need to punish a defeated South, and to impose upon them a new and unfamiliar set of beliefs.

Into this arena would walk a man basically unknown to

history, and in those instances where he is known, regarded largely as being imperfect and far less than a success when charged with the responsibility of leading his nation. His name was Andrew Johnson. Following in the footsteps of one of the greatest men that our nation has produced, as well as the first president to be assassinated, Johnson would be placed into an unfortunate set of circumstances, which would have seen the likely political demise of any individual afforded such similar conditions. Given the situation and the extreme animosity of the time, one can only ponder with what success, if any, Mr. Lincoln could have handled similar circumstances. After all, it was the election of Mr. Lincoln that brought about the determination of many of the southern states to secede from the Union, though in all likelihood the issue of slavery was just so contentious an issue that the same thing could have happened with the election of any anti-slavery president.

With the assassination of Lincoln, Andrew Johnson became the seventeenth President of the United States. As he himself was not elected to the office, the circumstances of his becoming chief executive can be regarded as being both fortuitous and unfortunate. Much of this probably had to do with the fact that in his bid to be re-elected as President in 1864, Lincoln had chosen Andrew Johnson as somewhat of a conciliatory measure, as the war was by this time regarded as being a contest in which the North would ultimately prevail and there would be an eventual need for reconciliation between North and South. The story of how Johnson became Vice-President is far more interesting. The story of his political demise is perhaps more interesting, as well as unfortunate. Beneficially for the country, there would be a number of individuals who possessed a level of wisdom and the political courage to save

Andrew Johnson from himself, and save the country from an unjustified assault on the Executive branch of our federal government.

As for Andrew Johnson the man, he was born December 29, 1808 at Raleigh, North Carolina. His early life would be one of almost unmitigated poverty, as his father died when Andrew was only three years old. His mother, finding herself in such an unpleasant set of circumstances, raised Andrew as best as she could until he could be apprenticed out to a tailor at the tender age of fourteen. When Andrew was seventeen the family departed Raleigh and moved to East Tennessee, settling in Greenville in September 1826. Relying upon his years as an apprentice, Andrew opened his own tailor shop. It should be noticed that at no time in his youth were circumstances so fortunate so as to allow him to receive any formal schooling. This is not to say that Andrew Johnson was illiterate as, like many during his time, he was able to acquire the basics of writing, especially from his wife whom he married when he was nineteen years old. Her name was Eliza McCardle and, similar to Andrew, her early years were not especially kind to her and she had been raised as an orphan. Two years younger than Andrew, she would be required to confer upon Andrew Johnson much of his ability to read and write.

Regardless of the unfortunate set of circumstances involved with his youth and his lack of any schooling, the young Andrew Johnson was fixated with a desire to improve his lot in life and at a very early age began to entertain thoughts of political service. For an individual who is often times regarded as being a failure politically, he was elected to political office early and often during his younger years. In 1829, he was elected alderman in his town; at age twenty-two he became mayor. His political fortunes would rise again when he was elected to the state legislature in 1835 and to the state senate in 1841. In 1843, the people of Tennessee elected him to serve in the United States Congress, "Ten years later, he was Governor of Tennessee."[60] During his years as Congressman and Governor, he is not remembered for any truly outstanding acts, though in Congress he was very much in favor of Homestead Legislation, and as governor he fought valiantly to raise the school tax. He was also a firm believer in the merits of public education, perhaps a reflection of the fact that such a luxury had been denied him. By 1857, his reputation and political views were such that he was elected to the United States Senate. This is where he would find himself when his home state of Tennessee seceded from the Union in the fateful year of 1861.

Like all men, Andrew Johnson was the possessor of a variety of personality traits. Many of these traits could be seen as good. In his time he was viewed as being a tireless worker, although in this habit he was without imagination and could be quite inflexible. Jefferson Davis, who also served as a Senator from the Antebellum South, once commented that "His habits were marked by temperance, industry, courage, and unswerving perseverance; also by inveterate prejudices or preconceptions on certain points, and these no arguments could change."[61] Andrew Johnson was also very methodical, as President he maintained an organized system of any business he transacted while in office, and his methods are thought to have revolutionized the administration of the executive office.

Andrew Jackson Johnson's father Jacob, who is little known to history, was regarded as being a man who, though poor, was noted for possessing the cardinal virtues of honesty and bravery. Andrew Johnson was to inherit these virtues from his father. It was said of Johnson at the time that, "He was eminently faithful to his word, and possessed a courage which took the form of angry resistance if urged to do or not do anything which might clash with his convictions of duty. He was indifferent to money, and careless of praise or censure, when satisfied on the necessity of any line of action.[62] Abraham Lincoln was fond of saying that he did not think of hardworking as being a quality in someone you would want to discourage. And, as for honesty, that quality certainly speaks for itself, especially in our more modern society where there is almost none of it and, it even seems that at times it has become fashionable to lie. Both traits, that of being hardworking and honest, can serve an individual well.

However, there were traits both personal and political which tended to hurt Andrew Johnson. As a Jacksonian Democrat, he was very fixed in his principles. Johnson himself once remarked that, "I have, during all of my political life, been guided by certain principles, I am guided by them still. They are the principles of the early founders of the Republic, and I cannot certainly go far wrong if I adhere to them, as I intend to."[63] He was fiscally conservative and well known for his tight-fistedness with what he regarded as the people's money. In Congress he had voiced strong opposition to increasing soldiers' pay during the Mexican War and was opposed to funding the Smithsonian Institute. He also tried to lower the salaries of government white-collar workers. His Jacksonian roots caused him to be ever vigilant against what he considered as extravagant government spending.

And then there was the issue of pride. Jefferson Davis once stated that Andrew Johnson had an almost morbidly sensitive pride and that he was guilty of "the pride of having no pride."[64]

Johnson had always regarded himself as having plebian origins, even taking some measure of pride in it. However, he always tended to be resentful of those who had much more than he did, which may explain why he always maintained an almost vehement hatred of the ante-bellum Southern aristocracy. His pride was such that in the political sphere, once he had taken a position on any given issue, he would view political opposition and dissimilar views as being an attack on himself. In many instances, if he believed himself to be in the right on any given issue, he could be both inflexible and intransigent. Existing in a country with a two-party political system, where the ability to seek compromise is at times almost absolutely essential, this firmness and rigidity of principle was a very serious handicap during his life.

One thing that could never be questioned about Andrew Johnson, by either friend or foe, was his loyalty and devotion to the Union. In the years prior to the Civil War, his loyalty was usually with his state and party, and he himself did not believe that the election of Abraham Lincoln as president would sever the Union. However, when it did, he broke with both state and party and remained in the U.S. Senate. He was the only Senator from a seceding state to do so. In terms of political courage it was an almost unprecedented act, as by doing so it ensured the animosity of his fellow Democrats from the South as well as all of his friends and relatives who sided with his home state of Tennessee. Although without a formal education, Andrew Johnson must surely have understood that his actions could have meant the end of his political career as well as a future of near solitude in his hometown. But he stood on principle and the years would prove him to be correct in his actions.

If siding with the Union against the will of his state was a courageous act guaranteed to win for him the animosity of many, the next step in his career could be interpreted as being even more controversial. With the outbreak of hostilities in the now divided nation came the need for the North to subdue the rebellious Southern states. Although it would take four years of bloodshed to accomplish this mission, it soon became clear that there would be a need to govern those areas that were gradually brought back within the control of the federal government. With this in mind, and forward thinking as he was, in March of 1862 Abraham Lincoln, through his Secretary of War Edward Stanton, had Andrew Johnson appointed as Military Governor of Tennessee. This act required Johnson to surrender his Senate seat, with Congress appointing Johnson as Brigadier General in his new capacity as overseer of the military government in the state. Johnson, therefore, surrendered "the soft cushioned seat in the Senate for the jolting saddle of the horse."[65]

Regrettably for Johnson, not only did his position carry much responsibility, it also carried much uncertainty. Although Abraham Lincoln had invested him with nearly unlimited powers, to include the power to appoint or suspend officials, to suspend the writ of habeas corpus, and to supervise elections, the military situation in Tennessee was tenuous at best. Union armies under Don Carlos Buell and then William Rosecrans did manage to gain control over much of the state. However, in September of 1863 at the Battle of Chickamauga, Confederate forces would win a substantial victory which obliterated many of the earlier Union gains.

What's more, slavery would also become an issue, as the benefits of the Emancipation Proclamation were not extended to the State of Tennessee. Runaway slaves inundated those sections of the state that were under Union control, and Andrew Johnson and the Union army were quick to seize upon this source of free labor to construct defenses and maintain roads over which the army would travel. Johnson himself would begin to view slavery as a direct cause for secession and often referred to slavery as a "cancer on our society." However, though he was opposed to slavery and maintained an especially virulent hatred of the South's slaveholding elites, it was clear that he was not entirely in favor of granting either citizenship or any form of political rights to the newly freed black slaves.

Yet, Johnson's biggest obstacle as military governor may have been himself. From the time of his arrival in Tennessee the pro-southern citizens of Nashville treated him with outright contempt, which was something a man like Johnson could never comprehend nor tolerate. As conditions worsened, "Johnson returned hatred with all the violent intensity of his nature. As the storm of abuse beat upon him, he became more and more bitter. With him, an affront took on something of the character of the feud, familiar, one may imagine, to his not too remote forbears; the debt must be repaid in full."[66] His opposite number, the Confederate Governor of Tennessee, Isham G. Harris, said of Johnson, "If Andy Johnson was a snake, he would hide in the grass and bite the heels of rich men's children."[67] There was a constant danger of either assassination or kidnapping which required such extensive fortifications around Johnson's capitol that it became known as "Fort Andrew Johnson." Relations in the state were so bad that the relationship between Johnson and the U.S. Army, which was there to subdue the rebellion and protect him, became very strained.

However, even though there were many who complained that his very combative nature was an extreme handicap in dealing with the many difficulties with which he was confronted, it can also be said that his indomitable will and firmness were required to control a nearly uncontrollable situation. As the election of 1864 neared, Lincoln would use the decision of Andrew Johnson to remain in the Senate in 1861, in opposition to his state, and his abilities as military governor for three years during the war, in order to gain for Johnson the nomination as candidate for Vice President under Lincoln on the National Union ticket. This was the name adopted by the Republican Party for the election of 1864, which also allowed the Democrat Andrew Johnson to be allowed as Vice Presidential nominee. It would be a fateful decision.

The Vice Presidency of Andrew Johnson is little remembered, perhaps due to the fact that it was the shortest term of any tenure with the exception of James K. Polk, who served in that capacity for only one month before President William Henry Harrison's death catapulted him into the position of chief executive. During his tenure as Vice President, Johnson made only two speeches; one on the occasion of his inauguration and one upon the news of the fall of Richmond. Much of his time would be consumed with issues of patronage and individuals attempting to secure from the government payment for property or services rendered during the war. On April 6, 1865, the newly inaugurated Vice President would travel to Richmond, Virginia, the fallen capital of the Confederate States of America, though by this time it was heavily damaged as a result of the war. Upon his return to Washington, Andrew Johnson would have his only meeting with Abraham Lincoln, when the two discussed the importance of punishing the rebel leadership, which had overseen the secessionist movement resulting in a divided country. The date of this fateful meeting was April 14, the evening of Lincoln's assassination at the hand of John Wilkes Booth. Andrew Johnson was supposed to have been a target of the plot as well, but escaped when his would-be assassin lost his nerve. With the death of Lincoln on the morning of April 15, Johnson was sworn in as seventeenth president of the United States by Chief Justice Salmon P. Chase at the Kirkwood House.

Just as Andrew Johnson had been thrust into unfamiliar territory when he became military governor of Tennessee, an unprecedented act, he now found himself on unfamiliar grounds again as the Reconstruction of a war-torn nation had not been attempted before in this country and there were no provisions for it in the Constitution. During the war, Abraham Lincoln had used his powers as Chief Executive to initiate his Ten Percent Plan, whereby if ten percent of the 1860 voters in one of the occupied Confederate states swore an oath of allegiance to the United States they could then create an electorate, could elect a convention to write a new state constitution, and seek re-admission to the Union. There were of course certain provisions. These occupied states would need to recognize such federal wartime measures as the abolition of slavery. Nevertheless, Congress refused to recognize Lincoln's Ten Percent Plan as binding, and when the first two states to complete the plan, Arkansas and Louisiana, sent their new representatives to Washington, Congress refused to seat them. Therefore, even before Andrew Johnson assumed his office, an imminent struggle between the Executive and Legislative branches of government had been initiated to determine who would oversee Reconstruction.

Shortly after Andrew Johnson became President on April 15, he put forth a plan for Reconstruction that was very similar to Lincoln's. First of all, he believed Reconstruction to be a function of the Executive branch. Like Lincoln, he also believed that it should be accomplished as rapidly as possible and with as little disruption as possible. However, Congress would assume an attitude against Johnson's plan, much as they had against Lincoln's, with their one major complaint being that Congress was not afforded a sufficient role in Reconstruction policies. There were a few dissimilarities between the two plans. Lincoln had only called for ten percent of the population that had voted in 1860 to swear an oath before Reconstruction could begin in one of the Confederate states. Under Andrew Johnson's plan, a majority of the 1860 voters would be required. With the Johnson plan there existed fourteen categories of individuals who could not receive amnesty by means of an oath, but rather had to apply directly to the President for a personal pardon. Many of the Confederacies civil and military leaders fell into this category, as did any persons whose pre-war worth exceeded $20,000. There were also to be temporary governors assigned to each of the eleven seceding states, governors who were to be appointed by Johnson himself. On the whole, Johnson's policies were probably wise, and under normal circumstances they may have even worked. However, Johnson may never have had his finger on the pulse of the nation as Lincoln had. With Lincoln, there was a wartime President with vast powers who had the backing of the army as well as much of the electorate of the North behind him. He was known to be lenient toward the South, which would also gain him some measure of support in that region. Andrew Johnson was a Democrat before the war, and even though he had remained true to the Union, he could expect some level of opposition from the Republican Party. Also, there was the fact that he had never been elected to the office which he now held, which denied him the right to claim that he had any kind of mandate from the electorate.

Initially, Johnson's plan was to meet with some level of success. By the autumn of 1865, reports were flowing north of renewed southern loyalty as well as a very healthy participation in the elections being held throughout the South. In Addition, the Executive office was being inundated with requests for personal pardons from former Confederates who fell into the fourteen categories of persons who were required to do so. His reconstruction efforts were proceeding so rapidly that he once remarked to a visitor, "that I sometimes cannot realize it. It appears like a dream."[68] There did arise some issues, naturally, as old habits die hard. In Mississippi there was reluctance to ratify a constitutional amendment abolishing slavery, as well as cases of individual states failing to repudiate the wartime debt. But on the whole, progress was being made.

Unfortunately for Johnson, conditions would change rapidly. As many of the former Confederates received their pardons, their political disqualifications were removed. Consequently, a large number of them were elected to office, which alarmed Republican leaders. In addition, many of the southern states were enacting Black Codes, which were laws created to govern the lives and labor of the newly freed slaves. Through much of this, Andrew Johnson remained indifferent, not wishing to interfere excessively in the affairs of the states. Therefore, when Congress assembled in December of 1865, it reacted quickly. It refused to admit the newly elected southern representatives and created its own Joint Committee of Fifteen to oversee Reconstruction. By these acts it had put the President on notice that Congress intended to reject his entire program of Reconstruction.

The President's reaction must have been very predictable. Commenting to his secretary William A. Moore, Johnson exclaimed, "Sir, I am right. I know I am right and I am damned if I do not adhere to it."[69] In his old style as a stump speaker from Tennessee he lashed out at his opponents as "a common gang of cormorants and blood suckers, who have been fattening upon the country."[70] However, his personal attacks on Republicans only served to alienate many of his former political allies, as well as those who had helped in his election as Vice President in 1864. During the elections of 1866, so many Republicans were elected that when the second session of the thirty-ninth Congress assembled in December of 1866, they held a two-thirds majority, which was nearly veto proof. The period of Presidential Reconstruction would end within months and Congress would gain control over Reconstruction of the former Confederacy.

With majorities in Congress, the Republicans were able to pass into law the Reconstruction Acts of 1867. By these acts Congress provided for the re-admission of the Confederate states to the Union upon their ratification of the Fourteenth Amendment. Though, added to this pre-requisite was a new stipulation, that Southern whites extend the right to vote to the newly freed blacks upon the same conditions. In addition, the provisional governments of the Southern states were to be supplemented with military administrators, as the former Confederate states were divided into five military districts. It was intended that the U.S. Army would remain in these areas as a means to protect the rights of southern loyalists and the newly freed slaves. In addition, the military was given authorization to remove any state officials who obstructed the military administration in the performance of its duty.

Also in 1867 the new Fortieth Congress passed the Supplementary Reconstruction Act, which authorized the military commanders of the five districts to supervise the election of new delegates to constitutional conventions. This would finally establish new state governments that would meet all of the requirements of the provisions set forth by Congress for re-admission to the Union. These acts did not pass without debate, however, for by now the Republican Party was beginning to divide itself between what were known as conservative Republicans and those more inclined toward a harsh treatment of the South, those known as Radical Republicans.

With the various acts of Congress superseding the Reconstruction efforts of Johnson, the ever stoic Johnson only became more intransigent in his efforts to control events. In denouncing the congressional measures, Johnson proclaimed that the acts were "without precedent and without authority, in palpable conflict with the plainest provisions of the Constitution, and utterly destructive to those great principles of liberty and humanity for which our ancestors on both sides of the Atlantic have shed so much blood and expended so much treasure."[71] The President's tendency toward using his veto was also a strong indicator of what lay ahead, as it became clear that there now existed a clear struggle for primacy between the Executive and Legislative branches of government. Before the national tragedy of the Civil War, it was the unwillingness to seek compromise that had caused the separation between the states. Lamentably, that same vindictive spirit would return in the aftermath of the war. It would usher in a new constitutional crisis and the first attempted impeachment of a sitting U.S. President.

In an effort to set aside the authority of Congress and to nullify the effects of the Congressional Reconstruction Acts, Andrew Johnson would further reveal his intransigent nature by removing political opponents from positions within the government. Between July and December of 1866, Andrew Johnson removed from federal service a total of 1,664 postmasters, 1,283 of them for reasons purely political.[72] In essence, Johnson intended to force government officials to endorse his policies on Reconstruction by using the power of patronage as an axe to be wielded over the heads of those who did not agree with him. In response to this challenge to their authority, Congress passed the Tenure of Office Act. The sole purpose of this act was to control Presidential use of the patronage system for political gain and to prevent his continued removal of Radical Republican officeholders in his attempts to hinder Reconstruction.

As could be expected, Johnson vetoed the Tenure of Office Act and sent his explanatory letter to Congress on March 2, 1867. Much of his argument was centered on his constitutional beliefs, for he regarded the power to remove officials without senatorial approval as being granted to the President in that document. He also attempted to justify his actions by using precedents established by both the founding fathers and his childhood idol Andrew Jackson. In both instances his arguments were firmly rejected and the Congress re-enacted the bill on the same day that Johnson's letter had been received.

Within the bill itself, however, there was one exception which may have saved Andrew Johnson from himself and saved the country from the indignity of having a president removed without just cause. When the Radical Republican proponents of the bill had submitted it to Congress, it was intended to protect all officeholders. Nevertheless, Conservative Republicans and Democrats insisted that the department heads within the Executive branch be exempted. This exemption would play a major role in the crisis that was to befall the country in the following year of 1868.

Edward M. Stanton had been appointed to serve as the Secretary of War by Abraham Lincoln after the removal of Simon Cameron from that office amidst charges of fraud and inefficiency. In some ways he could be very much like Andrew Johnson in that he was a tireless worker who could offend many of his colleagues by his very brusque, to-the-point manner. He could be very demanding at times but was not considered as being entirely inflexible like Johnson. By his efforts the War Department became very efficient and the United States Army became the largest, best-equipped military force the United States had ever seen. In a sense purely political, Stanton could at times be a liability. When he had served as Attorney General under James Buchanan, he was known to pass along information about White House activities to congressmen and to President-elect Lincoln. This habit would continue during his service as Secretary of War under Andrew Johnson, as he frequently passed along information to Radical Republicans in an effort to derail Johnson's policies toward Reconstruction.

By August 1867, the division between Johnson and Stanton was so great that in accordance with the Tenure of Office Act, Andrew Johnson suspended him from his office and replaced him with General of the Army, Ulysses S. Grant. As Congress had just adjourned, this provided Johnson with several months to justify his actions. When Congress returned to session it initially attempted to pass a resolution of impeachment against Andrew Johnson, which failed. When Johnson forwarded his explanation to the Senate as to why he had released Edward Stanton from his duties, the Senate voted not to "advise and consent" to Stanton's suspension. Unsure of the ramifications of this action, Ulysses S. Grant relinquished his position as Secretary of War, allowing Stanton to return. But this was not the end of the issue. Certain that the Tenure of Office Act was unconstitutional, Andrew Johnson once again fired Stanton, replacing him with Adjutant General of the Army, Lorenzo Thomas. This continued defiance of the Congress led to a second attempt at impeachment proceedings.

On February 24, 1868, the House of Representatives voted 128 to 47 in favor of Articles of Impeachment against President Johnson for "high crimes and misdemeanors." In total, eleven charges were filed against the embattled chief executive, eight of which involved the Tenure of Office Act and the replacement of Stanton with Thomas. The ninth article accused Johnson of violating the Army Appropriations Act, while the tenth argued that he had delivered "intemperate, inflammatory and scandalous harangues... as well against Congress as the laws of the United States." It was the eleventh charge, however, that may have revealed the Articles of Impeachment for what they truly were, a simple attempt to remove an unpopular President from office because his behavior was viewed as an impediment to congressional will. The eleventh charge was an obscure amalgamation of all the other charges intended to provide those who were in favor of impeachment but could not justify a guilty vote on the other charges with a catch-all. In accordance with the provisions of the Constitution, the House of Representatives alone could bring impeachment charges against the President. But the actual trial itself had to be conducted in the Senate, with the Chief Justice of the United States presiding. A two-thirds majority was required for conviction, and as the Southern states were not represented in the Senate, thirty-six of the fifty-four members would have to register a guilty vote. Even though Johnson was elected as a National Unionist and had served as Vice President under a Republican president, he was sure to receive votes of acquittal from all twelve of the senate Democrats. With forty-two Republicans in the chamber, conviction of the President seemed almost assured.

The trial itself was a unique affair because it was the first of its kind. At no time did the President attend the proceedings, although during the trial he did commit a daring, though unwise act by submitting the name of General John M. Schofield as a replacement for Stanton, knowing that Schofield was very popular among his political adversaries. Unfortunately for the Radical Republicans, just as the defendant was at all times absent from the trial, absent also was any substantial proof that Johnson had committed any real crime.

The trial would commence on the fifth of March 1868. From the beginning, nearly all of the focus was centered on the Senators and how they would vote. During a preliminary Republican caucus held in reference to the fate of Andrew Johnson, six Republican senators affirmed that in their opinion there existed a lack of sufficient evidence to convict the President under the existing Articles of Impeachment. One other individual, Senator Edmund Gibson Ross of Missouri, refused to declare his vote either for acquittal or conviction ahead of time. And it would be his decision as well as that of the other six defiant conservative Republicans that would be the focal point of the trial.

For six weeks the trial would consume the attention of the nation. Henry Stanbery would resign his position as Attorney General to head up the President's defense counsel. Prosecuting the President would be Radical Republicans Benjamin F. Butler, Thaddeus Stevens, Thomas Williams, John Bingham, James Wilson, George S. Boutwell and John A. Logan. All were known enemies and vocal critics of the President. As the trial dragged on, arguments would be brought forth by both sides in regard to issues ranging from presidential authority and constitutional rights to what powers and authority were held specifically by Congress. Finally, the Senate moved to vote on each of the articles separately, with May 16th being set as the date for the vote on Article XI. Even though the seven dissenting Republican Senators had been brought under extreme forms of pressure to ensure a guilty vote, when the roll was called on the Senate floor there were 35 votes for a conviction, 19 votes for acquittal, one shy of the two-thirds necessary. Seven very courageous Republicans had broken with their party. They were William Pitt Fessenden of Maine, James W. Grimes of Ohio, Joseph S. Fowler, Lyman Trumball of Illinois who had once defeated Abraham Lincoln for the Senate in 1852, Edmund Ross of Kansas, John B. Henderson, and Peter Van Winkle of West Virginia. All were condemned to political obscurity for their actions and none were ever re-elected to the Senate.

There would be subsequent votes on the other Articles of Impeachment as well, and each time the vote was the same, 35 guilty and 19 not guilty. By May 26th the trial was over and the Senate adjourned itself as high court of impeachment. Andrew Johnson would remain as President of the United States; Edward Stanton would relinquish his position as Secretary of War. It was a regrettable affair, but with an ending that turned out to be very favorable for the country.

It is written, and in all likelihood true, that those who had voted for the acquittal of Andrew Johnson were for a very long time the objects of scorn and abuse. Yet in the end their actions would be viewed in a true light, and they would be vindicated as having been right all along. In time, the newspaper The Nation, which had favored conviction, would write of the seven dissenting Republicans, "We believe, for our part, that the thanks of the country are due to Mssrs. Trumball, Fessenden, Grimes, Henderson, Fowler, Van Winkle, and Ross, not for voting for Johnson's acquittal, but for vindicating … the sacred rights of individual conscience."[73] Of the incident, Lyman Trumball would write, "The question to be decided is not whether Andrew Johnson is a proper person to fill the Presidential office, nor whether it is fit that he should remain in it … Once set, the example of impeaching a President for what, when the excitement of the House shall have subsided, will be regarded as insufficient cause, no future President will be safe who happens to differ with a majority of the House and two-thirds of the Senate on any measure deemed by them important … What then becomes of the checks and balances of the Constitution so carefully devised and so vital to its perpetuity?"[74]

There would also be some measure of vindication for Andrew Johnson. His political career would be ruined for a time, but unlike the seven gallant Republicans who had voted for his acquittal, he would return to public office. During the election of 1868, the Republican Party chose as its candidate Ulysses S. Grant. Wildly popular for having helped defeat the Confederate armies, thus ending the rebellion, it is unlikely that any other candidate for the presidency could have overcome him. In time, though, his Presidency would also see much controversy and would be remembered for instances of shoddiness and corruption. During the Grant administration Congress modified the Tenure of Office Act so as to afford the President greater latitude in removing public officials. In 1926, the U.S. Supreme Court would write that the Tenure of Office Act was unconstitutional. So it seems, that in his views, Johnson may have been right.

In the aftermath of the impeachment trial, Andrew Johnson was viewed as a political liability by his party. He had but ten months left in his term of office. In the election of 1868, the Democratic Party turned to the wartime governor of New York, Horatio Seymour, as their candidate. Seymour would lose to Grant in the Electoral College by a plurality, 214 votes for Grant, 80 for Seymour. Andrew Johnson would return to his home state of Tennessee, no doubt exhausted after thirty years of public service. For a time he would remain quiet, though events would require him to become involved in Tennessee politics once again. Initially his efforts would be centered on getting anti-radicals elected to office. In 1869 he stumped the state of Tennessee on behalf of W.C. Senter, who was running for governor of the state. Senter would win the election and a conservative legislature would be elected to serve in the statehouse. With this turn of political fortunes within the state, speculation began to rise as to the prospects of Andrew Johnson once again returning to the U.S. Senate, which had only recently attempted to end his Presidency through the Articles of Impeachment. In October of 1869, he would meet with one of the few setbacks in his political career when he lost a bid to become U.S. Senator from Tennessee to the Radical Republican Henry Cooper, fifty-five votes to fifty-one. It was believed at the time that much of the reason for his loss stemmed from the fact that his independent political views had made him unpopular with both the Radical Republicans and the ex-Confederates who had combined to foil his attempt for election.

In some measure he would gain his revenge a few years later. In 1872, under the provisions of a general redistricting bill, Tennessee was accorded the right to send an additional member to the U.S. Congress. Many in the state had hoped Johnson would be elected to hold this position as a congressman at large, rather than from a specified district. When it became known to Andrew Johnson that there were those who intended to submit his name as a candidate, he informed his aide Colonel Reeves that he was not interested in a congressional seat as he intended to run for U.S. Senate again in 1875. He told Reeves, "I would rather have the vindication of my state by electing me to my old seat in the Senate of the United States than to be monarch of the grandest empire on earth. For this I live, and will never die content without…"[75] He then instructed Reeves that if his name were submitted, to promptly withdraw it in his authority.

However, when General Benjamin Cheatham was nominated for the congressional seat by Democrats along with Horace Maynard by the Radical Republicans, Andrew Johnson suddenly reversed course. There was much speculation when Johnson announced his name as an independent candidate at large that his motives were simply to ensure that the ex-

Confederate Cheatham would not win the election. As events transpired, those who harbored such fears were correct, and although Andrew Johnson finished a distant third in the election, he did receive enough votes to ensure the defeat of the former general.

True to his words, in January of 1875, Andrew Johnson became a candidate to succeed Parson Brownlow as U.S. Senator from Tennessee. It was an uphill battle, as there existed six candidates in addition to Johnson. On the first ballot, Johnson received ten more votes than any of the other candidates. The other two leading candidates, Governor Neil Brown and General Bate became involved in a deadlock, with each determined that the other should not win. When Confederate war hero Nathan Bedford Forrest arrived in Nashville to act on behalf of General Bate, Andrew Johnson met with him and pronounced, "When the gods arrive, the half gods depart. If the people really wanted to send a Confederate military hero to the Senate, they would elect Forrest himself, instead of a 'one-horse' general."[76] A number of the candidates would withdraw, and after five days and fifty-four ballots Johnson would regain his old Senate seat by a majority of one vote, the same margin that had provided for his acquittal during the impeachment trial.

Much as the seven Republican Senators who had voted for Johnson's acquittal had been later vindicated, it would be a time of vindication for Johnson as well. Many of the newspapers that had formerly attacked him were now sympathetic to his cause. The St. Louis Republican considered his election as, "the most magnificent personal triumph which the history of American politics can show."[77] The nation, which had long been in favor of his impeachment during the crisis of

1868, now remarked that Andrew Johnson's "personal integrity was beyond question and his respect for the law and the Constitution made his administration a remarkable contrast to that which succeeded it."[78]

Andrew Johnson's return to the U.S. Senate would be poignant, triumphant, and brief. He would make only one speech, an attack against the policies of Ulysses S. Grant in regard to the President's decision to place by force an individual of disreputable character in the governor's chair in Louisiana. As a conclusion to his speech he remarked, "Give me the Constitution of my country unimpaired. …In the language of Webster, let this Union be preserved 'now and forever, one and inseparable.' Let peace and Union be restored to the land. May God bless this people, and God save the Constitution."[79]

Like all of the great characters on the stage of history, the time of Andrew Johnson would pass. When the Senate adjourned a few days after his speech, Andrew Johnson returned to Tennessee. He had once remarked to a friend that when his time on earth was at an end he wanted to go "all at once and nothing first." While visiting his daughter Mary Stover in Carter County he suffered a stroke. This first stroke, one of paralysis, would be shortly followed by another, which would render him unconscious. At two-thirty on the morning of July 31, 1875, the seventeenth president of the United States would pass away.

For a number of years history would remember Johnson as being a less than successful President, one who by his tough demeanor and intransigent spirit divided the country and worked to foil the efforts to re-unite the country in the aftermath of the Civil War. However, time has and will perhaps continue to vindicate his positions while in public office. As Governor of Tennessee he was a firm advocate for and a believer in public education. As a Congressman he worked for passage of the Homestead Act, the passage of which would assist in the creation of an economic boom in the country in the post Civil War years that transformed America from an almost purely agrarian society to the greatest industrialized nation on earth. As a Senator from the South, he remained true to the Union when every single one of his colleagues resigned their positions and sided with their states during the years of secession. And as President, he favored the more lenient Reconstruction policies of Abraham Lincoln in an attempt to re-unite the war-torn nation as quickly as possible and with as little interruption as possible. For these positions, which many would now regard as being correct, he was often castigated by friend and foe alike and sentenced to years of political obscurity.

But it would be neither easy nor just for the historian today to condemn Andrew Johnson for his actions. Many now regard the history of the United States as having two distinct and separate parts. There were the years before the Civil War when we existed largely as a conglomeration of states, and there are the years after the Civil War where we now exist under an omni competent federal government that reigns supreme with its authority over the states. Andrew Johnson fought very hard against Congressional Reconstruction, as he believed its terms to be harsh and unnecessary. The facts tell us that during the years of Congressional Reconstruction the five military governors of the South, known to Southerners as "satraps," ruled the region firmly and at times with a flagrant disregard for civil rights. Confederate veterans organizations as well as historical societies that championed Southern rights were suppressed. The governors of six states and thousands of other local officials were removed from office by the military governors, a move that today might be regarded as a form of dictatorship. Military tribunals often replaced the civil courts and state laws were either set aside or modified when they were not in harmony with the wishes of the Radical Republican Congress in Washington.

All of these things Andrew Johnson fought against. He was a firm believer in the Constitution and the rights of individual citizens. His belief in ordinary Americans was so great that he once told a young legislator, "What I have to say seems very simple and unimportant. But it is of the utmost importance to one who seeks favor of the public. If you should continue in public life, be sure of one thing… that you always strive to keep in touch with, and on the side of, the common people. With them for you, corporations and combinations may organize against you…. but they will war in vain… Keep the common people on your side and you will win."[80] Throughout three decades of public service Andrew Johnson remained true to himself and his country. No one could justly ask for more.

Chapter VI

¤

TO SAVE A NATION

The soldier. He has existed perhaps as long as mankind itself. He is known to history by his deeds, both collectively and individually. Even though there are many who may be ignorant of the deeds of those who are considered as history's great soldiers, there are few who are unfamiliar with the names of Alexander the Great, Caesar, Napoleon, or Frederick the Great. The soldier is, at times by his deeds, the noble redeemer of mankind's greatest sins and most violent acts. He may on occasion be the defender of his own people, or be the conqueror of his people's enemies. He does not go forth blindly, but rather at all times obediently and willingly to answer his nation's or his state's call in times of crises. Unlike the statesman and the politician, he is rarely involved in the decision to take up arms and seek conflict, yet it is he who must bear the burdens of war and every so often make the ultimate sacrifice. When victorious, he is the embodiment of all that is good, just, and heroic. When in defeat, he must bear the burden of all his country's sins. The soldier is, by his perseverance and courage, the most noble of all creatures.

Over the centuries, the soldier has also had to prove himself adaptable. He is periodically the actor on a great stage. But on the other hand, as the actor on the stage seeks the approbation of the crowd, wounds and death are the common currencies of the soldier. As man has transformed himself from his roots as a simple herbivore to become an almost lethal carnivore, the weapons that he once used to hunt his food became the weapons that he would use to hunt his fellow man. His art, that of warfare, has transformed itself from a contest of survival, to a sport of kings; to the simple business of slaughter, killing his enemies by the most efficient means possible. Whereas the technology of war once allowed him to kill his enemies by the hundreds, it has now progressed to the point where it allows him to kill his enemies by the hundreds of thousands. When mankind learned to walk erect and to cultivate crops, he began to live in clans or tribes that might sometimes go to war. With the arrival of city states such as those of the Sumerians in ancient Mesopotamia, we find the beginnings of standing armies and men aligned in formations. Eventually the Greeks would develop the phalanx, the Romans the legion. What's more, members of the animal kingdom would be asked to play a part in man's wars with the advent of cavalry and the war elephant. The club would be replaced by the spear; the spear by the sword; the sword by the longbow; the longbow by the gun; the gun by the cannon; the cannon by the bomb; and the bomb by the missile. Warfare has devolved from a contest between two combatants where the stronger of the two win, to an impersonal affair where a man might kill his enemy by the push of a button.

Because of these advances in war and the technology of death, the individual soldier has become a mere statistic. As the size of armies has steadily increased, so also has the number of casualties one could expect when armies meet on the field of battle. During the time of John Churchill, Duke of Marlborough, or of Napoleon, armies were limited to a certain size because the nations that raised them were limited in their agricultural and industrial capacity and could only produce so many weapons to arm their soldiers and so much food to feed them. By the twentieth century, the modern industrialized nation could produce nearly unlimited numbers of weapons and were restricted only by the amount of natural resources available to them. Then once again, the soldier became of less importance. Even so, there still can be times, though those times are rare, when the individual soldier can play a decisive role in the outcome of a battle. When Caesar invaded Britain in 55 B.C., we are told of an incident where the aquilifer, or standard bearer, of one of the legions leapt over the side of his transport and charged into the Britains who had waded into the surf to meet the invading Romans. His fellow legionnaires were so inspired and loyal that they leapt over the side as well and charged into the awaiting Britains, who were then routed. This is an example of personal courage by a common soldier that played a crucial role in the outcome of a battle. History books are filled with such examples of the exploits of very brave men in the face of battle.

Sometimes a soldier can have an impact, which may not only determine the outcome of a small attack or a large battle, but also an impact that determines the fate of a nation. Unfortunately, even though the soldier may choose the right path or course of action, if the conditions are wrong he may suffer immediate unpleasant consequences. He may even know this in advance and choose to follow the correct path anyway, at great hazard to himself. Just such an event would occur in the late summer and early autumn of 1914 "when the lights were going out all over Europe."

Charles Lanrezac was born July 31, 1852. He was a native of Guadeloupe in the Leeward Islands of the West Indies. Little is known of his youth, although he started his military career very early when he entered the military school at Saint-Cyr in 1869. When the Franco-Prussian War of 1870 began he left the school and joined the French Armée de la Loire as a lieutenant. In January of 1871 he was transferred from the Army of the Loire to the Armée de l'Est, or Army of the East. The Franco-Prussian War would not be a pleasant experience for Charles Lanrezac, or any other of France's soldiers.

The Franco-Prussian War of 1870-1871 may be regarded as a war of suspicion and, like so many other wars, another needless expenditure of human lives. For centuries Germany had existed as a coalition of Germanic states loosely tied into a confederation. Prussia had always been one of the more dominant and more successful of these states. During the Seven

Years War of 1756-1763, Frederick the Great had put on display for the world the abilities of the Prussian Army when he repeatedly defeated the combined armies of Austria, France, Russia, Sweden and Saxony. During the years of Napoleon Bonaparte, the Prussian Army would be defeated by the armies of the Emperor many times, though they did play a crucial role in his defeat at Waterloo in 1815. But the instinct for national survival and the military efficiency and spirit that accompanies it remained. When Otto Von Bismarck became Chancellor at the beginning of his twenty-eight years in power, he had stated that, "Since the treaties of Vienna, our frontiers have been ill designed for a healthy body politic. The great questions of the time will be decided, not by speeches and resolutions of majorities, but by iron and blood."[81] Although at the time this statement received much criticism, it turned out to be both accurate and prophetic.

The Statement would also be indicative of his personal beliefs and how his policies would fall into line. Much of von Bismarck's efforts were spent into rallying the north German states into a North German Confederation, which was very anti-French in its policies. The policies of Von Bismarck were not only anti-French, however. On June 14, 1866, Austria would make a firm denunciation of what they regarded to be overly aggressive Prussian power politics in the aftermath of Prussia's occupation of Holstein. In response, Bismarck dissolved the Germanic Confederation and mobilized Prussia for an immediate war against both Austria and the south German states that supported Austria's position. The result would become known as the Austro-Prussian War, or Seven Weeks War of 1866. As Prussia had proven its military prowess under Frederick the Great during the Seven Years War, it would prove it again within seven weeks during June and July. Their effort would culminate with the decisive Battle of Kōniggrätz on July 3, 1866. In a pitched battle fought in the driving rain, the Prussian troops who were armed with their state of the art breech-loading needle guns would prove superior to their Austrian counterparts who were still armed with muzzle-loading rifles. Prussia suffered 10,000 casualties, but they inflicted 45,000 casualties on their Austrian foe.[82] Two days later, Napoleon III of France offered to act as mediator between the two opposing countries. Prussia would accept the offer of mediation and with the resulting Treaty of Prague of August 23, 1866, Austria would be henceforth excluded from German affairs and the German states north of the river Main would form a new North German Confederation under Prussian leadership. Those German states south of the river were left to form a confederation of their own.

Having accomplished his goal of furthering Prussian interest in 1866, Bismarck set about to expand Prussian influence beyond the borders of the new confederation. In 1870, he initiated an effort to place a Hohenzollern prince on the throne of Spain. In the eventuality of a future war between France and Prussia, this could present France with the possibility of having to fight a two-front war. Therefore, with the mistaken belief that the French army was somehow invincible, Napoleon III pre-empted this possibility by declaring war against his neighbor to the east and mobilized for offensive action against Prussia. His decision to initiate war would prove to be just another of mankind's unwise decisions and as such it would cost his nation dearly.

As the Austro-Prussian War had proven to be a brief conflict with Prussia securing a quick victory, the Franco-Prussian War would also become known for its brevity. In addition to overestimating the strength of his own army, Napoleon III would underestimate the political fallout of his actions. With his declaration of war, the southern German states that were formerly opposed to Prussia now joined her in the defensive war against France. No doubt having studied the recently concluded American Civil War, Prussian military preparations were efficient, utilizing railroads to the fullest. In contrast, French preparations were both haphazard and inefficient.

To encounter the French assault, Prussia and its German allies could rely on a well equipped army of 380,000 men, all concentrated on the frontier west of the Rhine River. France would initiate hostilities against this force with an army of about 224,000 men who were organized into eight army corps.[83] It is generally assumed in most military circles that in order to succeed in an offensive operation that an attacking army should have a superiority of almost 3 to 1. How the French emperor intended to succeed against an army far larger than his own is not known. However, the French army at this time was known to be overly confident in its reliance on offensive military operations and possessed very poor intelligence of its enemy.

Even worse for the average French soldier in 1870, the French army had a very poor command structure. Perhaps mistakenly believing his military abilities to be comparable to those of his namesake Napoleon Bonaparte, Napoleon III placed himself in supreme command of French military operations. In contrast, Prussia had a very competent general staff under the direction of General Von Moltke. Whereas the French plan of battle called for nothing more than a general assault towards the east, the Prussian plan was based upon military realities; the destruction of the French field armies followed by the occupation of the French capital once this had been accomplished.

In the contest to follow, Prussian efficiency and superior planning would prevail. Whereas the Prussian army had needed a mere seven weeks to defeat Austria in 1866, it would need a little more than nine months to defeat France. Although the Franco-Prussian War of 1870-1871 is not as noteworthy in history as the wars which have transpired since then, the outcome and implications for future relations between France and Germany were infinitely more important than the war itself.

The war would begin with an initial skirmish at Saarbrucken on August 2, 1870, which resulted in Napoleon III regrouping his troops into two armies, the Army of Alsace and the Army of Lorraine. This was to be another fateful decision, the consequences of which would extend far beyond the war itself. Two days later a Prussian army would encounter the southernmost of the French armies at Weissenburg, driving it back and forcing the French to recognize that they would have to abandon any further attempts at offensive action. Almost simultaneously, Prussian forces attacked the Army of Lorraine in the north, sending it into headlong retreat as well. By August 12, the reality of the situation forced Napoleon to relinquish command of the French armies, although the gesture was unimportant as the military situation was by now so favorable to the Prussians that there was little hope of French recovery or victory. On the first of September 1870, the decisive Battle of Sedan was fought when the Army of Alsace attempted to come to the aide of its sister army of 115,000 men that had become trapped near Metz. Unfortunately, the Army of Alsace would itself become trapped in a bend of the River Meuse along the

Belgian frontier.

What followed could be considered in some ways as a precursor to the events of 1914 to 1918. The Prussian Army would mass artillery around the entrapped French Army and begin a day-long bombardment of the town. In an attempt to break out of the encirclement, the French launched a series of four cavalry charges against the Prussian forces. As could be expected, cavalry had little chance against massed infantry armed with modern bolt-action rifles and machine guns. The result was a needless slaughter of both man and animals. By 5 pm the situation had become so desperate that the ailing emperor had himself rouged so that he could formally surrender himself to Wilhelm I. It was one of the most humiliating defeats of the nineteenth century. With the capture of the emperor, the French empire collapsed after a popular uprising in Paris, and a new Third Republic was proclaimed under a provisional government.

With half of its field army captured at Sedan and the other half besieged at Metz, the war was for all intended purposes over. As planned, the Prussian Army encircled Paris and initiated a siege, which was intended to starve the city into submission. The French would continue to resist the Prussian invasion, relying on guerilla warfare in the areas overrun by the Prussian Army, while hoping that the army at Metz might somehow break out. Eventually Metz would fall, as would Paris in January of 1871. There would be one final siege at Belfort where a French army of 17,000 men held out for 105 days against the Prussian onslaught. Eventually the French General Assembly ordered the garrison to surrender, ending any further hostilities.

On May 10, 1871 the Franco-Prussian War ended with the

signing of the Treaty of Frankfurt. As conditions of the treaty, France was required to pay an indemnity of five billion francs, was forced to surrender Alsace and northwestern Lorraine to Prussia, while a Prussian army of occupation was to remain in France until such time as the indemnity was paid. If one wonders why France was so determined to impose such harsh terms against Germany with the Treaty of Versailles at the conclusion of the First World War, they need look no further than the humiliating terms which France had to endure following its defeat during the Franco-Prussian War.

As both French field armies had been captured during the war, Charles Lanrezac became a prisoner of war and was interned in Switzerland. However, the unfortunate set of events of the Franco-Prussian War did not dissuade him from his desire to pursue a military career. Perhaps they only caused him to crave revenge against the more powerful German state which had arisen in the aftermath of the war.

In 1876, Lanrezac was promoted to captain and In 1879 he gained entrance into the École Militaire. Upon graduation from that institute, he would resume his career by serving in numerous staff positions with the 113th Infantry Regiment, as well as serving on a brigade staff in Tunisia. In 1902 Charles Lanrezac was promoted to Colonel and given command of the 119th Infantry Regiment. Command at the regimental level was to be followed by command of the 43rd Infantry Brigade stationed in Vannes. He was also awarded the rank of brigadier general, as befitting of his new position.

Upon his completion of brigade command, Charles Lanrezac was to see a break in his career as an infantry commander. Having himself been a graduate of École Militaire, he would return there as an instructor. Regarded as being an outstanding lecturer, as an instructor he was looked upon as having the character fault of being very distemperate. Around this time he also began to formulate ideas as to how France should conduct its operations in the event of a future conflict with its long time archrival, Germany. His theories would begin to place him in opposition to the other high ranking officers within the French general staff. He was a firm opponent of Ferdinand Foch's belief in the offensive a l'outrance, writing "If every subordinate commander has the right to ram home an attack on the first opponent it sees, the commander in chief is incapable of exercising any form of direction." No doubt having served in the Franco-Prussian War, and having seen the disastrous results of France's blind belief in the offensive during that war, would cause him to view things from a different perspective.

In 1911 his career as an infantry officer would resume when he was given command of a division. His reputation was by now well known and he was often referred to as the "Lion of the French Army." In 1912 when the position of Deputy Chief of the General Staff became vacant, Charles Lanrezac's name was placed on the very short list of three men being considered for the position. However, his career was to follow a different path, for he was given command of the French XI Army Corps in Nantes. In April 1914 he was again promoted, being named as a successor to Joseph Gallieni as a member of the French Supreme War Council and receiving command of the French Fifth Army. It would be this assignment that would put Charles Lanrezac in the crosshairs of history.

In the early years of the twentieth century the world began to see rapid changes that would transform it forever. In terms of technology, the automobile began to free mankind of its reliance on horse drawn transportation and the invention of the airplane had freed man from his restriction to the ground. Electric lights began to become commonplace in urban areas and in time the telephone would replace the telegraph. Mankind was beginning to change its views as to how it should be governed as well. For centuries the aging empires of Europe had been governed by families with names such as Romanov, Hapsburg and Hohenzollern. Russia had experience the outbreak of revolution in 1905 and Tsar Nicholas II was forced to use the Russian army to suppress his own people. He was not unique in his approach.

Industrial growth was accompanied in most of the nations of Europe with increases in population and enlightened social legislation. However, this did not mean that stratification of European societies was ended. The rich were still very rich, the poor still very poor. In many of the European countries the governments of the various nations were as fearful of their own populations as they were of the populations of other nations. Whereas the inventions of the telegraph and telephone, of the typewriter and steel filing cabinet had been devised for one purpose, they would be combined with increasingly larger police forces as a means to control people. The reaction to this tendency in the years prior to World War I was an increase in anarchism and anti-government beliefs. In the two decades before the outbreak of war, an American president, a premier of Italy, and an Austrian archduke were all assassinated. Socially, it would become a more violent age.

The governments themselves would act to destabilize the situation in Europe. In the years after the Franco-Prussian War, the Prussian Chancellor Otto Von Bismarck had followed a policy of maintaining peaceful relations with Russia in the east while seeking reconciliation with France in the west. Given that

Europe had experienced centuries of warfare between the various monarchies he sought to avoid a war on two fronts at all cost. In 1878, he had presided over the Congress of Berlin, which had overseen the fate of the Turkish territories in the Balkans and had granted independence to Serbia, Montenegro and Romania. It was perhaps one of the defining moments of his illustrious career. For a number of decades the Bismarckian foreign policy worked to prevent another major war in central Europe. Unfortunately, when Kaiser Wilhelm I was succeeded by Wilhelm II, the new Kaiser released Bismarck from his duties in 1890. Wilhelm II had decided to assume the role of acting as his own minister of foreign affairs, with disastrous consequences.

In an attempt to maintain peace between the various nations of Europe, a system of alliances was created during the years before the outbreak of war. France, still with memories of Sedan to consider, formed an alliance with Russia in the east. The preliminaries of this agreement were signed in 1891, and further strengthened by military conventions in 1892 and 1894. Through the diplomatic process France was able to confront Germany with the possibility of a two-front war, which was a serious threat in case of the outbreak of a major European war. It had been the possibility of a two-front war that had caused Napoleon III of France to initiate hostilities against Prussia in 1870. Also of a very destabilizing effect was the creation of the Triple Alliance between Germany, Austria-Hungary and Italy in 1882. As it had since the time of William of Orange, England followed a path of relying on its naval supremacy to keep it secure, while at the same time playing off other nations to guarantee that no single power on the continent would gain an ascendancy over the other nations. However, England had signed a treaty in 1839 along with France, Russia, Prussia and Austria, guaranteeing that Belgium would remain an "independent and perpetually neutral state." Under Lord Palmerston it had pledged itself to war if Belgium's neutrality was violated by any of the other powers on the continent. It would be an arrangement that would place Britain in a very tenuous position in the late summer of 1914.

It has been said of Charles Lanrezac that he possessed the gift of a Cassandra and had the ability to foresee future events. As commander of the French Fifth Army he was given control of the left wing of French defenses along the Belgian frontier. As the system of alliances had grown in the years prior to the outbreak of war, nations began to arm themselves on an increasingly larger scale and developed war plans so as to be prepared for the outbreak of any future hostilities. In the event of a war with Germany, France had developed what was known as Plan XVII. It called for five French armies to be deployed between neutral Switzerland and the Sambre River on the border with Belgium. If hostilities were initiated by Germany, the French armies were to begin immediate offensive operations with two major attacks to be launched into Alsace and Lorraine from the north and south of the Theonville-Metz fortified area. As Alsace and Lorraine had been surrendered to Germany after the Franco-Prussian War, Plan XVII betrayed itself as an overt attempt to recover these two provinces at the outbreak of hostilities and hence to gain some measure of revenge. It was also intended that, by initiating offensive action at the outbreak of hostilities, this would demonstrate to Russia a display of good faith in keeping with the terms of the mutual defensive pact just signed in 1891. However, the plan completely discounted the possibility of any German attack through neutral Belgium, as French intelligence and its general staff did not believe that Germany possessed the manpower reserves to launch any attack from the north that could reach west of the Meuse River. Unfortunately Plan XVII was both unrealistic and completely unsound.

Germany had developed its own war plan that was to be initiated upon the outbreak of any future hostilities. Completed in 1905 by Count Alfred Von Schlieffen, who was then the head of the German General Staff, the Schlieffen Plan was devised as a response to the possibility of having to fight against France and Russia at the same time. The plan comprised a number of basic elements, "A minimum force, together with any help Austria could provide, was to hold the Russians in check on the Eastern Front."[84] In the west, seven German armies would confront the French. In the south, two armies would initiate an attack in an attempt to induce the offensive-spirited French to launch their own attack into that heavily fortified area. To the north, five German armies comprised of about thirty-five and one-half army corps were to attack west through neutral Holland and Belgium and then swing west and south around Paris in an effort to drive what was left of the French armies to their destruction against the five army corps, which comprised the left wing of the German Army. It was a sound plan that not only recognized the realities of the terrain on which the war would be fought, but also took into account the known French tendency to attack in all circumstances and exploited the weakness of the fullest. If the plan had been left unaltered, a German victory most likely would have occurred within months. Unfortunately for Germany, Schlieffen retired in the latter half of 1905. His successor, General Helmuth von Moltke, retained the plan but altered the balance of forces by weakening the troops on the right and placing some of the units in the south so as to alleviate his concerns that the forces there were insufficient to repel the expected French assault. However, the right wing of the German Army still comprised the bulk of the available German forces, and if war did take place they would come thundering down on the French Fifth Army and its commander Charles Lanrezac.

Ironically and unfortunately, in the years prior to World War I, there were attempts by some within the French military establishment to avert the impending crisis which would occur in the event Plan XVII was placed into action. In 1911 General Michel became chief of the French Army. He was convinced that if war broke out between Germany and France, any future German offensive would come through neutral Belgium where the terrain was far more favorable for maneuvering large field armies. He also regarded the regions of Alsace and Lorraine as being unfavorable for a French attack. Therefore, his plan called for reorganization of the French Army with a French assault to be launched through Belgium. Then again, this plan would have necessitated a French breach of Belgian neutrality, which the government was not willing to do. Therefore, General Michel was relieved from command and his plan was removed from consideration. It is interesting to note that if his plan had been retained, when the German forces attacked through Belgium in 1914, they would have encountered the bulk of the French Army.

General Michel was not alone in his belief that in the event of war Germany would attack through Belgium. Beginning in June of 1914, Lanrezac started making predictions relating to a war that most people were starting to view as becoming more and more imminent. On June 23, 1914, Lanrezac stated that he did not believe that the German armies would come west of the River Sambre, but believed that they would make a much wider turning movement, after going through neutral Belgium. Again on July 31, just prior to mobilization, he warned that he still believed that any possible German attack would come through Belgium. As Plan XVII called from the French Army to launch an all out assault against German forces, he also stated that the forces available to him in the form of the Fifth Army were not sufficient for him to launch any kind of an assault against what he thought would be much larger German forces. Events would prove both General Michel and Charles Lanrezac correct.

Even though Wilhelm II had released Otto Von Bismarck as Chancellor in 1890, one of Bismarck's predictions would live on after him. Recognizing the volatile nature of European politics with its ever changing borders and the problems associated with ethnic nationalism, Bismarck had once stated that the next major conflict in Europe would be initiated due to "some damned foolish thing in the Balkans."[85] It was a prediction that would one day come back to haunt the German nation. In June of 1914 the heir to the Hapsburg throne of Austria-Hungary, the Archduke Franz Ferdinand, was in Sarajevo, Bosnia-Herzegovina with his wife the Countess Sofia. Ironically, he was there to watch the summer maneuvers of the Austro-Hungarian army. Unfortunately for the archduke and for history, members of "Young Bosnia," a secret society that was determined to end Hapsburg rule over the Slavs in the region, were present as well. After an initial assassination attempt failed, another member of the gang named Gavrilo Princip, a Serbian nationalist, fired his pistol into the open-topped car carrying the archduke and his wife, killing both of them.

Of itself, the incident need not have touched off another war.

However, after years of turmoil in the region, Austria-Hungary viewed the incident as an opportunity to crush Serbia and punish the Serbian nationalist believed to have been behind the assassination plot. But before acting on its own, the Austro-Hungarian government sought assurances from its ally to the north in accordance with the terms of the Triple Alliance, which had been formed during the days of Bismarck. On July 5, 1914, the Austrian ambassador in Berlin was assured that Germany would give Austria its "faithful support" in whatever course of action it took against Serbia, even if it meant that Russia would be drawn into events in support of its interest in the Balkans. The decision by Kaiser Wilhelm II to support his Austrian ally was not the singular event that would lead to war, it was just one of a series of diplomatic mistakes that would accelerate events and force the ancient states of Europe into a corner from which they could not escape.

On the 23rd of July, Austria handed Serbia an ultimatum that would have ended with Serbia surrendering its sovereignty as a state. Many of the conditions Serbia was willing to accede to so as to prevent war. There were two provisions however, that Serbia could not assent to. One involved Austrian power to interface with a Serbian inquiry into the events of the assassination; the other would have allowed Austria a hand in the internal affairs of Serbia. Serbia suggested that the disputed demands could be decided by a tribunal in the Hague or by a decision rendered by representatives of the Great Powers. With German assurances already in hand, the Serbian attempts to avoid war were rejected and Austria declared war on Serbia on July 28. On the 29th of July, Austrian guns began to bombard Belgrade, that same day Russia began to amass its forces on the Austrian-Hungarian border. On the 30th both Austria-Hungary and Russia ordered general mobilizations. The following day Germany would send an ultimatum to Russia to demobilize in twelve hours and make a declaration to that effect. The ultimatum would go unanswered; war, with all of its horrors and destruction was now inevitable.

In the west, Germany had decided to strike first. Although August 2nd was a Sunday, the diplomats of the Great Powers were still hard at work both preparing for war and trying to prevent it. On that evening the German government demanded from Belgium the right of passage over Belgian soil for its troops. In one of the more courageous acts of the war, tiny Belgium rejected the German demand and started blowing up bridges and tunnels along its eastern border with Germany. Belgian resistance was something that was not anticipated in the Schlieffen plan, which had envisioned easy passage through the Belgian countryside and the encirclement and defeat of the French Army. It sounded like an impossible task, but it should be remembered that in May and June of 1940 this same feat was accomplished in exactly 43 days.

The most fateful day of the war was August 3, 1914. On that day Germany declared war on its western neighbor France. As Germany had already declared war against Russia on August 1st, the long dreaded yet highly anticipated war on two fronts would become a reality for the Second Reich. On August 4th, one and a half million German troops began their westward march, the first of them crossing the Belgian frontier in the early hours of the morning. Learning that Belgian neutrality had been violated, Great Britain sent an ultimatum to Germany to remove its troops from Belgium by midnight or face the possibility of a war declaration from Great Britain. As with all of the ultimatums sent by the various governments during those dark days in the summer of 1914, this ultimatum went unheeded. As Charles Lanrezsac awoke on the morning of August 4, 1914, he would find himself in the unenviable position of not only discovering that his nation was at war, but also that he was in command of a Fifth Army that was directly in the path of one of the largest field armies ever assembled. In total, 35½ corps of the German Army would comprise the hammer blow that was intended to destroy the French Army.

It has been long said that if you want to hear the gods laugh, tell them your plans. So it would be with the German invasion of Belgium and France. The initial Schlieffen Plan had called for the German armies to violate Dutch neutrality as well. For reasons most likely political, this was changed. Instead of having a wide area to travel through "the two northernmost (and strongest) of the five enveloping German armies would be crowded and slowed up through the Liege bottleneck in Belgium."[86] It was the first of but many mistakes. Once into Belgium, the German army was slowed by the unexpected resistance of the tiny Belgium army of King Albert.

Although Belgium had always attempted to maintain strict neutrality, this did not mean that it had neglected its national defenses. Having been a witness to the Franco-Prussian War of 1870, King Leopold II had ordered the construction of a series of forts along the Meuse River at Liege, and at Namur near the confluence of the Meuse and Sambre Rivers. At Liege there were twelve forts, six of which were large pentagonal structures, while the other six were triangular in construction and somewhat smaller. At Namur there were an additional nine forts, five of which were larger, with four smaller forts distributed among them. They were designed by Henri Brialmont in the 1870s and would remind one of the intricate forts designed by the great French military engineer Sébastien de Vauban in the 1600s. It was intended when built that they would serve as strongholds, with the ground units of the Belgian army dug in between them. However, the German assault caught the Belgians so completely off guard that the fortresses would be asked to fend off the German assault on their own. Initially the valiant Belgians in the forts would succeed in holding off the German assault regiments of General von Emmich, but when the German army deployed its larger 305 and 420 millimeter howitzers, the forts were pulverized to dust.

Although the six divisions of the Belgian army had no chance against the three German armies that were unleashed against it, they did provide the French army with two commodities of great importance: time and an example. As the Schlieffen Plan had been devised to be exact right down to the number of trains needed to deploy the one and a half million troops that would assault Belgium and France, time was of critical importance. It had been expected that the Belgian army would offer no resistance, or perhaps only a token resistance to the German advance. However, the last fort at Namur never surrendered until the 24th of August, twenty days after the first German units crossed the border into Belgium. With the Belgium army defeated, the Fifth Army of Charles Lanrezac and the Fourth Army of General Fernand Langle de Cary were squarely in the path of the German juggernaut.

As the German invasion of Belgium had resulted in a British declaration of war against Germany, four divisions from the British army were rushed to France to join their new allies in France. This British defense force is known to history as the British Expeditionary Force, or BEF. They were to form into the line of battle to the left of Charles Lanrezac's Fifth Army; and there, they certainly would be needed. Even though it was now known that the German army was in Belgium, due to an element commonly referred to as the "fog of the war," what was not known was the strength of their forces and their ultimate objective. King Albert of Belgium was the first to recognize that his army was facing at least five corps (it was actually 16) and that the German army might be trying to envelop the left flank of the French army. He also believed that this possibility might be avoided if his army was reinforced by the British and the French. However, the French overall commander, Joseph Jacques Cesaire Joffre, still had his mind made up concerning a French offensive to recover Alsace and Lorraine, and would have none of it. For this lack of strategic insight there would one terrible consequence. Instead of the war being fought in Belgium on terrain that had existed as the theatre of operations from the first moments of the German invasion, for the next four years the countryside of northern and eastern France would become the scene of unmitigated destruction.

On August 6th, three French Cavalry divisions under the command of General Sordet moved into Belgium to reconnoiter and ascertain the strength of the German forces there. Unfortunately, they moved too far, too fast, and failed to encounter the bulk of the German armies, which had been slowed by the resistance of King Albert and his tiny but determined Belgian army. Because of this, General Joffre was further slowed in his recognition of the strategic situation and decided to press ahead with his assault on Alsace and Lorraine.

However, Charles Lanrezac was not so easily deceived. On August 8th Lanrezac sent his chief of staff, Hely d' Orssel, to

Joffre's headquarters, or Grand Quartier General (CQG) at Vitry-le- Francois, to warn them of the impending crisis. Again, Joffre and his staff dismissed Lanrezac's concerns as being unrealistic and overly cautious. By August 9th, the first British troops began to land in France and were being sent directly to the front on the left of Lanrezac's army. However, the British high command had not yet decided on how far forward they should be deployed. In accordance with provisions of Plan XVII, Lanrezac's Fifth Army was still facing toward the northeast, with instructions to attack into Belgium once the Germans had violated that country's neutrality. If, however, the German assault came down from the north and west of the Meuse, Lanrezac's left flank would be left undefended and subject to a flanking movement.

Events in Belgium continued to plague Lanrezac during that second week of August 1914. As the cavalry of Sordet had been unable to unravel the mystery of what German intentions were, on August 11th, Colonel Adelbert of GQG was sent as a personal emissary to King Albert of Belgium imploring him to hold firm until the Fifth Army of Lanrezac and the British troops could reinforce his six divisions, which were now being asked to contain 34 German divisions. He was informed by the King that events continued to unfold as he expected, that he would not let his army be surrounded, and that he would retreat to Antwerp. On the following day, the 12th of August, the Germans would launch an all out cavalry assault against the Belgium forces at Haelen. Just as the French had been so fool hearty as to launch cavalry squadrons against the German positions at Sedan, now the finest cavalry squadrons of Von Marwitz's Uhlans were launched against the Belgians. The result would be the same, as lances and sabers were no match for the repeated volleys from Belgian rifles. Much as reports out of Belgium had been exaggerating the success of the Liege and Namur forts in repelling the Germans, the repelling of the assault at Haelen was reported as being a decisive event in the war. Colonel Adelbert would compound the situation, writing to GQG that it could regard "the retreat of the German cavalry as final and the projected attack through central Belgium as postponed or even abandoned."[87] Nothing could have been further from the truth.

From the southwest, the quarter of a million men that comprised Lanrezac's army began moving into Belgium toward Dinant and into the angle between the Sambre and Meuse Rivers. On August 14th, the lead regiments of Lanrezac's forces reached Dinant. Early the next morning they would begin to receive incoming fire from artillery. A young lieutenant who would one day become leader of the Free French Army and President of France named Charles de Gaulle, was involved in that action. While advancing toward the enemy, de Gaulle became aware that "something struck my knee like a whiplash, making me trip. I dropped, and Sargeant Debout fell on top of me, killed outright. There was an appalling hail of bullets all around. I could hear the muffled sound of them hitting the dead and wounded scattered all over the ground."[88] If nothing else, the action at Dinant should have proven to GQG that, contrary to the report of Colonel Adelbert, the German advance was real and continuing. Although the cavalry sortie of Sordet had "blundered about in the forest of the Ardennes for over two weeks in August without finding hair or hide of its opponents,"[89] fresh reports from French airmen and out of Belgium were reporting long lines of grey-green clad German soldiers crossing through central Belgium northwards and toward the exposed left flank of Lanrezac's army.

In July of 1863 at the Battle of Gettysburg during the American Civil War, after two days of fighting, General Robert E. Lee launched 13 brigades of Confederate troops toward the center of the Union forces believing that to be the weakest point in the Union army, resulting in dire consequences. As the southernmost components of the French army had met with strong resistance in Alsace and Lorraine, and as reports started streaming in of large concentrations of German forces in Belgium, General Joffre would make this same mistake. Now believing that the center of the German armies in Luxembourg and the Ardennes were the weakest point, he ordered the nine corps of the Third and Fourth Armies to attack between Charleroi and Verdun, with Lanrezac receiving orders to attack at the Sambre. These orders show a complete lack of strategic knowledge of the impending crisis, as well as a total disregard for the lives of the average poilu (soldier) of the French army. As the British army had still not deployed all four of its divisions to the left of Lanrezac, it further imperiled the entire French army.

On the morning of the 22nd of August, elements of the Third and Fourth Armies moved into the Ardennes. Initially their movements were concealed by fog. When the fog cleared, the French soldiers who were still clad in the blue coats and red pantaloons, which the French soldiers had worn in Sedan, were suddenly exposed to their German enemies. At Virton the Cavalry of the 12th Hussars, still armed with the Polish lance that Napoleon had adopted in 1807, were mown down by concentrated rifle and machine gun fire. All the other units of the Third and Fourth Armies suffered equally at the hands of an efficient Germany army that was possessed with weapons of such a destructive nature that the leaders cf neither side yet understood or appreciated. During the first day of the Battle of the Somme in July 1916, the British army was reputed to have had 19,000 men killed on the first day of the battle, the greatest one day loss ever suffered by the British army. In comparison, the decision of Joffre to attack into the Ardennes cost the French army 27,000 men killed, with equal numbers being wounded or taken prisoner. In all, the failed French offensives of Plan XVII cost the French somewhere between 270,000 and 300,000 casualties. But this would only become an indication of things to come.

It would be at this juncture of the battle that Lanrezac would decide to disregard his orders from GQG to go on the offensive with the Fourth and Third Armies, and begin to fight a withdrawal back south of the Sambre. He was wise to do so, as more and more units of the First German Army of Alexander von Kluck continued to come on line. By this time the 100,000 British troops that comprised the four divisions of the BEF were on Lanrezac's left flank. On the evening of August 22nd units of the BEF would encounter advance units from von Kluck's army near the town of Mons. When the Fifth Army of Lanrezac had received a bloody nose at Charleroi north of the Sambre, they began to give ground. As the BEF was still moving north, this left a gap of nine miles between the left of Lanrezac's army and the right flank of the British second corps.

Although Lanrezac still did not know the exact number of the German forces descending down upon him, he did realize, unlike Joffre, the danger that the Fifth Army and the BEF were in. The Fifth Army comprised a total of 13 divisions, with four divisions of the BEF to his right. As the Belgian army had been forced to retire to Antwerp, there remained only a single Belgian division at Namur. Coming down directly upon them were 30 divisions from von Kluck's and von Bülow's First and Second Armies. In addition, during the two-day fight at Charleroi, many of Lanrezac's units had been severely cut up. Some units lost most of their officers. Two French colonial regiments had been completely destroyed while making frontal assaults against the bridgeheads over the Meuse, which had been taken by the Germans. On the night of the 22nd of August, Lanrezac sent a message to the commander of the BEF, General Sir John French, asking if he could relieve the pressure on the Fifth Army by wheeling ninety degrees to the right and attacking the right flank of Karl von Bülow's Second Army. Fortunately French declined, as this would have left his own left flank open to attack. As events turned out, the British would have their own dilemma to deal with on the 23rd and 24th of August when the bulk of von Kluck's First Army attacked their position at Mons along the Conde Canal. Initially the German infantry units suffered severe casualties at the hands of the British with their Short Magazine Lee Enfield rifles and Vickers machine guns. However, when the as always efficient German artillery found its range on the British positions, the troops of the BEF were forced to retire. With the German Second Army still exerting pressure against Lanrezac's Fifth Army, the only possible course of action was a withdrawal to the south. The BEF was to fight another day-long battle at Le Cateau on the 26th of August.

The Fifth Army of Lanrezac would continue its withdrawal south towards the Aisne River. The British to his left were fighting a withdrawal of their own. On the 28th, Joffre appeared at Fifth Army Headquarters with instructions for its commander. Its fighting withdrawal was to be temporarily halted and the next day the Fifth Army, or what was left of it, was to counterattack toward Guise and Saint-Quentin. It was a tall order to mandate, especially in light of the fact that the British Commander in Chief had determined that his forces could not render any assistance in the action because they needed a day's rest. Under the explicit threat of being relieved of command if the Fifth Army did not attack, Lanrezac ordered his forces forward. The left formations of his army were to attack the First Army of von Kluck, the right were to attack von Bülow. An English observer at Lanrezac's headquarters wrote, "He manipulated his units with the skill of a master at the great game of war, but he played his hand without zest or faith."[90] The attack met with some measure of success around Guise, but at Saint-Quentin the French assault encountered heavy casualties. Charles Lanrezac then sent a new request for British support on his left, which was again denied. That night Major General Henry Wilson drove to Reims to meet with Joffre. After explaining the situation, Wilson implored Joffre to allow the BEF to continue its withdrawal. This, Joffre agreed to do. Due to the order for the Fifth Army to attack at Guise and Saint-Quentin while the Fourth Army on his right and the BEF on his left continued their withdrawal, the Fifth Army was left exposed and a day's march behind the other forces. Recognizing this, Lanrezac would call GQG and ask for permission to retire. The order would be given on the evening of the 29th but, due to a mix up at staff headquarters, the message was not received by Lanrezac until the following morning.

Much of the fault for the continued retreat of the Fifth Army could be attributed to a dispatch sent on August 30th by Sir John

French to Joffre at GQG that his intention was to pull the BEF
all the way back to the Seine River. It would leave the Fifth
Army with no choice but to follow, or be destroyed by von
Kluck's army, which would be free to roll up its left flank.
Therefore, the southward movement of the entire left flank of
the French armies would continue.

Fortunately however, even though the tactical situation for
the French and British armies was still critical, the strategic
situation was beginning to change. Even though the German
armies still held a numerical advantage, after a month of
fighting they had traveled several hundred miles from their
starting points. Their lines of communication and supply were
stretched very thin, and gaps were starting to appear between
each of the armies. Whereas the Schlieffen Plan had originally
called for the right flank of the German armies to swing west
and then south to Paris, by the end of August the situation was
beginning to change. A new Sixth Army was being formed to
the left of the BEF under General Joseph Manoury, and General
Joseph Gallieni had been appointed as military governor of
Paris. Although these forces were organized for a defensive
purpose, that situation would soon change. It would change
because the condition of General von Kluck's First Army was
becoming critical. By the beginning of September two-thirds of
the First Army's motor lorries had broken down. When the
First Army had started its journey into Belgium it had 84,000
horses to transport its artillery and supplies, which required a
daily diet of two million pounds of fodder a day.[91] The German
soldiers were dead on their feet after a month of marching and
fighting. As had occurred in Belgium with the city of Antwerp,
von Kluck now decided Paris could be left to conquer later,
after he had destroyed Lanrezac's army.

Therefore, when Lanrezac's army continued its withdrawal south and east of Paris, von Kluck followed. By the first of September, aerial reconnaissance began to discover what came to be known as von Kluck's Turn.

Recognizing what perhaps von Kluck did not realize because he assumed the British army was beaten and he was unaware of the existence of the new Sixth Army on his flank, Joffre and Gallieni both began to see an opportunity to finally hit back at the German right wing. To stiffen its resolve, Joffre issued orders to his commanders that any man caught deserting the army or their unit was to be shot. On the third of September changes were made in the command structure of the army. On that day Joffre would relieve Charles Lanrezac from command of the Fifth Army. He would not go alone, as Joffre also relieved two other army chiefs, ten corps commanders and thirty-eight division commanders.

As to whether or not the decision to relieve Lanrezac was justified, that is a verdict which history must render. He was one of the first generals on the western front to recognize the strategic situation when hostilities opened at the beginning of August 1914, and he understood what the intention of the German army was from nearly the beginning. When Joffre decided to launch the attacks at the center of the German line in Luxembourg and the Ardennes, Charles Lanrezac was opposed to the attacks and thought they would result in the needless slaughter of French poilus. His decision on the 23rd of August probably saved the Fifth Army from being destroyed and denied the Germans the decisive engagement they sought which could have ended the war.

Personal perception and Charles Lanrezac's character may have had much to do with his dismissal. Tuchman wrote that, "while the rest of the French army charged to the east, he saw himself left to guard France's unprotected flank from the blow he believed was designed to kill her. He saw himself given the heaviest task – though GQG refused to recognize it as such with the smallest means."[92] His army had to traverse the greatest distances of the campaign and he was asked to operate alongside the Belgian and British armies, over which he exercised no control. Not only were the armies of Britain and Belgium under independent command, but there existed a language barrier between the BEF and Lanrezac's army. To compound that situation, Charles Lanrezac and the commander of the BEF, Sir John French, did not get along well at all. French has been described as being, "arrogant, combative and mercurial."[93] He also maintained a very low opinion of his French counterparts. During a meeting between French and Lanrezac on the 17th of August, when Lanrezac informed the British commander that German forces had been discovered at the Meuse River near Huy, in broken French the field marshal inquired as to what they were doing there and what their plans were. Lanrezac, no doubt short of patience after weeks of campaigning responded, "Mais pour pêcher dans la riviere," they are probably going there to fish.[94]

Much of the failure to get along may well have been beyond Lanrezac's control. When the BEF had been sent to France, Sir John French had been given strict orders from his direct superior Horatio Herbert Kitchener, "that your command is an entirely independent one, and that you will in no case come in any sense under the orders of any allied general."[95] At the August 17th meeting between French and Lanrezac, French informed his counterpart that the BEF would not be prepared to go into action until the 24th, when their assistance was needed then. When Lanrezac was ordered by Joffre to counterattack at Guise and Saint-Quentin, French refused his assistance. On the fateful morning of August 28, when Lieutenant General Sir Douglas Haig of the First Corps of the BEF was willing to assist Lanrezac in his counteroffensive but was countermanded by French, Lanrezac exploded and referred to the act "C'est une félonie." He was also to add comments, which were described as "terrible, unpardonable things about Sir John French and the British army."[96] In these expressions, he may well have been both justified and correct. In the end Lanrezac was caught between an unrealistic commander who recognized too late the strategic situation unfolding before him, and a very unsteady ally in Sir John French who had difficulty understanding both the unfolding series of events and the need for cooperation between the armies.

When Joffre relieved Lanrezac of his command on the 3rd of September, he would write to the newly appointed military governor of Paris, "He was a remarkable professor who in wartime does not live up to the hopes placed in him. Do what you want with him."[97] One would have to wonder what Gallieni would think of this comment, as he had himself opposed Joffre's plan to attack into Alsace-Lorraine on the 14th of August along with Lanrezac.

Personal views or animosities aside, what cannot be disputed were Charles Louis Marie Lanrezac's actions during that dreadful August which had seen so many setbacks for the French army in what the Germans referred to as "Die grosse Zeit." He recognized the strategic situation from the start, and he and his Fifth Army fought at a distinct disadvantage a much larger German force, over far greater distances than the other

French armies. On numerous occasions he had extricated his army from perilous situations so that it could remain intact for later use. He would be denied a role in the Battle of the Marne that would be fought in the first weeks of September 1914, which would strike at von Kluck's exposed right flank and drive the Germans back to the River Aisne. Nevertheless, he did a great deal prior to the battle to guarantee its success.

Both Joseph Joffre and Sir John French were vocal critics of Lanrezac, perhaps because he was a vocal critic of them. They would survive in command for a time, although their shortcomings would lead to their demise. Sir William French would continue to make his blunders and he would be replaced by Douglas Haig in December 1915. Joffre would be succeeded by the hero of Verdun, Robert Georges Nivelle in December of 1916.

After his dismissal from the Fifth Army, Lanrezac would remain in retirement. In 1917 his country attempted to call him back to its service, but he declined the offer. After the war he published a book, "Le Plan de campagne Francaise et le Premier mois de la Guerre, I Aout – 3 Septembre 1914." Later, recognizing the prudence of his actions during that dreadful August of 1914, he was made an officer of the L'egion d' honneur in July 1917. In 1923, the nation of Belgium would recognize his efforts and he was awarded the Grand Cross of the Order of the Crown. The following year France would award him the Grand Cross of the L'egion d' honneur. Though well deserved, these awards were probably little compensation for a man who may have saved his nation.

Charles Lanrezac died in January of 1925. At his request no military honors were afforded at his funeral.

Chapter VII

¤

WAGING PEACE

Peace. The all-elusive state of tranquility that mankind yearns for yet is unable to obtain. In its absence we find years and even decades of death, destruction and the most violent acts that mankind has ever perpetrated. There are those who abhor war on moral grounds, who seek to avoid it by acts of protest or pacifism. But they are not always either successful or alone in their efforts. Surprisingly, there are those who are opposed to war who, by profession, are involved in the conduct of it. Many times it is the soldier who assumes the lead role in trying to secure the avoidance of war. This only seems natural, as it is the soldier who has seen and experienced the horrors of war first hand and who, in the event of war, will be asked to make the extreme sacrifice in the currency of the lost years of his life or even of his blood.

Although man has been an occupant on this planet for tens of thousands of years, longer if we consider our primitive ancestors, we have only existed in organized societies for a mere fraction of that time period. Yet during this period of supposed civilization we have developed a certain fixation with conflict that permeates our very existence. Irregardless of the reasons why we fight, be it over land or borders, personal slight or vengeance, for money or for glory, the fact remains that we fight. During the course of human events, those who are most known to us and that have been the greatest actors on our stage have been great soldiers and makers of war, such as Alexander the Great, Caesar, and Napoleon. It is an unfortunate fact that throughout our history there are instances where the actions of a handful of individuals can work to overcome the will of the many and plunge the world into war.

But just as there have always been those who want only to take up the sword or beat the war post, there have always been those who have been opposed to violence. Their views and their methods differ, so that at times those who are against war actually become enemies in their fight against it. In the years between the world wars of 1914 to 1918 and 1939 to 1945, there were many who took a stand against a potential war in Europe they feared might develop. In England, Prime Ministers Stanley Baldwin and Neville Chamberlain followed a path of appeasement in their attempts to avoid war, a path that was very popular and eventually guaranteed that war would come.

Yet their political adversary Winston Churchill also sought to prevent a war. His policies, if followed, may have actually prevented war. However, he was portrayed as, and regarded to be, a warmonger by the very people who sought the same ultimate goal. Here we find one of the root causes of war, a failure of diplomacy.

There have been throughout history those who have attained greatness and respect for their efforts towards peace, yet have failed in their desire to achieve that end. After his election to the Presidency of the United States in 1860, Abraham Lincoln sought to avoid the Civil War. In his first inaugural address he implored the nation to avoid it by stating, "I am loath to close. We are not enemies, but friends. We must not be enemies. Though passion may have strained, it must not break our bonds of affection. The mystic chords of memory, stretching from every battlefield and patriot grave to every living heart and hearthstone all over this broad land, will yet swell the chorus of the Union, when again touched, as surely they will be, by the better angels of our nature." Unfortunately, the bitter angels of his countrymen's natures would prevail over their better angels, and the most destructive war in our history would soon follow.

The attempts of Lincoln to avoid war are perhaps one of the more recognized of such actions throughout history. Then again, there are many others who staked everything they had to avert mankind's most violent acts. Unfortunately, many of them are either unknown or are only barely known to history. They have existed in all ages. John Jay sought to avoid a war between Great Britain and his infant nation and was vilified for it. As second President of the United States John Adams risked public support and the chance of re-election so as to keep the

United States out of a war with either Great Britain or France during the years of volatility in Europe after the French Revolution. The path of the pacifist can be a lonely one if it runs contrary to popular will.

Of all the periods of violence known to mankind, and there have been many, the two most violent and perhaps needless of all, were the two world wars of the twentieth century. The two decades between these events were times of both political and social upheaval, the consequences of which were fatal to the future. These years are known to us primarily as the years of economic dislocation due to the Great Depression, and as the years of the rise of Nazism, Fascism, and totalitarianism. Yet, those very same years that were to see a steady march of the forces of violence, hatred and intolerance were the same years that would see a number of individuals, great and small, who would try to arrest the march toward war and place the world on a more solid footing. Though the very nature of mankind doomed their efforts to failure, their stories are worth remembering.

When Woodrow Wilson became the twenty-eighth President of the United States on March 4, 1913, he inherited a nation that was experiencing explosive growth and had not been involved in a major conflict since the war with Spain that had lasted from April to December of 1898. True, the Philippine Insurrection had continued until 1902, but there had still existed a decade of peace. When war broke out in Europe in August of 1914, Wilson resisted the urge to lead the United States into an arena of madness, which the United States neither initiated nor stood to gain from. Although events beyond his control, such as the German decision to initiate unrestricted submarine warfare, eventually forced his hand, it was with reluctance and wisdom that he led his nation to war. During his first term in office Woodrow Wilson had proven himself an able leader with a record of legislative accomplishments. During his two terms in office, "His legislative accomplishments included the Federal Reserve, the income tax, the Federal Trade Commission, the first child labor law, the first federal aid to farmers, and the first law mandating an eight-hour workday for industrial workers, as well as the appointment of Brandies to the Supreme Court."[98] Yet when he ran for re-election in 1916, the slogan, "He kept us out of the war" may have helped him prevail in one of the closest presidential elections in U.S. history.

Shortly after his second term in office began, Germany would announce to the world on February 1, 1917 that it was initiating its policy of unrestricted submarine warfare. In response to this act, the United States was to sever relations with Germany on February 3, 1917. However, even though German actions were causing the nation to drift towards war, as soon as it became apparent that he would secure a second term in office, Woodrow Wilson began to lay down the groundwork for a multi-faceted peace initiative which he hoped would bring the bloodletting in Europe to a close. His proposal was for an American mediation of the war, first to be revealed through diplomatic channels and later to be released to the public. Even at that early stage, Wilson's well developed mind was formulating plans to establish a league of nations to further secure world peace once hostilities had ceased and the reasons for its cause resolved. On January 22, 1917, he publicly announced his intention to lay out a plan for "a peace without victory," which would be non-punitive, would seek territorial adjustments in Europe so as to satisfy and remedy issues of ethic nationalism, and the establishment of a league of Nations which would enforce peace once it was again established. Given the nature of the senseless slaughter which was at that time occurring in the trenches on the Western Front, it was a very forward thinking approach to a problem that had plagued mankind, and Europe in particular, for centuries.

Regrettably, external events would derail Woodrow Wilson's attempts for an early resolution of the war. The depredations of Germany's U-boats were beginning to turn public favor away from a position of U.S. neutrality in regard to the war, when in March of 1917 the Zimmerman Telegram became public knowledge. This note, which had been forwarded to the German Minister to Mexico by the German Foreign Secretary, Arthur Zimmerman, contained proposals for a German defensive alliance with Mexico that provided for Mexico re-conquering territories in New Mexico, Texas and Arizona in the event of a war between the United States and Germany. It further insinuated that Mexico urge Japan to join the Central Powers in the conduct of war. Initially, this message was intercepted by British Naval Intelligence, who then forwarded it to Walter Page Hines, who was at that time serving as U.S. Ambassador to Britain. Once it had been verified by U.S. intelligence sources and released to the public, it would further incite public opinion against Germany and the Central Powers.

In further response to German aggression on the high seas, on March 13, 1917, both the State and Navy departments announced the decision by Woodrow Wilson to arm U.S. vessels that would be passing through the war zone. As Germany continued its policy of unrestricted submarine warfare in its attempt to impose a blockade on England and

France, and as U.S. vessels continued to be sunk, Woodrow Wilson finally decided to ask Congress for a declaration of war against Germany. On April 2, Wilson would issue his war message to that body, "It is a fearful thing to lead this great powerful people into war, into the most terrible and disastrous of all wars, civilization itself seeming to be in the balance. But the right is more precious than peace, and we shall fight for the things which we have always carried nearest our hearts — for democracy, for the right of those who submit to authority to have a voice in their own governments, for the rights and liberties of small nations, for a universal dominion of right by such a concert of free peoples as shall bring peace and safety to all nations and make the world itself at last free."[99] On the morning of April 16, 1917, Congress voted on the measure to take up arms against a belligerent Germany. The vote was 373 for war, 56 opposed to it. Curiously, the measure did not declare war against Germany's ally Austria-Hungary. That event would occur eight months later on December 17, 1917 when the United States declared war against that nation.

As a war president, Wilson was to be both firm and effective. For a nation of abundant natural resources, the most important resource of all was the number of males of military age out of a then population of 103 million, the largest of any of the war's combatant nations with the exception of Russia. Those men would be needed, for shortly after the American war declaration, mutiny would break out in the French army from April 29 to May 30, 1917. For some months the Western Front was nearly denuded of French combat troops. The situation was remedied by a British offensive in the north, which occupied German attention until the new French commander Henri Petain was able to restore order. The extent of the mutiny and the severity of the situation were not made known to the public for a period of ten years.

An even greater threat was to confront the allies on the Western Front. In March of 1917, Czar Nicholas II of Russia was forced to abdicate and his government was replaced by the much more moderate government of Alexander Kerensky. In September 1917, the Germany army launched its Riga Offensive in the east, the result of which was to topple the new Russian government. In November, the Bolsheviks seized power and promptly concluded terms of peace with Germany in February 1918. No longer fighting a war on two fronts, this allowed Germany to shift all its manpower resources in the east to the Western Front, thus giving them a ten percent advantage over France and Britain in terms of the number of available troops. With this new numerical superiority, Germany was able to employ a new style of tactics devised by General Oskar von Hutier and launch a series of five major offensives on the Western Front that very nearly won the war.

In his message to Congress on April 2, 1917, Woodrow Wilson stated, "We have no selfish ends to serve. We desire no conquest, no dominion. We seek no indemnities for ourselves, no material compensation for the sacrifice we shall freely make. We are but one of the champions of mankind. ...We enter this war only where we are freely forced into it, because there are not other means of defending our rights."[100] On January 8, 1918, President Wilson would further outline a specific set of objectives for peace with his Fourteen Points. These points were to include:

(1) Open covenants openly arrived at.

(2) Absolute freedom of navigation alike in peace and

war, except as the seas might be closed by international action to enforce international covenants.

(3) The removal so far as possible, of all economic barriers.

(4) Adequate guarantees that armaments would be reduced to the lowest point consistent with domestic safety.

(5) An impartial adjustment of all colonial claims on the principles that the interest of the population must have equal weight with the claims of government.

(6) The evacuation of Russian territory and the free determination of her own political and national policy.

(7) Evacuation and restoration of Belgium.

(8) Evacuation and restoration of French territory and righting the wrong done to France in the matter of Alsace-Lorraine.

(9) Readjustment of the frontiers of Italy along clearly recognizable lines of nationality.

(10) Opportunity for autonomous development for the peoples of Austria-Hungary.

(11) Evacuation and restoration of Rumanian, Serbian, and Montenegrin territory, together with access to the sea for Serbia.

(12) The Turkish parts of the Ottoman Empire to be given a secure sovereignty, but the other nationalities to be given an opportunity for autonomous development, and the Dardanelles to be permanently opened to the ships of all nations under international guarantees.

(13) An independent Poland, to include territories indisputably Polish, with free and secure access to the sea.

(14) A general association of nations to be formed to afford mutual guarantees of political independence and territorial integrity to great and small states alike.[101]

If these fourteen simple points had been adhered to, the world may have been spared another of its great catastrophes in 1939.

Whereas Congress had made its declarations of war against Germany and Austria-Hungary, the task of mobilizing for war and ending hostilities would need to be completed before Wilson's attempts at a lasting peace could be made. With a peacetime army of but 200,000 men, which included 65,000 National Guardsmen who were stationed along the border with Mexico, much needed to be done in order to recruit, train, equip, and transport an army to Europe that would be sizeable enough to turn the tide of war in favor of the allies. Woodrow Wilson would oversee this effort with nearly amazing results.

General John Pershing was named as overall commander of the U.S. forces to be sent to Europe. Initially he would ask for an army of three million men. However, through a combination of volunteer enlistments and a successful peacetime draft, the actual figure would be four million, or twenty times its original size at the time of our declaration of war. It was the largest armed force raised by the United States up until that time. While it was twice the size of the Union Army of 1861-1865, it only cost one-twentieth as much to recruit. It was also recruited and trained quickly. By the time of the Armistice in the autumn of 1918, forty-two divisions, each of about 28,000 men, had been equipped and sent to France.

Having never served in the military, as had so many of the

previous presidents, one would think Woodrow Wilson might be lacking in those qualities necessary to be a wartime president. But just the opposite held true. As with all things in his life, he was decisive and wise enough to surround himself with men of talent and to delegate authority. Immediately after convincing the Congress to declare war, he was able to lobby for the Selective Service Bill, stating, "there is a universal obligation to serve and that a public authority should choose those upon whom the obligation of military service shall rest."[102] This bill was far more successful than that which had been passed during the Civil War, as it provided for local draft boards comprised of local civilians instead of military men. Notably absent from the bill were provisions for individuals to purchase or provide a substitute for themselves.

Recognizing also that the American Expeditionary Force would need to be fed and supplied with everything from bullets to blankets at the end of a 3,000-mile chain of supply, Wilson instituted policies toward making America more efficient agriculturally and industrially. It was Wilson's intention to cause America to "correct her unpardonable fault of wastefulness."[103] To that effect, male high school students were released from classes so as to work the family farms, and in the cities and suburbs the practice of having "victory gardens" was established.

As the civilian and military establishments of the United States had anticipated that the next war the United States would participate in would require an army of about 500,000 men, the American Expeditionary Force found itself woefully short of weapons. Although the U.S. Army possessed the best battle rifle of its day, the 1903 Springfield, only about 600,000 were in existence. Although the United States also possessed the Browning automatic rifle and the Browning M-2 heavy machine gun, also the best of their time, these existed in few numbers as well. The U.S. Navy, which had been the pride and joy of Theodore Roosevelt, had a sufficient number of heavy warships, and was sent into action immediately. As the airplane had become an important instrument of a war the United States had remained out of prior to 1917, when the Aviation Section of the U.S. Army Signal Corps went to war it had but 130 trained pilots, with 1,000 enlisted men and 55 serviceable aircraft.[104]

Accordingly, the effort to equip a force eight times as large as what the available supply of weapons would permit required a Herculean effort as well as new unproven methods. Woodrow Wilson would prove to be a master of the situation. A "Council of National Defense" was created from among half a dozen Cabinet Secretaries. It was to work with the Advisory Commission of the Council of National Defense for "the coordination of industries and resources for the national security and welfare."[105] A War Industries Board was also established so that military leaders could coordinate with the leaders of private industry for the purchase of much needed war supplies.

In Wilson's efforts to prepare the country for war, almost nothing would escape his attention. A committee on Public Information was established so as to help promote the "Gospel of Americanism." With an initial budget of 100 million dollars, the CPI was intended by the twenty-eighth president to capture the public's hearts and minds. By war's end, more than 750,000 speeches would be made on behalf of the CPI, reaching an audience of more than eleven million people. Just as the "Victory Garden" would become a visible symbol of the effort to win the war, another product of the CPI would also become iconic. When the CPI initiated a campaign to distribute window cards and posters intended to bolster morale, a recruiting poster created by James Montgomery Flagg was introduced to the public. It depicted a white-haired Uncle Sam with a star spangled top hat and the slogan "I Want You for U.S. Army." It may well be one of the most recognized images in our long history.

As the antithesis of the CPI, Wilson was also partially responsible for the Espionage Act, which was passed by the Sixty-Fifth Congress on June 15, 1917. Woodrow Wilson had initially voiced concerns on such matters as espionage during his 1915 State of the Union Address when he spoke of the danger of naturalized citizens "who have poured the poison of disloyalty into the very arteries of our national life."[106] In appealing to Congress for the authority to deal with measures of espionage "with a firm hand of stern repression." Wilson may have been thinking of the actions of Abraham Lincoln who had suspended the Writ of Habeas Corpus on numerous occasions and also relied on the use of martial law when necessary. When challenged by the Supreme Court on such measures, Lincoln even threatened to have Chief Justice Roger B. Tanney thrown in jail. It is curious that Wilson followed this chain of thought, especially given that when war was declared he remarked to his cousin, "Fitz, thank God for Abraham Lincoln."[107] When asked about the reason for the comment, Wilson further stated, "I don't want to make the mistakes he did."[108] During the early years of the Republic when John Adams was president he proposed the Alien and Sedition Acts, which were hugely unpopular. Ironically, the Sedition Act of 1918 was passed in order to prohibit "disloyal, profane, scurrilous, or abusive language about the form of government of the United States."

The Espionage and Sedition Acts aside, as the forces of the American Expeditionary Force came online in Europe, the effect would be to turn the tide of war. Even though the spring offensives of Erich Ludendorff nearly won the war for Germany, they also further depleted the already much diminished capacity of the German nation to fight. Perhaps recognizing that the German Army had punched itself out, the French Marshall Ferdinand Foch, who became Supreme Allied Commander in April 1918, recommended a series of immediate counterattacks against the tiring German Army. Between the 18th of July 1918 and the end of the war, three allied offensives were launched on the Western Front. They would be launched at Aisne-Marne, at St. Mihiel, and finally at Meuse-Argonne. As an indication of the importance of the American Expeditionary Force to the final war effort, during the Meuse-Argonne offensive 1,200,000 U.S. troops participated in the action, with 120,000 of them becoming casualties of war.

Of equal note, as early as October 2, Erich Ludendorff began reporting to his government that due to the arrival of sufficient numbers of American troops coupled with the lack of any further German reserves, victory for Germany was no longer possible. His recommendation was that the German government seek peace. Acting upon this advice, the German government immediately contacted President Wilson and asked for peace along the terms of his Fourteen Points. Unfortunately, Woodrow Wilson lacked the authority to negotiate terms on behalf of the other allied governments. For the time being, hostilities would continue.

In a fatal and desperate act, the military leadership of

Germany asked its navy to relieve the pressure on the German army by sailing out to engage the Royal Navy. As the plan was devised, the cruiser squadrons of the High Seas Fleet would raid along the Strait of Dover and at the mouth of the Thames River. When units from the Royal Navy responded, the Germany submarine fleet would join the fray, to be joined by the battleships and battle cruisers, which would engage the heavy units of the British fleet off the Dutch coast. Unfortunately, after four years of near inactivity, the sailors of the German navy decided to mutiny instead of engaging in what they considered to be a near suicidal mission. The mutiny would not be restricted to the vessels of the High Seas Fleet, though. For, within a number of days the sailors gained control of most of the cities of northern Germany where the fleet was stationed. By November 5th the situation had become so untenable that representatives were sent to Ferdinand Foch to receive the terms upon which the Germans would need to agree in order to surrender.

On the evening of November 7, 1918, the German Secretary of State Matthias Erzberger crossed the front lines under a white flag of truce to meet with Foch at his traveling headquarters near Compiegne. At that time, the American commander John Pershing wanted to continue fighting until the Germans were forced to lay down their arms in the field. He would be overruled on this point, though the terms of the armistice that were agreed to were so severe that Germany could not have resumed fighting after its terms took effect. At 1100 hours on November 11, 1918 the terms of the Armistice went into effect. Germany was forced to surrender all occupied territories within two weeks. It had to surrender its means to fight on land, to include handing over 5,000 pieces of artillery and 25,000 machine guns. All sixteen of its capital ships plus eight cruisers and fifty destroyers were to be interned in either neutral or allied ports. All of its submarines were to be surrendered as well and its troops were to evacuate the west bank of the Rhine River, creating a 6-mile wide demilitarized zone. In addition, Germany was forced to surrender 5,000 locomotives, 150,000 railroad cars and 5,000 trucks, so that it would be destitute of any means of transport or to supply an army.

When the guns fell silent in November 1918 and the "war to end all wars" had been fought to its terrible conclusion, the task of establishing a lasting peace was just beginning. True enough Woodrow Wilson had proposed terms for a lasting peace with his Fourteen Points. Nevertheless, old animosities die hard and the problems of ethic nationalism were difficult to solve in a Europe where borders were always shifting and populations always moving.

For Woodrow Wilson, the greatest challenge in his efforts to secure peace would not come from enemy bullets or bombs; it would come from an established two-party political system. In early 1917 when Woodrow Wilson determined upon a policy of "armed neutrality" and asked Congress to pass legislation authorizing him to arm merchant ships, he was met with resistance in the U.S. Senate by Senators George Norris and Robert LaFollette. When hostilities ended in November 1918, The New York Times had written of Wilson that his "clear vision of the moral objects for which nations took up arms against Germany … won for him very early acknowledged pre-eminence as the spokesman of the allied cause."[109] Yet within weeks of the Armistice opposition to Wilson' policies and plans were taking form under the leadership of Theodore Roosevelt, who may have been contemplating a run for President in 1920. Roosevelt referred to the Fourteen Points and a League of Nations as a "product of men who want everyone to float to heaven on a sloppy sea of universal mush."[110] When Wilson had asked for a war declaration in 1917, Roosevelt was all in on the request, even asking Wilson to allow him to enter service at the head of a regiment he intended to raise. Yet as soon as hostilities ended, he marched in a direction opposite that of the man he had proclaimed support of.

Opposition would come from foreign leaders as well. Of the "Big Three," France, England and the United States, Woodrow Wilson was the only leader who had served throughout the war. David Lloyd George had become Prime Minister of England in 1916. Georges Clemenceau had served as Premier of France from 1906 to 1909, and then was recalled to office during the dark days of 1917. At seventy-eight years of age he was still often referred to as the "Tiger" of France. When Wilson had first announced his Fourteen Points, Clemenceau was to comment, "God was satisfied with Ten Commandments. Wilson gave us fourteen."[111]

Wilson would have better luck with Lloyd George. On January 4, 1918, David Lloyd George had made a speech at the Trade Union Conference in London during which he had stated that the basis of any territorial settlement in Europe after the war must be based upon "government by consent of the governed."[112] Although Woodrow Wilson is often considered as being the originator of the term "self-determination," it was Lloyd George who coined this phrase during his speech. However, Woodrow Wilson was never one without his own verbal firepower. When word reached the United States that the terms for the Armistice had been agreed to, Wilson was to declare, "A supreme moment of history has come," and "The hand of God is laid upon the nations. He will show them favor, I devoutly believe, only if they rise to the clear heights of His own justice and mercy."[113]

In the events to follow, justice and mercy would prove to be two qualities sadly lacking in his contemporaries. From the first, it became increasingly obvious that some of the leaders of Europe were not anxious to have Wilson attend any peace conferences, especially in light of that fact that he desired equal representation for all nations, large and small alike. Given the nature of the posturing that was occurring in Europe since the Armistice had taken effect, and probably also realizing the long shadow of Sedan in the upcoming peace talks, Wilson believed that the European powers would insist upon "a peace of force and vengeance, whereas he believed that only upon a "peace of justice could a stabilized Europe be rebuilt."[114] Wilson was also of the opinion that if the United States simply sent an ambassador to the peace conference, he would be upstaged by the more prominent premiers of the allied powers and that hence America's role would be much diminished. It was decided that Wilson would go to Europe and both represent his country and be the champion of his belief in a new League of Nations.

Before departing for Europe Woodrow Wilson addressed the U.S. Congress so as to ask for its united consent during his forthcoming mission for peace. But the plague of the two-party system would act as a plague against peace. On December 3, 1918, Philander Knox of Pennsylvania introduced a resolution to restrict any peace settlement "to the reasons for which the United States had gone to war and postpone for separate consideration any discussion for a League of Nations."[115] Knox was not to be his only critic, for soon the chorus against U.S. participation in any such league grew.

On the same day that Knox introduced his resolution, Woodrow Wilson and his wife Edith boarded a train for Hoboken, New Jersey, where they would embark on a ten-day voyage to France aboard the ship George Washington. Wilson was not to be alone in his attempts at securing peace, for he assembled a team of four Peace Commissioners to assist him. Among them were General Tasker Bliss and Secretary of State Robert Lansing.

When Wilson departed for Europe, no doubt he did so with both a sense of reality, recognizing that his efforts would meet with political opposition at home and abroad, and with a tragic sense that the expectations being placed upon him were unrealistic. While walking on the deck of the George Washington one evening he commented to a member of the peace mission, George Creel, "You know, and I know, that these ancient wrongs, these present unhappinesses, are not to be remedied in a day or with the wave of a hand. What I seem to see — with all my heart I hope I am wrong — is a tragedy of disappointment."[116]

When Wilson and his party arrived at Brest on December 13, he was met with a reception befitting a conquering hero or a national savior. During a time when it was still safe to do so, Wilson and his wife rode through the streets of Brest in an open-topped car, amidst throngs of French and American soldiers. Such receptions were to continue. When Wilson arrived in Paris the next day he was greeted at the train station by French President Raymond Poincare, Premier Georges Clemenceau and members of the French cabinet. Of the joyous crowds that greeted him, Wilson's former student Raymond

Fosdick would note, "The French think that with almost a magic touch he will bring about the day of political and industrial justice."[117] Being the first sitting President to travel abroad for an extended time period, Wilson and his wife were afforded stately accommodations at Murat Palace.

A Similar reception would await Wilson at some of the other ancient capitals and cities of Europe as well. He would spend the last five days of 1918 in London, where he met with the Queen Mother, the King, and with David Lloyd George and Foreign Secretary Arthur Balfour. He would also be afforded the opportunity to meet future Prime Minister Winston Churchill, and to tease the former head of the Admiralty about the American contribution to the war at sea, as the policy of convoying merchant ships which helped win the war was the creation of American Admiral William S. Sims.

It may be, however, that Wilson's reception in Rome at the beginning of 1919 was the one to top them all. Wilson and his wife were to travel from Paris to the Eternal City by means of the King of Italy's train. Joyful crowds lined the tracks along the way. When the train reached Rome, Secret Service Agent Edmund Starling described the reception as "exceeding anything I have seen in all my years of witnessing public demonstrations."[118] As Wilson was the first President to leave the country while in office, he was also the first to meet with a Pope, doing so when he traveled to the Vatican to meet with Pope Benedict XV. In the same way as the people of France had greeted him as a conquering hero, in Rome he was regarded as "The God of Peace." In a sense purely political, much of the enthusiasm that greeted him in Italy may have had to do with the fact that he would soon play a part — a very important part — in redefining the borders of Italy. It should be remembered that Italy had once been a part of the Triple Alliance with Germany and Austria-Hungary, and had entered the war on the side of the allies hoping for territorial gains at war's end. However, at the Battle of Caporetto in October and November of 1917, its army was decisively beaten and it had nearly been knocked out of the war. In the upcoming peace talks, Italy would not be bargaining from a position of strength.

Upon returning to Paris, Wilson and his colleagues resumed the business of peace. From the start, Wilson had taken the stand that his proposal for the League of Nations must be tied to any peace agreement. There may have been various reasons for this. Primarily, "he knew that the temper of the Allied and Associated Powers was not, in that January of 1919, such as to render possible a settlement of true moderation, and he hoped, in the Covenant, to provide an instrument by which, when saner councils prevailed, the Treaty could be modified and rendered less punitive. He knew also that the League of Nations would not be able completely to fulfill its high mission unless the direct impulse, the ultimate moral, physical, and above all financial force, were provided by the United States."[119] In addition, as it had become obvious even before his departure for Europe that his efforts would meet with stiff resistance in the Congress, Wilson thought the treaty might stand a better chance of ratification if there existed a connexus of the Treaties of Peace. Although he was largely correct in both assumptions, this decision would guarantee that the peace negotiations would be lengthy.

There would be other difficulties as well. Even before the representatives of the various nations had met, Georges Clemenceau had traveled to London on December 2nd and 3rd to meet with representatives of Her Majesty's government.

Although no formal agreements were reached, it was decided that a committee should be appointed to examine Germany's capacity to pay war reparations, to decide if the Kaiser should stand trial before an International Tribunal, to allow representatives of Great Britain's dominions to attend meetings of the conference which might pertain to their specific interest, and that a committee should be established for the purpose of supplying relief to the areas devastated by war.

Although the armies of Europe had long since trampled on the soil of North America during the years of colonization, World War I was the first time an American army had become involved in a major European war. Therefore, there would be a conflict of methods involved. Essentially the new diplomacy and idealism of Woodrow Wilson was to clash with the old ideas of diplomacy of the European nations. Whereas Wilson sought a permanent peace based on justice for large and small nations alike, the European leaders were more concerned with the division of the spoils of war and with indemnities and reparations. Add to this the difficulty of language. Whereas Clemenceau wished to have the treaty written in the precise language of France, Wilson and Lloyd George wanted it to be in English. As the fourth member of the Council of Four was Premier Orlando of Italy, who spoke neither English nor French, the treaty would end up being trilingual.

On January 12, 1919, two months after hostilities with Germany had ended, the first meeting between the representatives of the various nations met to consider questions of procedure. Much as had happened when the representatives of the thirteen original states had met to draft the United States Constitution, it was decided to deny admission to the press. They would be allowed to attend the Plenary Sessions, but for most of the conference they were denied access. As Woodrow Wilson had always been a successful legislator and was both a very good speaker and successful writer of state papers, this move no doubt removed a possible ally in his quest for peace.

Out of this first meeting, which was essentially nothing more than a meeting of the Supreme War Council, came a working organization for the conference in the form of a Council of Ten. This group consisted of the foreign ministers of the United States, Great Britain, France, Italy, and Japan, together with President Wilson and the Premiers of the other four nations. Eventually, this council would be replaced by the Council of Four, which was composed of Woodrow Wilson, David Lloyd George, Georges Clemenceau, and Orlando of Italy. There was also a Plenary Conference, which consisted of the representatives of twenty-seven nations who were called into session to ratify the findings of the executive as well as fact finding bodies. There were to be no representatives from defeated Germany and its allies. They would only learn the provisions of the treaty once it had been completed.

At the Council of Ten meeting on January 13, the members of the various nations began to formulate an agenda concerning those topics they wished to discuss, including the creation of new states, the disposition of German colonies, and the adjustment of frontiers and borders. As Great Britain, Japan and Italy were already formulating their own ideas as to the division of the German colonies, Woodrow Wilson wisely used this issue as an argument that the issuance of territories should come under the jurisdiction of a League of Nations and that its creation should be placed as the first priority of the Conference. France, as could be expected, placed the division of spoils as a first priority, the creation of the League as coming last. Great

Britain would offer a compromise, stating that it would be best if the question of the League was taken out of the Council and placed before a special committee. On January 22, the Council of Ten accepted a set of four resolutions:

(1) It is essential to the maintenance of the world settlement, which the Associated Nations are now met to establish, that a League of Nations be created to promote international cooperation, to insure the fulfillment of accepted international obligations, and to provide safeguards against war.

(2) This treaty should be created as an integral part of the general Treaty of Peace, and should be open to every civilized nation, which can be relied upon to promote its objects.

(3) The members of the League should periodically meet in international conference, and should have a permanent organization and secretariat to carry on the business of the League in the intervals between the conferences.

(4) The Conference therefore appoints a committee representative of the associated governments to work out the details of the constitutions and functions of the League.[120]

When these resolutions were unanimously accepted by the Second Plenary Session on January 25, it appeared that Wilson's dream of world peace might actually have a chance to succeed. Speaking on that occasion, Wilson stated that he sought no territorial gains for his country and that his purpose for being in Paris was a desire to not have his country return to war. He said he viewed the League "as the keystone of the whole program which expressed our purpose and our ideal in this war, and which the Associated Nations have accepted as the basis of the settlement."[121]

Unfortunately for Wilson, his keen mind and strong sense of moral obligation with regard to peace was not shared by many of his European contemporaries. The very same plenary session which had accepted the resolution toward creation of the League, was devoted to setting up committees to investigate reparations and damages from the war, with the internationalizing of waterways, and to establish "the personal guilt and responsibility of the authors of the war." Lord Curzon of Great Britain would write his contemporary Lord Derby that in his opinion the creation of the League "had nothing whatever to do either with the war or with the immediate task of concluding peace." Having been able to persuade the Council of Ten to establish a League Commission, the next step was to determine its membership. As accepted, the Commission was to consist of nineteen members, two from each of the four major powers, plus one member from each of the nine smaller powers. Woodrow Wilson was to serve as chairman, with Lord Cecil of Great Britain as vice chairman. As many of the members were favorable to the concept of the League, it was another positive sign for the aspirations of Wilson.

During an informal meeting with Lord Robert Cecil and the South African Prime Minister on the evening of January 19, Woodrow Wilson informed his two contemporaries that he hoped an informal Anglo-French-American group would be able to draft a plan for the League which could be presented in two weeks. Given the differing views of the various committee members, it was a great deal to ask for. However, on February 14, 1919, Woodrow Wilson was able to present a draft of the Covenant for the League of Nations to the full conference at the Quai d' Orsay, which was the unofficial term for the French Foreign Office. The fact that this draft was completed in a mere four weeks while having to overcome the barriers of differences in language and national interest is a true testament to the abilities of Wilson, as he was the most firm advocate and proponent. It was a vindication of his decision to attend the Conference personally, against the advice of many of his American contemporaries.

Though far from perfect, the draft did contain many of the elements Wilson thought of as being essential in the formation of the League. Wilson had once confided to an advisor that he hoped the Covenant could be on par with the Declaration of Independence or the U.S. Constitution in setting a new direction for the course of humanity. It contained an article calling for national independence and territorial integrity in accordance with the problems of ethnic nationalism then existing. Provisions were made for the establishment of a permanent Secretariat that would reside in Geneva. It was to be the permanent seat of the League, if accepted. A Permanent Court of International Justice was to be established so as to resolve issues between nations without the need for war. Perhaps most importantly, there were provisions within the Articles of the draft Covenant that would allow member nations to impose sanctions against other member nations who violated the provisions of the League.

With the draft Covenant completed and submitted, Woodrow Wilson returned home so as to conduct the necessary business of the Chief Executive, signing into law those bills that had been passed by the Sixty-fifth Congress during his absence. Leaving France on February 15, 1919, Wilson would arrive in Boston eight days later. When the President had left for France, it was apparent even that at that early stage he would meet with Congressional resistance in his desire for an equitable peace and the creation of the League of Nations. On his last night at sea, he confided to his physician, Dr. Grayson, "The failure of the United States to back the League would break the heart of the world."[122] Speaking to a crowd of between seven to eight thousand people, the President would offer similar sentiments the next day.

Before leaving Paris, Wilson had asked those members of the Senate Foreign Relations and Foreign Affairs Committees to withhold comment until he could return to Washington and explain the provisions of the draft Covenant to them. They would do so, to some extent, perhaps grudgingly, but several Senators were already formulating arguments against the League. In his farewell address, George Washington had advised against the new nation becoming involved in entangling alliances. He would write, "Europe has a set of primary interest, which to us have none, or very remote relation. Hence she must be engaged in frequent controversies." He would add, "Hence therefore it must be unwise in us to implicate ourselves, by artificial ties, in the ordinary vicissitudes of her politics, or the ordinary combinations and collisions of her friendships, or enmities."[123] In essence, Woodrow Wilson, in advancing the cause of the League, would be taking on the advice of the first occupant of the esteemed office which he now held.

The Republican adversaries of Wilson, such as Henry Cabot Lodge, Frank Brandegee, Philander Knox, and Robert

LaFollette would also fall back on other documents from the past, claiming that if the United States were to join a League of Nations that it would undermine the Monroe Doctrine and effect everything from trade to immigration. On the evening of February 26, Wilson set another precedent when he invited members of the Foreign Affairs and Foreign Relations committees to the white house for an informal dinner and discussion of the draft Covenant. As could be expected, without any regard for the proposals or possibilities within the Covenant, both favor and dissent began to materialize along mostly party lines. The nation's newspapers would follow this trend, with pro-League papers such as the New York Times and The World speaking favorably of the President and others, such as the New York Sun, being critical of the man who sought peace. The country would divide geographically as well, with Democratic strongholds in the south and east being in favor of the League, and the mid-west and west being opposed to it. Just as Wilson would be dealing with very short sighted and somewhat provincial minds in Europe, he would find himself dealing with much the same in his own nation.

On Sunday, March 2, the three most vocal opponents of Woodrow Wilson, Senators Lodge, Knox, and Brandegee, met to draft a statement opposing the draft Covenant as then written. On Monday March 3, Lodge read this resolution on the Senate floor, also taking time to announce the names of thirty-seven senators and four senators-elect who had affixed their names to the resolution. Others not present could be expected to do the same. If the remaining senators, in a U.S. Senate that comprised ninety-six members, held their position, the two-thirds majority needed for the Senate to ratify the proposed treaty would be lacking.

In his arguments against the League, Senator Lodge was to state, "We are all striving for a like result: but to make any real advances toward the future preservation of the world's peace will take time, care, and long consideration. We cannot reach our object by a world constitution hastily constructed in a few weeks in Paris in the midst of the excitement of a war not yet ended. The one thing to do… and that which I now wish above all others, is to make the peace with Germany."[124] He was also to declare, "That which I desire above everything else, that which is nearest to my heart, is to bring our soldiers home."[125] Though he sounded sincere in his arguments, the reality of the situation was quite different. Regarding "a war that had not yet ended," the reason Germany asked for the Armistice in November 1918 was because the nation no longer possessed the ability to not only wage war, but to defend itself. As for Lodge's desire to bring the troops home, as soon as hostilities ended, the decision was made to leave an occupation force of eight of the forty-two divisions sent over and to bring the others home. By the early spring of 1919, the flow of soldiers from the American Expeditionary Force returning home reached more than 300,000 per month, which was greater than the eastbound flow when the A.E.F was being deployed to Europe. By the summer of 1919, only 6,800 men remained as part of the occupation force. Given also that the United States has maintained a military presence in Europe since the conclusion of the Second World War, the arguments of Lodge seem almost irrelevant.

In response, the President would retort, "…and I am amazed, not alarmed but amazed, that there should be in some quarters such a comprehensive ignorance of the state of the world. These gentlemen do not know what the mind of men is just now. Everybody else does. I do not know where they have been closeted, I do not know by what influences they have been blinded, but I do know they have been separated from the general currents of the thought of mankind."[126] After a mere ten days in America, Wilson again set sail for the Peace Conference in France. In that short space of ten days the situation at the Conference had changed dramatically. On February 19, Premier Clemenceau had been shot by an anarchist and was now confined to his bed. David Lloyd George and Jan Smits were also gone, having been replaced by Lord Balfour and Winston Churchill. As negotiations had continued in his absence, Wilson found that in his absence Colonel Edward House had surrendered on several important points. Of this surrender, Wilson would remark, "He has compromised on every side, and so I shall have to start all over again and this time it will be harder... He has yielded until there is nothing left."[127]

Even more disconcerting, in his absence Arthur Balfour had put forth a resolution so as to proceed without delay the consideration of peace terms with the new German Republic to include establishing the frontiers of Germany and the disposition of its colonies. The colonies in the Pacific were a particular problem, as both Japan and Australia stood to gain from Germany's loss. When President Wilson asked the Australian Prime Minister W.M. Hughes if he intended to violate the spirit of the Peace Conference in a naked attempt to grab some of the German archipelagoes in the Pacific Hughes responded, "That's about the size of it, Mr. President."[128]

As Germany had found itself fighting a war on two fronts during the hostilities of 1914 to 1918, Wilson was now forced to fight a war on two fronts as well. When he had returned to the United States for ten weeks, his authority at the Council had been severely curtailed. Now that he was back in France, Republican opposition in the United States would continue unabated. In order to ensure passage of the provisions of the treaty and acceptance of the Covenant of the League of Nations, Wilson was forced to submit certain amendments to the draft Covenant. Although a Republican and a close friend of Senator Lodge and a member of Wilson's Peace Commission, Henry White had asked his friend in the Senate to forward him the exact phraseology of the amendments which might allow the Covenant to be accepted by the Republican members of the Senate. White believed two things, "that unless we form part of any League of Nations which may be set up, there will be none; and secondly, that if no agreement for a League of Nations can be arrived at, we can only revert to the old and only final method of settling international disputes, namely war."[129] Perhaps softening to the President's views on peace, White would also add, "I cannot but feel that a strenuous effort must be made to try to prevent a return to the barbarous methods hitherto prevailing, which will, of course, be even more barbarous hereafter in view of the constant scientific improvement in weapons for the destruction of human life."[130] Given the events of 1939 to 1945, a more accurate prediction could not have been made.

From the time of his return to France until his departure on June 28, Wilson continued his two-front war against Senate opposition in the United States and the old evils and prejudices of European politics. France was to be particularly stubborn due to its efforts to secure its own safety while weakening Germany both economically and militarily. It wanted the Rhineland to be separated from Germany and to use it as a permanent military barrier in case of future hostilities. France also wanted not only heavy reparations but was demanding that it be given the Saar Valley which was rich in coal. Italy wanted to gain control of the Adriatic by acquisition of Dalmatia and the city of Fiume. Japan, which had played almost no role in the European War, wanted Germany's Pacific Islands as well as Shantung. Great Britain, having seen American industrial might during the war was seeking to preserve its centuries old naval supremacy by placing restrictions on the growth of the U.S. Navy. As Woodrow Wilson had just celebrated his 62nd birthday on December 28, the years of toil were beginning to take their effect. While he was in France it had become normal for him to put in as many as fifteen hours a day. This schedule would exact a toll on a man half his age.

On April 3, 1919, after conferring with King Albert of Belgium during an afternoon meeting of the Council, the President became seriously ill and had to return to his room where Dr. Grayson found him complaining of severe head and back pains as well as coughing spells. With a fever of 103 degrees, Wilson was forced to spend the next four days in bed. Although it is impossible to diagnose an illness a century after the fact, what was then interpreted as the onset of influenza may well have been a minor stroke. As the President had a long history of cerebral vascular disease, this scenario is not entirely without credibility. When Wilson returned to his feet on April 7, he requested the ship George Washington be brought to Brest for his return to the United States, in effect threatening to break up the Peace Conference. Whether the act was a threat or medical necessity, the call for the George Washington had a sobering effect on many who were involved in the negotiations as well as leaders in the United States. Clemenceau, who had since returned after the assassination attempt seemed willing to seek compromise, while many in Washington considered it "as an act of impatience and petulance on the President's part."[131]

Perhaps now tiring from the constant adversity, President Wilson began to also relent in his demands. While the Rhineland was not to be amputated from Germany, it was to be occupied for a period of fifteen years. The Saar was not to become part of France, either, though the French were to get control of the coal mines there for fifteen years as well, after which time its eventual fate was to be decided by plebiscite. France was also granted reparations, though Wilson fought to have the matter decided by a Reparations Committee representing both the Allied and Associated Powers, and based upon what the new German republic could reasonably be expected to pay over a thirty-year period. Italy was not to receive the city of Fiume, though they did receive South Tyrol from Austria. Japan did not succeed in its efforts to have a statement of racial equality placed in the treaty, but it would receive Shantung, though this was on condition that the province would be returned to China at a future time. Although the provision for Shantung would cause Wilson no end of grief when disclosed in the United States, the President believed, "the settlement was the best that could be had out of a dirty past."[132]

One of the great tragedies of the treaty was that its clauses were based largely on the theory that Germany was responsible for the war. Upon the treaty's completion, delegates from the new German republic were invited to come to Versailles on May 7. The leader of the German delegation was Count Brockdorff-Rantzau. Upon reading the conditions of the treaty they would spend 21 days protesting its various provisions as being violations of the pre-armistice agreements. Though they were correct in their beliefs that Germany was not alone in its guilt for the outbreak of the war, the economic and political situation in Germany left them little alternative other than to sign the Agreement. On June 28, the German delegates affixed their signatures to the Versailles Treaty, although Germany itself was not allowed to become a member of the League of Nations until 1926. After having been away from the United States for four months, Woodrow Wilson began his journey home to face the difficult task of getting a very obdurate U.S. Senate to ratify the treaty.

Unfortunately for the President, certain conditions were to conspire against him in his search for senatorial ratification of the Treaty and League of Nations. In 1920, there was to be another round of public elections to include that of President. As Woodrow Wilson had won the election of 1912 due to the split in the Republican Party between W.H. Taft and Theodore Roosevelt and his Bull Moose Party, the senate republicans felt a certain urgency to remain united against the President. If it meant that defeating Wilson's attempt at peace was bad for America, Europe, or the world, so be it. All that was important to Senator Henry Cabot Lodge and his group of "irreconcilables" was political expediency.

To that end Lodge and his contemporaries decided upon a certain strategy. When Woodrow Wilson returned home in June of 1919, a majority of the populace was in favor of the Treaty and the League. But the ratification of treaties was not decided by popular vote; it was decided by two-thirds majority in the Senate. Even before Wilson had departed for Paris, Henry Cabot Lodge and Theodore Roosevelt had decided to cripple any attempt at ratification of the treaty by means of subtle attacks on its flanks, attacking its structure one piece at a time to create doubts in the public mind as to the dangers the Treaty might hold in regard to American diplomacy and freedom of action, to also wear the process down by means of further amendments, and finally to delay any vote on ratification until a sufficient number of votes had been acquired so as to ensure failure of ratification. In addition, public support was another means by which to attack the Versailles Treaty. Americans of German descent came to regard the Treaty as being too harsh against Germany. Italian Americans found dissatisfaction with the Treaty because Fiume had been denied to Italy. Whereas the Treaty failed to make any provisions for the independence of Ireland, Irish-Americans also found fault with it. Determined to win at all cost and deny the President any claim to have been successful in his aims at peace, these were to be the Republican's lines of attack.

Even more unfortunate for Wilson, not only was Henry Cabot Lodge serving as the Senate Majority Leader, he was also chairman of the Foreign Relations Committee. Although delay was a major component of his anti-Wilson policy, he would also stack the membership of the committee with those who held an unfavorable opinion of the League. When the list of appointments to the Committee was completed, the Republicans and Republican sympathizers held ten votes to only seven for the Democrats. It did not portend well for the President.

As early as May 19, Lodge began to hint at his intended method of delay when he released a statement to the press announcing, "It is obvious that it will require further amendments if it is to promote peace and not endanger certain rights of the United States which should never be placed in jeopardy."[133] As soon as Woodrow Wilson presented the Treaty to the Senate for ratification, Senator Lodge moved that the Treaty be sent to the Foreign Relations Committee, which he now controlled with a firm hand. Although it was dispatched immediately to the Public Printers office, it would be a full three days before any of the committee members received a copy of the text. Lodge then announced that a series of extensive public hearings would be held, hearings that could take as long as a month, possibly longer. To further delay the process, Lodge decided to read the entire Treaty of Versailles in the Committee. As the 264-page Treaty contained 440 articles, divided into fifteen sections, this effort required another two weeks. Not until July 28, 1919 would Lodge complete this word-by-word reading of a treaty that his sole purpose in life had become to derail.

If, in the years prior to 1919, Senator Lodge and his group of irreconcilables had attempted to impede the President in his efforts, it would have seemed as though a group of jackals were attacking a lion. But after his illness of April 3, the lion was now much weakened, both physically and mentally. No doubt Woodrow Wilson recognized this himself, even if he made pretenses otherwise. Unfortunately his adversaries were beginning to recognize much the same, and as with jackals, it only further encouraged their efforts.

Recognizing as well that his Republican adversaries could not come to acknowledge the issue of the Treaty according to its merits, Wilson decided to invite the Senate Foreign Relations Committee to the White House so as to answer any concerns they might have. At ten o'clock in the morning on August 19, the members of the Committee met with the President in the East Room of the White House. The meeting itself lasted three and a half hours and could have been viewed as little better than a barrage of hostile questions. Although it would be difficult to ascertain what was on the President's mind or what his mental abilities were as compared to his existing state before the illness of April 3, many viewed his performance that day as containing both lapses of memory and mental mistakes. Senator Lodge stated privately that on that occasion the President "displayed ignorance and disingenuousness in his slippery evasions."[134] There was much dissent during the meeting in regard to Article X of the Treaty, which stated:

> *The members of the League undertake to respect and preserve as against external aggression the territorial integrity and existing political independence of all members of the League. In case of any such aggression or in case of any threat or danger of such aggression the Council shall advise upon the means by which this obligation shall be fulfilled.*

As the U.S. Constitution reserved the authority to declare war exclusively for the Congress, the Republican irreconcilables used that as but one of their arguments against ratification of the peace treaty. However, it was by now quite obvious what the Republicans were up to. In one of its editorials, the New York Times would write, "The Foreign Affairs Committee has laboriously read the document, line by line, paragraph by paragraph, to the end of the eighty-seven thousand words it contains. It conducted the readings not in the spirit of men intent upon a sympathetic examination of the great charter of peace and liberty for all nations, but rather like a body of the Inquisition hunting through an Erasmian pamphlet for heterodox utterances, or a gimlet-eyed church committee bent upon convicting the parson of heresy. The members of the Committee are no wiser than they were before. The hearings go on, the speechmaking continues. Republican Senators, prompted by no other motive than their dislike of President Wilson, consume days in denouncing a document they are not competent to expound or elucidate."[135] As if the reading of the Treaty word-for-word was not an obvious tactic of delay, once the reading was complete the Republican members of the Committee decided that what was necessary next was a rewriting of the League Covenant. This rewriting of the Covenant would consume several more weeks, so that by the time the Foreign Relations Committee made its first report to the Senate, it was the second week of September. In its report, the Committee stated:

> *The Committee believes that the League as it stands will breed wars instead of securing peace. They also believe that the Covenant of the League demands sacrifices of American independence and sovereignty which would in no way promote the world's peace but which are fraught with the greatest dangers to the future safety and well being of the United States.* [136]

In its rewriting of the Covenant, the Foreign Relations Committee added nearly fifty amendments, plus four reservations.

As it was the intention of Henry Cabot Lodge to deny the President and the Democratic Party any chance in the upcoming election to claim either success in getting the Treaty ratified or of securing any kind of lasting peace, the addition of the amendments and reservations destroyed the League Covenant as a Wilsonian document. The President made one last appeal for ratification with the Senate when he gathered together a group of twenty of the Republican Senators who held mild reservations about the Treaty, only to discover they were subject to the party lash and therefore obligated to support whatever decision was made by their party's leadership. There were many who advised President Wilson to accept the rewritten Treaty with the amendments and reservations, but the ailing President simply could not bring himself to compromise the nearly seven months of hard work he had completed while in France.

As a remedy to the situation, Woodrow Wilson decided to take his case before the people of the nation. As he had not fully recovered from the ill effects of the illness he had suffered while in Paris, it was a fateful decision to make. His physician, Admiral Grayson, advised him against such a trip, as did his wife and many of the individuals within his own party who were loyal to him. In September 1912, Wilson wrote, "I would rather lose in a cause that I know will someday triumph, than triumph in a cause that I know some day will lose."[137] In September of 1919, the month he began a tour of the western portion of the nation so as to secure ratification of the Treaty, he would write, "I can predict with absolute certainty that within another generation there will be another world war if the nations of the world do not concert the method by which to prevent it."[138] If one considers the time of difference between generations as twenty years, the prediction was spot on.

The announcement of the President's speaking tour came on August 27, 1919. As scheduled, the President's speaking tour would cover ten thousand miles with stops in twenty-nine cities. The trip would be by train with Wilson spending much of his time in a private rail car named the Mayflower. For a man in the President's state of delicate health, it would be an extremely difficult trip. Nevertheless, in speaking to his wife Edith he exclaimed, "I promised our soldiers, when I asked them to take up arms, that this was a war to end wars; and if I do not do all in my power to put the Treaty into effect, I will be a slacker and never be able to look those boys in the eye. I must go."[139] The Presidential train departed from Washington, DC on September 3, 1919 with the first of its stops occurring in Columbus, Ohio on September 4. At one of the city's municipal auditoriums the President addressed a crowd of 4,000 people. In defense of the Treaty he was to declare, "the terms of the Treaty are severe, but they are not unjust."[140] In defense of the League of Nations, Wilson would proclaim, "The League of Nations is the only thing that can prevent the recurrence of this dreadful catastrophe and redeem our promises."[141]

The President would make forty speeches over a twenty-one day time period, including his speech in Columbus. Even in his weakened state and having little if any time for preparation, the President was able to give his speeches extemporaneously, in near perfect English, and without having to engage in undue repetition. Still, given the vices of a two-party system, the President's appeal to the people was not to go unchallenged. No sooner had the President left Washington, than a phalanx of Republican Senators, to include McCormick, Borah, Johnson, Reed, and Poindexter, began a speaking tour of their own throughout the various regions of the country. They were joined in their efforts by the violently anti-Wilson Hearst newspapers, which had a daily circulation of nearly 2½ million copies. In an age before television and radio, the presidential appeals could only be heard by the limited number of individuals who could hear his voice, a voice that was beginning to show signs of extreme fatigue. On the 25th of September he would deliver what was to be the longest speech of the tour. He would conclude this speech with:

> *Now that the mists of this great question have cleared away, I believe that men will see the truth, eye to eye and face to face. There is one thing that the American people always use to rise to and extend their hand to, and that is the truth of justice and liberty and of peace. We have accepted that truth and we are going to be led by it, and it is going to lead us, and through us the world, out into pastures of quietness and peace such as the world never dreamed of before.*[142]

Not only would this be perhaps the President's finest speech of the tour, it would also be his last. After departing Pueblo that evening, the train made a brief stop about twenty miles outside of the city so that the President could stretch his legs. He would receive as a gift a head of cabbage and some apples from a passing farmer who happened to recognize him, and take time to greet a former solder of the Great War who was sitting on a porch located not far from the road. It was another act of deference for the young men that he had been forced to send to Europe in that fateful summer of 1917. Although the walk seemed to have had a remedial effect on the exhausted President, later that evening, Admiral Grayson was summoned to the President's room where he found Wilson on the verge of a complete physical breakdown. The next morning he was able to return to his feet, with Grayson finding him in the act of shaving. However, by this time it was obvious to all who were near him that the speaking tour, or "swing around the circle" as it became known, would have to be discontinued. Mr. Wilson would protest, determined to fight on for the cause in which he so firmly believed. By mid-morning he had not recovered sufficiently so as to continue the tour, and Dr. Grayson informed the President's closest advisor and right hand man Joseph Tumulty that the balance of the tour would need to be canceled. Tumulty then ordered the train to depart for Washington, D.C., where it was to arrive on Sunday, September 28. For the next three days the stricken President went into seclusion, as Admiral Grayson thought rest as being the best treatment at that time. On October 1, the President would be further stricken with what neurologist Francis X. Dercum was to diagnose as a "severe organic hemiplegia, probably due to a thrombosis of the middle right hemisphere."[143] In more simplistic terms, the President had suffered a stroke which rendered his left arm and leg useless, with the left side of his mouth also being affected. No announcement was made to the public concerning the President's condition. As Woodrow Wilson had been the great champion of the League of Nations and the driving force behind the campaign to have it ratified, with his involuntary silence the chance of the League Covenant and the Treaty of Versailles being passed by Congress was reduced to nearly nothing.

Some years ago Barbara Tuchman was to write, "A phenomenon noticeable throughout history regardless of place or period is the pursuit by governments of policies contrary to their own interest. Mankind, it seems, makes a poorer performance of government than of almost any other human activity. In this sphere, wisdom, which may be defined as the exercise of judgment acting on experience, common sense and available information, is less operative and more frustrated than it should be."[144] With the debate over ratification of the

League Covenant and the Treaty of Versailles raging in the chambers of the U.S. Senate in the autumn of 1919, this very same phenomenon was to occur. With President Wilson debilitated from the thrombosis of October 1, the debate became more and more of a one-sided affair. The Republican irreconcilables would make every effort to claim the Treaty as their achievement by virtue of all of their added amendments and reservations. Though much weakened, the President would remain firm in his resolve to see the Treaty ratified as presented to the Senate on July 10. In a country that had once prided itself on its democratic foundations and its ability to seek compromise, that ability would be absent when most needed during the debate over ratification. Many of Wilson's closest advisors urged him to accept the Treaty with the Lodge reservations. When Mrs. Wilson pleaded with her husband to accept the terms he was to reply, "Can't you see I have no moral right to accept any changes in a paper I have signed without giving to every other signatory, even the Germans, the right to do the same thing. It is not I that will not accept; it is the nation's honor at stake. Better a thousand times to go down fighting than to dip your colors to dishonorable compromise."[145]

On March 19, 1920, the U.S. Senate held the final vote on the Treaty with the recently revised reservations. By the conclusion of the vote, 49 Senators had voted aye, 35 had voted nay. Even though a majority had voted in favor of ratification, they were still seven votes short of the necessary two-thirds majority. Naturally, the President would be bitter to see all those months of effort in Europe come to nothing. The Republican irreconcilables and the Hearst newspapers would regard the failure of ratification as a victory. History tells us otherwise. For his efforts at peace Woodrow Wilson would receive the Nobel

Peace Prize. When the Republican majority in Congress attempted to end the war by a joint resolution of Congress, simply reversing the war declaration of 1917, Woodrow Wilson vetoed the resolution.

Although his efforts to secure American involvement in the League of Nations and the ratification of the Treaty of Versailles failed in his own country, when the League held its first assembly at Geneva, Switzerland, 42 nations were represented. Even Germany, upon whom much of the blame for the war was afforded joined the League in 1926.

Of his experience during the drafting of the Treaty of Versailles, British statesman Harold Nicolson was to write, "Given an America united in support of the whole Wilsonian doctrine, we felt confident that we could embark on a secure voyage to the Islands of the Blessed. It was only when we realized that we were being given but a patchwork Wilsonism that anxieties assailed us. These anxieties were trebled as soon as it dawned upon us that in the maintenance of this patchwork we should receive no support from the United States.

The New World having failed to answer the call of its own herald, we turned back in panic towards the balance of the old. Inevitably we sought to regain the firm familiar ground of the old Europe which, with all its dangers, was at least a territory which we knew."[146] It was a clear statement as to what may have been possible had the leadership of Wilson been allowed to fulfill its true promise and potential. The South African Prime Minister Jan Christian Smuts would write of Wilson, "Probably to no human being in all history did the hopes, the prayers, the aspirations of so many millions of his fellows turn with such poignant intensity as to him at the close of the war. At a time of the deepest darkness and despair he had raised aloft a light to which all eyes turned. He had spoken divine words of healing and consolation to a broken humanity."[147]

The price of speaking to a broken humanity for Wilson was a broken body and a broken spirit. In the fight for ratification of the Versailles Treaty Woodrow Wilson had expended what remained of his health. He would finish his second term in office, though in a much diminished capacity He would never recover the necessary strength to resume his crusade for peace. He was succeeded as President by Warren G. Harding, who had been an implacable foe of the League Covenant and Treaty of Versailles. However, Warren Harding would succumb to a heart attack in 1923, to be replaced by his Vice President Calvin Coolidge, whom Woodrow Wilson regarded as being a good man. In the later years of his life, Wilson would meet with two of his political antagonists from the Peace Committee, Georges Clemenceau and David Lloyd George. Old differences of opinion would be forgiven. As with most former presidents, Woodrow Wilson was to see his popularity rise after his departure from office, as perhaps by that time people had sufficient time to digest all of the things he had done for his country, even at the cost of his own health. In 1923, Wilson delivered a speech of approximately eight paragraphs to his countrymen on the eve of Armistice Day. The speech was delivered to the public by means of public radio and was the first time the former President ever addressed a crowd by such means. Always an elegant speaker, one has to wonder how much public radio could have helped Woodrow Wilson during the Treaty debate if that means had been available to him. The next day, 20,000 well-wishers descended upon the former President's house at No. 2340 S Street. As his physical condition precluded any lengthy address that day, the former President offered only a few words from his doorstep. Three times during his remarks Wilson was interrupted by overwhelming applause from his captive audience. During his brief remarks he would heap encomiums upon General John Pershing and the men of the American Expeditionary Force who had fought to secure peace in Europe. He spoke of the Armistice of 1918, referring to it as an "armed standstill," and also told the crowd that day, "I am not one of those who have the least anxiety about the triumph of the principles I have stood for. I have seen fools resist providence before and I have seen the destruction and contempt. That we shall prevail is as sure as that God reigns."[148]

The twenty-eighth President celebrated his sixty-seventh birthday on December 28 of that year. As a special gift and in recognition of all that he had sacrificed for his country and all that he had done for it, he was presented with a new Rolls-Royce Silver Ghost six-passenger limousine for him and Mrs. Wilson to enjoy on their daily excursions. The car was black with a removable top and had the former President's initials monogrammed on the rear doors in orange, the color of his alma mater. Wilson would have his photo taken in the vehicle that day. It would be the last picture ever taken of him. That same day, future four-term President Franklin Roosevelt announced that the Woodrow Wilson Foundation was to begin accepting nominations for its first annual $25,000 prize, which was to be awarded "to the individual who has rendered within the year the most unselfish public service of enduring value." Regardless of the value of the prize, it would be difficult for any individual to live up to the public standards of the man for whom the prize was named.

The following month the now hemiplegic former President

was to see further declines in his already failing health. On the 16th of January 1924, roughly 200 members of the Democratic National Committee made a pilgrimage to visit the ailing former President at his home on S Street. Woodrow Wilson summoned the strength to shake hands with all of his guests and made personal remarks to each of them. On January 29, the former President's longtime physician Admiral Grayson would leave Wilson's side to go hunting in South Carolina with Bernard Baruch, who had played such an instrumental role in transitioning the United States economy from a peace time to a war time setting during World War I. He was not to be gone very long, for no sooner had he departed than he was recalled to Wilson's side when the President's health took a sudden turn for the worse. Initially Grayson was not alarmed, believing that the former President might be suffering from an indigestive attack. When Dr. Grayson examined his patient again on the morning of February 1, however, he concluded that the former President was getting worse, for his bodily functions were beginning to shut down. Recognizing that the end was near, family and friends would begin to gather at the residence and when news of Wilson's condition was released to the public, a national vigil was begun. President Calvin Coolidge sent a cordial note to Mrs. Wilson stating, "I join in the universal prayer that there may very soon be a change for the better."[149] But the years of strenuous effort had taxed Woodrow Wilson's body beyond the point of recovery. On February 2, 1824, Woodrow Wilson slipped into a state of unconsciousness. On that day he would utter his last word, "Edith." On Sunday morning, February 3, the United States would lose one of its greatest Presidents and the world would lose one of the greatest peacemakers of all time. There would be no great state funeral for Woodrow Wilson, but rather a short service at his home, followed by another at the Washington National Cathedral where the former President's funeral was held before a group of 300 guests, which included President and Mrs. Coolidge. The Bethlehem Chapel of the National Cathedral was to be the final resting place for the man who had risked it all to ensure peace for future generations.

With the death of the 28th President, the future possibility of the United States considering its position in regard to the Treaty of Versailles and the League of Nations vanished. The ramifications for this would be serious for the United States and disastrous for the rest of the world. Throughout the peacemaking process of 1919, Woodrow Wilson had recognized that his dream of peace was not perfect. He knew that the Treaty would be flawed, just as the people who were charged with the responsibility of writing the Treaty were flawed. However, he believed that these shortcomings in the Treaty could be compensated for with the creation of the League of Nations. When the founding fathers drafted the United States Constitution, they created what was known as a living document. Living, in that it held provisions within it so that it could be changed. Wilson believed that with a League of Nations in place, future exigencies could be remedied due to provisions within the League Covenant, which could fulfill a similar role.

Not all of those individuals who participated in the drafting of the Treaty of Versailles and the creation of the League of Nations shared his idealism or his optimism. General Tasker Bliss, who was one of Wilson's four Peace Commissioners, wrote Secretary of War Newton D. Baker that the next war would come in "thirty years." Marshall Foch would perhaps be a little more accurate in his predictions when he said of the Versailles Treaty "This is not peace. It is an armistice for twenty years." As for the financial burdens that had been placed upon defeated Germany, Winston Churchill regarded them as being both "malignant and silly." It wasn't that the victorious nations were not sincere in their desire for peace, they were. However, out of their sincerity and their anger, they would arrive at a peace that was so stringent that it was guaranteed to provoke and not prevent the next war. The new territorial delineations which sought to remedy the problems of ethnic nationalism and to ring Germany with a host of nations old and new to confine it within its boundaries was a sure way to provoke war. Especially when one considers the creation of the Polish Corridor, that narrow strip of land which split East Germany from the rest of the nation. And it is unlikely that anyone could have even predicted the severe levels of social unrest that would result from the financial distress that prevailed after the war. True enough, for a time there was a period of great economic growth in the United States during the 1920s, but in post war Germany and what was left of Austria-Hungary, times were very lean. In September of 1919, a former corporal in the German army attended his first meeting of the new National Socialist Workers Party, hence becoming its seventh member. When Germany suffered from an inflationary panic in 1923, Hitler and his fellow Nazis would reach for power in what was to become known as the Bear Hall Putsch. When it failed, Hitler was arrested and sentenced to Landsberg Prison. But no sooner was he released in 1924, then he was proclaiming "In this struggle of ours there are only two possible outcomes – either the enemy passes over our bodies or we pass over theirs."[150] To anyone listening, his comments should have come as a warning, for a very violent future.

As the victors of the first truly global war, the United States, France and England had a responsibility to the future to preserve peace. In this obligation they would fail dismally. Not only had the U.S. Senate refused to ratify the Treaty of Versailles, it also failed to ratify a Wilson sponsored treaty aimed at collective security which would have provided for assistance to England and France if they were again attacked by Germany. Following on the heels of this breach of collective security, the members of the "Big Three" would fail in their efforts toward national security as well. In a dither of pacifistic dreams, the United States and Britain would reduce the size of their standing armies to a mere fraction of what they had been. France, forgetting the lesson of the Great Wall of China, would seek security behind its Maginot Line, which the Germany army of 1940 would simply go around instead of through.

But where most of the world returned to a state of near somnolence, there were a few who were able to perceive what the future held and were duly alarmed by it. As World War I had become known as "the war to end all wars," much of the civilian populace of the United States had become blinded by unrealistic visions of a perpetual peace. The carnage and slaughter of the Western Front had been so hideous, that it was difficult for any rational mind to believe that the world would ever be so foolish as to allow itself to repeat the mistake. This belief was perhaps natural, but also naïve. Therefore, if the alarm bells were to be rung, those who would suffer most in the event of future war would be forced to become the voice of reason.

During World War I, a new theatre of operations had been added to the conflict due to the invention of the Wright

Brothers. Initially, employed as scout observation aircraft, a role that the balloon had served in the American Civil War, the pilots of these aircraft soon began carrying sidearms with which to shoot each other. In the natural evolution of things, the planes themselves soon began to be armed with rapid firing machine guns so as to destroy enemy aircraft. From there it naturally followed that if they could carry guns, they could also carry bombs to be dropped on enemy combatants. During the war a number of U.S. aviators had fought in the skies over the Western Front. One of them had been born into a wealthy mid-western family in the 1870s who had joined the army at an early age and had served during the Spanish-American War. During World War I he served with distinction as a pilot, at one time "leading the largest armada of airplanes ever to attack an enemy force, returning as a dashing young general with a chest full of medals and the radical belief that airpower would be the only decisive instrument for future wars."[151]

As with all great warriors who transitioned from war to peace, the experiences he learned during the war were not lost to him. They simply reinforced his already deep-seated beliefs and made him an advocate of those things in which he firmly believed. And what William "Billy" Mitchell believed in most was that his country had a responsibility to assume a mantle of power in the world, and that airpower was now as essential to a nation's ability to project power as the Royal Navy had been during the years of British dominance, and the U.S. Navy had been during the Spanish-American War. Billy Mitchell was also very vatic, in that he believed one day the aircraft would replace the ocean liner in carrying passengers back and forth across the oceans. He would be fairly accurate in believing it could be done in as little as six hours. He also believed that one day Japan would attack Pearl Harbor in Hawaii, and that eventually rockets would allow nations to engage in intercontinental attack.

But the problem for Billy Mitchell was that his outspokenness ran contrary to the political currents of his country. They would run especially counter to the beliefs of President Calvin Coolidge, who history has always regarded as being a very do-nothing or laissez faire president. As with all men, however, when placed in a position of authority he was not partial to having his authority undermined.

In 1919 Brigadier General William Mitchell began a one-man campaign to secure an independent air service. In 1921 Mitchell secured for himself and his proposed air service a resounding victory when he used a fleet of Martin MB-2 bomber planes to sink the 22,800-ton ex-German Navy Battleship Ostfriesland, ending the mythology that the battleship was still the predominant weapon in naval warfare. Of sixty-seven 2000-pound bombs dropped on the ship, only sixteen would hit the target. But that was enough. Afterwards Mitchell would claim, "Air power has completely superseded sea power or land power as our first line of defense."[152] He also predicted that the battleship would become "as obsolete as knights in armor after gunpowder was invented."[153] As the Navy had long been considered as the nation's first line of defense, his actions and comments were sure to make him an enemy of all those who still were advocates of a battleship navy.

Perhaps even worse for Mitchell were the remarks he made when he often criticized both the Army and Navy high commands for the way they managed the nation's defenses, especially in regard to its airpower. Several times he had testified before Congress as to the inadequate state of the nation's air defenses. In 1925 he released a book entitled *Winged Defense* on the very subject. John Weeks, who was Secretary of War under Calvin Coolidge, had declined to reappoint Mitchell as Assistant Director of the Air Service because he considered Mitchell's comments to be almost insubordinate. Mitchell was also reassigned from Washington D.C. to Fort Sam Houston in Texas.

Even though the U.S. government had severely reduced the U.S. military after the Armistice and restricted its budgets, there were still some attempts at modernization and experimentation. For the U.S. Navy there was the experimental rigid airship program. The program was fairly expensive, the airship Shenandoah had cost 2.7 million dollars to build, plus an additional 3 million for its hangar at Lakehurst, New Jersey. Its sister ship Los Angeles had a similar cost. The program was not without its setbacks, as the airships Akron and Macon were both lost to inclement weather. On September 3, 1925, the Shenandoah herself would fall victim to a line squall over Caldwell, Ohio. At an altitude of 6,200 feet, the severe winds of the storm broke the 682-foot long airship's keel, tearing it apart and sending the remnants to be scattered about Noble County, Ohio. Fourteen of the airship's crew would perish during the incident.

For Billy Mitchell, the incident was not only an unfortunate accident, but also further proof of the woeful state of aviation in the United States and just another example of why America needed a unified air service to bring order out of the chaos that was military aviation. Always outspoken, on Saturday, September 5, Colonel William Mitchell released a statement of 6,080 words to reporters from the Houston Press and San Antonio Evening News. His statements were extremely critical of the military establishment. He declared, "These incidents are the direct result of the incompetency, criminal negligence, and almost treasonable administration of the national defense by the Navy and War Departments."[154] In his statement, Mitchell was to criticize everything from the lack of adequate weather stations in the country to the expenditure of hundreds of millions of dollars on a battleship fleet that would become a useless component of national defense in future wars. He would conclude by stating, "As far as I am personally concerned, I am looking for no advancement in any service." He also added that, "I have had the finest career that any man could have... I owe the government everything. The government owes me nothing." However, "as a patriotic American citizen, I can stand by no longer and see these disgusting performances by the Navy and War Departments."[155]

In his statements, Mitchell was in all likelihood correct on many of his observations, but when the national media published his statements all over the country, it was too much for the administration in Washington D.C. to ignore. To many people, Mitchell was a prophet trying to awaken his country from its slumber in regard to the state of its national defense. To others he was insubordinate and disrespectful of his superior officers. Major General Ernest Hinds, who commanded the Eighth Corps at Fort Sam Houston was so enraged over Mitchell's comments that he cabled Washington D.C. with a request that he be allowed to relieve Mitchell as the Corps Air Chief. The War Department in Washington approved the request. Of a far more serious nature, Billy Mitchell was to be brought before a Court Martial for violating Article 96 of the Articles of War. Of the eight specifications within the Article, Mitchell's September 5th statement to the press was supposed to be in violation of four of them. His formal arraignment was to take two hours. Colonel Mitchell, defiant as ever, remained standing for the entire time. Perhaps even more defiant, when the Tribunal began at the end of October 1925, Mitchell's attorney, Republican Congressman Frank Reid of Illinois, challenged three members of the Army's high command who were to act as jurors and had them removed for cause.

The trial itself was to last for seven weeks, the longest court martial for a senior officer up to that point in time. It was an exhausting affair, with the prosecution calling 58 witnesses and the defense calling 41. At the end of what could be considered as essentially a political trial, Colonel Billy Mitchell was found guilty of violating Article 96 of the Articles of War. He was sentenced to be suspended from rank, command and duty for a period of five years. This suspension was accompanied by a loss of all pay and allowances for a period of the same five years. As the verdict did not remove Mitchell from service, it created a serious problem for the now convicted air officer, for he was to be without pay, and Army regulations prohibited moonlighting. As President Calvin Coolidge was Commander in Chief of the armed forces, he was entitled to review Mitchell's case, which he did. The guilty verdict was to stand, although with his revision of the terms of punishment, Coolidge determined that Mitchell should be allowed to draw half pay during his sentence as a means to support his family. At the time, this was to be $397.67 per month. With both his vanity and pride wounded, Mitchell chose instead to resign his commission as an officer in the United States Army, to take effect February 1, 1926.

Although Billy Mitchell was alone and was punished for his harsh criticism of the military establishment and the nation's military preparedness, he was not alone in his views. Major General Douglas MacArthur, who served as one of the jurors during Mitchell's court martial, had written to a friend barely four months earlier that, "Conditions in the Army are more or less chaotic." He added, that "a general sense of instability and lack of confidence in the higher command seems to permeate the rank and file. The War Department itself is a madhouse."[156] One has to love the irony that the day would come when MacArthur would be relieved of command in Korea by President Harry S. Truman for speaking out against the policies of the Truman administration during the Korean War.

Just as Billy Mitchell had predicted, war would come to the Pacific and it would begin with an attack against the U.S. Fleet at Pearl Harbor. Though his crystal ball was not clear enough to predict the use of aircraft carriers in the attack, he did predict that it would occur in the morning and that it would involve the use of pursuit planes attacking the airfield while bomber planes attacked the nearby fleet. As tensions grew between the island nation of Japan and the United States during the years prior to the outbreak of hostilities on December 7, 1941, each nation attempted to circumvent the outbreak of war while at the same time employing diplomatic means that would guarantee the eventuality of such a war. In the early spring of 1940, Navy Headquarters had ordered Commander in Chief of the United States Fleet, Admiral James O. Richardson, to forward deploy the bulk of the Pacific Fleet to Pearl Harbor, Hawaii for maneuvers. This intended show of force was supposed to deter Japan from any further acts of aggression. When these maneuvers were concluded, Richardson believed he would be allowed to return with the fleet to its permanent moorings on the West Coast. He was to be disappointed in his expectations.

As the year 1940 lingered on, the U.S. Fleet would remain on in its stay at Pearl Harbor. Due to the narrow entrance to the harbor which only permitted one vessel to pass at a time, Admiral Richardson began to regard Pearl Harbor as little better than "a God-damn mousetrap,"[157] He was also concerned about the ability of the heavy units of the fleet to operate away from the West Coast for extended periods of time for mostly logistical reasons. However, the War Department decided to keep the fleet at Pearl Harbor indefinitely in the wake of a recent Russian-Japanese agreement to reconcile their differences, as they feared it left Japan with the ability to attack eastward in the event the fleet was moved back to the West Coast. Richardson therefore began to view the role of the fleet as no longer being an implement of national security controlled by the Navy, but merely as a diplomatic tool to be used by the State Department to thwart Japanese aggression. Since Richardson had served in the Navy for many years, he believed that the Japanese knew enough of U.S. Naval dispositions so as to not regard the fleet as the deterrent the War Department believed it to be. Therefore, in October of 1940, he traveled to Washington, D.C. where he would meet with Secretary of the Navy Frank Knox, as well as President Franklin D. Roosevelt. When the President spoke of the deterring effect on the Japanese, which he believed the fleet posed, Richardson's captious tongue responded, "Mr. Roosevelt, I still do not believe it, and I know that our fleet is disadvantageously disposed for preparing for or initiating war operations."[158] Perhaps even worse for Admiral Richardson, he voiced the opinion that, "Mr. President, I feel that I must tell you that the senior officers of the Navy do not have the trust and confidence in the civilian leadership of this country that is essential for a successful prosecution of a war in the Pacific."[159] Though it is understandable how a man in the military profession could make such a statement if he were speaking to someone within his own profession, it was a grievous error to make such a statement to a politician. To further inflame his now precarious position, when informed by Secretary Knox that the President wanted to establish a picket line of light ships extending from Hawaii to the Philippines and from Samoa to the Dutch East Indies, Richardson responded that his fleet was in no way disposed "to put such a plan into effect, nor for the war which would result from such a course of action, and that we would certainly loose many of the ships."[160] This position would place Richardson at odds with Secretary Knox who responded to the Admiral's objection by stating, "I am not a strategist: if you don't like the President's plan, draw up one of your own to accomplish the purpose."[161]

There exists an old naval adage that, "loose lips sink ships." If that is so, sometimes loose lips can also sink an admiral. Having rattled the President's cage and then having crossed swords with the Secretary of War, it should have come as no surprise to Richardson when he was relieved of his command on Sunday, January 5, 1941. Although he was absolutely right in his convictions, as no Japanese carrier force could have made it all the way to the West Coast of the United States to attack the fleet without being detected, Admiral Richardson found himself being expendable for reasons purely political. As a career officer in the U.S. Navy he took his dismissal professionally, although he did travel to Washington, D.C. so as to question the reason for his dismissal. At a meeting with Secretary Knox on March 24, he was not given a specific reason for the act, other than Knox alluding to the fact that, "The last time you were here you hurt the President's feelings."[162] As to whether or not the events of December 7, 1941 would have been altered if Admiral James O. Richardson had remained in command of the Pacific fleet at Pearl Harbor is another one of history's "what ifs." But his not being present on that fateful Sunday morning did spare him the indignity of having to bear responsibility for the disaster. As Richardson was perhaps more oracular than most, maybe, just maybe, he could have spared his country the loss of its fleet and left the United States in a much stronger position during the initial phases of the Pacific war of 1941 to 1945.

During those crucial years between the two world wars there were other men in other nations who had the ability to accurately decipher the events of the time and attach to them the importance that they would hold towards future events. Unlike Billy Mitchell and Admiral J. O. Richardson, they were not all military men, although they seemed to comprehend the dangers involved from inaction and what the terrible consequences of this inaction would be. Most, if not all, are aware or at least should be, of the terrible ordeal suffered by Winston Churchill as he struggled to awaken a somnolent England from its voluntary myopia in the years prior to World War II. He would succeed in his efforts and awaken them, in the nick of time, though he would not succeed in his efforts to keep England from losing its empire.

Like all great actors on life's stage, and Churchill was a great actor, there are always those who are needed as co-stars or co-actors. As Churchill was both a focal point and a vocal point in the attempt to overcome the disadvantages of appeasement and stating the need to stand up to an increasingly bellicose Adolf Hitler, he could not have succeeded without a supporting cast who supplied him with the necessary information so as to make his speeches in Parliament which were critical of the administration of Stanley Baldwin so effective. There were others who served in the government of Great Britain who were also instrumental in Churchill's return to influence and power before and during the war. All of them deserve credit for their insight and for supporting an unpopular cause and an unpopular man. Although history is unclear as to how many of life's actors assisted Churchill, and the number is believed to be perhaps twenty, there were a few who joined his efforts sooner as opposed to later who had a definite effect on Churchill's ability to succeed in the face of adversity. Brendan Bracken was a self-made man who had been elected to the House of Commons in 1929 who would serve as Churchill's parliamentary private secretary as well as becoming minister of information in 1941. He was one of but three staunch supporters of Churchill in Parliament. The other two would be Churchill's own son-in-law Duncan Sandys, and Robert Boothby who had served as Churchill's parliamentary private secretary when he was Chancellor of the Exchequer. They would be his sole source of public support until the German invasion of France in May 1940 would lead to the downfall of Prime Minister Neville Chamberlain and his replacement with Churchill.

There were others, perhaps as few as four, who worked behind the scenes to provide Churchill with the means to work for the re-arming of Great Britain during those crucial years when Nazi Germany was so determined to march along the road towards war. One of them was Desmond Morton, who lived within a mile of Churchill's home and great keep, Chartwell Manor. Churchill had become acquainted with Morton years earlier as both were veterans of the Great War. Morton had served on the personal staff of Field Marshall Sir Douglas Haig and was an artillery officer who was fortunate enough to survive being shot through the heart. In 1919 when Churchill became Secretary of State for War and Air, he appointed Desmond Morton to a vital position in the Intelligence, a position which would allow him access to important information. When Ramsay MacDonald became Prime Minister in 1929. Morton obtained permission to maintain his association with Churchill and to keep him informed of all matters military, including estimates of German military strength.

It was this association with Desmond Morton that would lead to Churchill's friendship with Ralph Follett Wigram, a longtime member of Great Britain's Foreign Office. Educated at Eton and the University College of Oxford, Ralph Wigram had served the Foreign Office abroad both in Paris and in Washington D.C. Over a twenty-year time period he had risen from Temporary Secretary in Washington, D.C. in 1916, to First Secretary at the British Embassy in Paris from 1924 to 1933, to Counselor at the Foreign Office and head of the Central Department by 1934. In the last position, Ralph Wigram was to find himself working under the supervision of Permanent Under-Secretary Sir Robert Vansittart, another individual of prescient qualities who was becoming alarmed by the re-militarizing of Nazi Germany. Although Vansittart could never be regarded as being a close associate of Winston Churchill, he was in sympathy with some of his views and, if he never urged his colleague Wigram to assist Churchill in his efforts against the Baldwin cabinet, he most certainly never did anything to discourage the relationship.

As for Wigram himself, Churchill regarded him as being, "a charming and fearless man, and his convictions, based upon profound knowledge and study, dominated his being."[163] Valentine Lawford, who served under Ralph Wigram at the Foreign Office, stated that his first impression of Wigram was one of "gentleness, young looks, shyness, modesty, economy of language."[164] Churchill's biographer William Manchester would regard Wigram's information as relayed to Churchill as being, "hard, precise, and tersely told."[165] Not only that, Wigram had the ability to decipher the information which he had gathered and to predict what the chain of events would be as Adolf Hitler continued to gain influence in the now defunct Weimar Republic. When the Reichswehr stopped publishing its annual list of the officers serving in the German military, Wigram correctly deduced that this was an attempt to conceal the size of the German Army, which was restricted to 100,000 men by the terms of the Treaty of Versailles, as more officers meant a larger army. He also warned of the influence of the Generalstab, or General Staff, for many of them were holdovers from the day of the Kaiser, and this collection of high ranking officers had been outlawed by the Versailles Treaty. Wigram was to write Churchill in October of 1934 that the Nazis were "working for an army of offensive strength: in two years they expect to have 1,000 warplanes ready for combat."[166] Although he thought England safe for the time being, he also predicted that by 1938, "we shall be faced by a very, very much stronger Germany."[167] Almost as if he could read the Reichs Fuhrer's mind, he predicted that as German military strength rebounded, Hitler would begin demanding concessions from the signatory nations of the Versailles Treaty and would initiate a policy of intimidating the other European nations by showing off his modernized army. He predicted also that with each concession and Nazi gain, that Germany would become "increasingly arrogant and definitely aggressive. Instead of emitting protest and airing grievances, Germany will make demands and assert rights."[168] He even recognized that when Hitler felt his position strong enough, or that of France and England weak enough, that he would work for the absorption of Austria, Czechoslovakia and the rest of central Europe.

It had been Woodrow Wilson's dream to see a Versailles Treaty and a League of Nations, which would prevent future conflict in Europe. The failure of the United States to ratify the 1919 Treaty had been the first domino to fall in the chain of events which would lead to a less than perfect union of the victorious nations of World War I. Ralph Wigram was also a believer in the power of the League of Nations, and on many instances recommended its use in curbing the influence of a resurgent Germany. When German troops marched into the Rhineland on March 7, 1936, an act clearly in violation of Articles 42, 43 and 44 of the Versailles Treaty, Wigram was to be proven correct in many of his predictions about Hitlerian intent. On the following Monday, March 9th, Ralph Wigram traveled to Paris along with Anthony Eden and Lord Halifax to consult with England's cross-channel ally as to what response should be given to the latest German breach of the Versailles Treaty. Initially, it was intended that a meeting of the League should be convened in Paris, although this plan was amended so that the French Foreign Minister, Pierre Flandin would come to London instead. Ostensibly, the reasoning for this change of itinerary was because it was believed that perhaps the French Foreign Minister would receive firmer support if the discussions were to take place in London. At the meeting that did occur in Paris between the British, French and Italian diplomats, no action was taken. It had been the intention of Flandin for the united strength of the three World War I allies to eject the token German force in the Rhineland with force, but the Italian ambassador reminded his colleagues that Italy was already under League sanctions for its invasion of Albania and Abyssinia. And Eden, while sympathetic of Flandin's cause, did not want to see any direct action taken. As the meeting ended, Flandin would say to Eden, rather prophetically, "Negotiations will end in nothing, or rather, they will sanction a new retreat. And this time the retreat will be decisive, for it will generate a whole series of retreats."[169] Again, a prescient remark that would go unheeded and would ultimately be proven true by future events.

When Flanden did travel to London for meetings with the Chancellor of the Exchequer Neville Chamberlain and Prime Minister Stanley Baldwin, his appeal for assistance would be met with clammy hands. Neither of the two proponents of British appeasement was willing to risk any action that might incite the Reichs Fuhrer. Much of this may also have had something to do with Victorian attitudes towards the French. In the words of Sir Robert Vansittart, "Victorians were vaguely convinced that nineteenth century France had too good a time: that France laughed too much and cooked too well for this vale of tears."[170] Furthermore, when Hitler attempted to conceal his blatant act of aggression with a proposal for a 25-year nonaggression pact, the British press, with the Times of London and the Daily Herald leading the charge, expressed their belief that Hitler was sincere in his desire for peace. Combined, with the heads of state in opposition to his plans and the British press directing public opinion away from the crisis at hand, Flandin found himself facing insurmountable odds.

Himself aware of the dangerous road which lay ahead, and recognizing the need to stand up to German violations of the Treaty before they became nearly epidemic, Ralph Wigram decided to take action even if his own government would not. Therefore, perhaps even to the consternation of his superior Robert Vansittart, Ralph Wigram called for a press conference at his Lord North Street home where he turned the floor over to the distressed French minister. Flandin would implore Great Britain to take a stand alongside France, stating, "The whole world and especially the small nations turn their eyes toward England. If England will act now she can lead Europe. You will have a policy, all the world will follow you, and thus you will prevent war." For this act of opposition to the British government, it was thought at the time that perhaps Ralph Wigram would face the party lash. It was by this time known that Ralph Wigram was in opposition to the policies of Stanley Baldwin and the Conservative Party. In fact, at one point Walter Runcimen, who was an ardent Baldwin supporter and President of the Board of Trade, was sent to speak to Wigram's wife Ava in an attempt to get her to persuade her husband to leave off in his crusade against Baldwin and his nearly pro-German policies. This, she would not do.

Unfortunately, Stanley Baldwin and the Conservative Party would need not seek retribution against Wigram. His highly intelligent, very quiet and somewhat sensitive nature would be of his own undoing. With England and France refusing to take action against resurgent Germany after the occupation of

Rhineland, Wigram seemed to lose hope. His wife Ava would later write Churchill, "After the French delegation had left, Ralph came back, and sat down in a corner of the room where he had never sat before, and said to me, 'War is now inevitable, and it will be the most terrible war there has ever been. I don't think I shall see it, but you will. Wait now for the bombs on this little house'."[171] He went on to state that he believed, for whatever reason, that he had failed to raise awareness of the British people to the danger that now lurked on the other side of the channel. Ralph Wigram would continue in his efforts, but his spirit was broken. On December 31, 1936, Ralph Wigram passed away at the tender age of forty-six. Churchill would write, "His untimely death in December 1936 was an irreparable loss to the Foreign Office, and played its part in the miserable decline of our fortunes."[172] Ralph Wigram would leave behind a wife and son, as well as some controversy as to his cause of death. His death certificate listed Pulmonary Hemorrhage as the cause of death. But a letter of the time from Henry Pelling would speculate that his death was a suicide from the result of severe depression. Wigram was buried at Cuckfield, in Sussex. His funeral was sparsely attended by the members of the Foreign Office, with the Churchills, Sir Robert Vansittart and Brendan Bracken being the only members of government to attend. Like a handful of others from his time, his voice was the disregarded voice of a Cassandra. His death was unfortunate, perhaps needless. Unknown at the time and largely forgotten, he had taken all of mankind's sins upon his shoulders, and had carried them for some time. True to himself to the end, he should always be remembered as an example of what true public servants are intended to be.

Chapter VIII

¤

A MOST DIFFICULT DECISION

An ever turbulent world. When Woodrow Wilson, the greatest peacemaker of his time passed away in 1924, with him died also the chance for a lasting and successful League of Nations that might have prevented the human disaster of 1939 to 1945. Granted, there were others of his generation who cherished the thought of peace and worked ardently toward that end. For a time, they and their efforts would be forced into the shadows of an ever more violent age. However, when President Harry S.

Truman decided in favor of using the newly developed atom bomb against the Japanese to end hostilities in the Pacific War in 1945, a new age dawned in the affairs of mankind. Likewise, as the uranium bomb of the 1940s was replaced by the hydrogen bomb of the 1950s, it finally brought mankind to the time and place where he had the technological ability to destroy the planet upon which he lived, and hence, himself. Even though the decades after the Second World War would be dominated by a new Cold War and a nuclear arms race, they were also to evidence a new realization by mankind that the need for peace was now more important than it ever had been before. During the Thirteen Days of October 1962 when the world stood on the brink of nuclear war, saber rattling between two nuclear superpowers over the introduction of Soviet Intermediate Range Ballistic Missiles in Cuba came within an inch of reducing the world to ashes. Fortunately, in John Fitzgerald Kennedy, the United States and the world would see an uncommon wisdom and a man possessed of unparalleled nerve who was able to bring the world back from the edge of total destruction.

As the year 1924 had seen the death of one great peacemaker, it was to also see the birth of a man who, like Wilson, was willing to spend his life energy working for peace and who, like John F. Kennedy, may have had the foresight to avert what could have escalated into an ordeal similar to those of August 1914 and September 1939.

His name was James Earl Carter, Jr., and he was born in a small farming town named Plains, Georgia. Like Kennedy, Carter had served as an officer in the U.S. Navy. His education was somewhat different than the Princeton graduate Woodrow Wilson or the Harvard graduate John F. Kennedy, for he had just attended Georgia Southwestern College and Georgia Tech before enrolling in the U.S. Naval Academy at Annapolis in 1943. Upon graduation Jimmy Carter spent seven years in the Navy, two of which were spent working with an old battleship, which was being used as a test platform, and five years spent working with submarines. It was during his tenure with submarines that Carter became acquainted with Admiral Hyman Rickover, who would be a pioneer of and proponent for the Navy's new atomic submarines. It may have been these years in the Navy that would later formulate his ideas in regard to national defense and weapons procurement during his years in the White House. As his path of education was slightly different than that of Wilson and Kennedy, his path to the presidency would differ slightly as well. During their political careers neither Woodrow Wilson nor John F. Kennedy ever suffered an electoral setback. After leaving the Navy Jimmy Carter would serve on a number of local municipal boards before running for Georgia State Senate in 1962, a position he would be elected to by a margin of 1,200 votes. However, when his political aspirations caused him to pass up a potential seat in the U.S. House of Representatives so as to run for Governor of Georgia in 1966, he would suffer a humiliating defeat that caused him to enter into a brief period of depression in his life. To his credit, he never let it get the best of him, and in 1970 he ran again for the same office. In his second quest to be governor of Georgia he would be successful, although as a negative to his electoral success the campaign was a very tough one both mentally and physically. In addition, his campaign had proven to be one of expediency as "Carter afterward told some of his friends that he 'felt bad' about his actions, and it was known that he had prayed for forgiveness for some of the things that he felt he had had to say and do to get himself elected."[173]

As governor of Georgia, Jimmy Carter would prove to have chameleon-like qualities. As a candidate Carter had run a campaign with racist overtones which garnered for him much of the electorate who had voted for and supported George Wallace. Yet during his inaugural address he was to declare, "I say to you quite frankly that the time for racial discrimination is over. Our people have already made this major and difficult decision. No poor, rural, weak, or black person should ever have to bear the additional burden of being deprived of the opportunity of an education, a job, or simple justice."[174] It was a remarkable transformation for an individual who as a county school board member had shown himself to be every bit as segregationist as other white southerners of the time.

As governor of Georgia from 1970 to 1974, Jimmy Carter again proved himself difficult to nail down on any given position or any given issue. For example, during his tenure as governor from 1970 to 1974, he made numerous attempts to dissuade other governors from speaking out against American involvement in the very contentious Vietnam War. And as Governor of Georgia he was also known to support the administration in Washington's request for further appropriations with which to fight that war. This was a very interesting position to take, as during his presidential campaign in 1976 he spoke against the war as being both immoral and being beyond the control of the American people. Furthermore, when First Lieutenant William L. Calley Jr. was convicted of premeditated murder in the slaying of twenty-two South Vietnamese non-combatants at My Lai on March 16, 1968, Governor Carter was in favor of President Richard M. Nixon's decision to have Lt. Calley released from the stockade at Fort

Benning, Georgia while he personally reviewed the case before final sentencing was carried out. As candidate for the presidency during the nation's bi-centennial year, Carter would regard the massacre as just another of the manifestations of an unjust war.

Perhaps the most recognized and controversial aspect of Carter's term as governor of Georgia was his policy of what was regarded as zero-based budgeting and his attempt to reorganize the state government by reducing the number of state agencies from approximately 300 down to 22, although many of the agencies which were consolidated were either out of date or were so minor as to require no budget at all. According to Carter, this reorganization of state agencies had the potential to save the state approximately 50 million dollars. However, there were several flaws in Carter's plan, the effects of which were not recognized until later. Whereas the proposed zero based budget was intended to slow growth within the state budget, as events actually transpired between 1971 and 1974 the state budget actually increased by 58 percent.[175] In addition, whereas Carter had proposed that the consolidation of state agencies would reduce the size of state government, in actuality the number of state employees grew by 14.5 percent, from 34,322 to a total of 39,298. Nevertheless, when Jimmy Carter ran for president in 1976, he still portrayed his reorganization of the state government as having been somewhat of a success, even though the facts were to say otherwise. And facts, when they choose to be, can be stubborn things.

Shortly after his inauguration as the 76th Governor of Georgia on January 12, 1971, Carter began to be noticed by the national media. Much of this may have been the result of his statements in regard to discrimination during his inaugural address. Part of this may also have been the result of the fact that during the 1970 election cycle a number of "progressive" governors had been elected in the southern states, to include Rubin Askew of Florida and Linwood Holton of Virginia. In the eyes of the national media there seemed to be in its infant stages a new level of moderation in the political views of the old South. In May of 1971, Time magazine ran an issue in regard to this new phenomenon, featuring a cover illustration of James Earl Carter as representing this new movement. It would also write of Carter as "a South Georgia peanut farmer who is both product and destroyer of old myths. Soft-voiced, assured, looking eerily like John Kennedy from certain angles, Carter is a man as contradictory as Georgia itself, but determined to resolve some of its paradoxes."[176]

As desegregation was an important national and state topic of the time, Jimmy Carter found himself in the rather unenviable position of having to placate those of segregationist views who had helped elect him, as well as trying to adhere to the policies of anti-discrimination which he had enunciated in his inaugural address. To these ends, he hired the African-American woman Rita Jackson Samuels to assist him in his attempts at expanding the number of black state employees and public officials. He also placed a portrait of Martin Luther King Jr. in the Georgia state capital building. Yet in stark contradiction to these measures, at the National Governor's Conference in 1971, he co-sponsored an anti-busing resolution with none other than George Wallace.

As can be said of all ambitious men and political animals, the climb up the social ladder to become Governor of Georgia had only served to whet the appetite of Jimmy Carter in regard to higher political office, or in this case, the highest political office in the land. Being somewhat of a representative of the "New South," Jimmy Carter was to receive visits from several key national political aspirants at his governor's mansion. During these discussions and meetings it became clear to Carter that they were of no greater abilities than he, although he regarded many of their social habits, such as drinking to excess, as being well below his level of behavior. For these and no doubt other reasons, sometime around 1972 Governor Jimmy Carter began to formulate plans to become President Jimmy Carter. In that same year of 1972 Governor Carter served as a delegate to the Democratic National Convention. At this convention he endorsed U.S. Senator Henry "Scoop" Jackson, as opposed to the eventual nominee George McGovern, who was at that time considered as being very liberal. As with all things in Jimmy Carter's life, things did not go his way at all. An attempt to become chairman of the National Governor's Association ended badly and, as the Presidential election of 1976 approached, his name recognition among likely voters was a mere two percent.

Although things sometimes did not always go well for Carter personally, events transpiring around him, which were well beyond his control, began to auger well in regard to his future aspirations. During the latter half of his term as governor, it was noticed that he was becoming more and more of an absentee governor. Some of this may have been due to his aspirations for higher office. Furthermore, some of it may have been due to the fact that in his attempts at reorganizing state government he found himself dealing with a very intransigent state legislature as well as a lieutenant governor in the form of Lester Maddox who felt he had betrayed his supporters and political base with his attempts at social reform. But if things did not always go well for Jimmy Carter, they were going much worse for others around him. In Washington the conviction of Vice President Spiro Agnew, after he agreed to plead nolo contendere to a felony count of failure to pay his taxes, led to his resignation on October 10, 1973. As the Twenty-fifth Amendment contained provisions for the filling of a vice-presidential vacancy by presidential nomination followed by House and Senate confirmation, Gerald R. Ford was to assume the office of Vice President of the United States.

Of even greater importance both to the nation and the future of Jimmy Carter, the resignation of Spiro Agnew would be shortly thereafter followed by the resignation of President Richard M. Nixon in the wake of the Watergate scandal. The Vietnam War was nearing its dreadful conclusion and the health of the national economy was very poor due to a condition now referred to as stagflation. In the months after Gerald Ford became President of the United States, inflation would spike at seven percent and the North Vietnamese Army would violate the Paris Peace Treaty and march into South Vietnam. In addition, as an aftershock of the Yom Kipper War, energy costs would skyrocket, affecting the personal finances of every American worker and family. This accretion of unfortunate circumstances had a telling effect on American confidence in its affairs and its government.

Fortunately for the nation, although unfortunately for himself, in Gerald Ford the United States had a man of known integrity who quietly went about the process of trying to right the ship of state and set the country on the path of forward progress again. It was a daunting task, as he was forced to proceed without having gained popular support or even a mild consensus by process of popular vote in a public election. It was written of him at the time that, "Ford had a quality rare in politician: he could come close to separating his own political gain from what he believed to be the national interest"[177] It was as if political and national wisdom did exist for a few days as Gerald Ford was easily confirmed by the Senate and House by votes of 92-3 and 387-35. Not only that, but within weeks of assuming his new role as President, Gerald Ford could claim an approval rating of 71 percent

The task before him, of healing the nation's wounds and putting Watergate behind the country, placed Ford in a position where he would be forced to make a very tough decision that spared the country much indignity yet may have cost him his office. On July 27, 1974, the House Judiciary Committee voted to recommend the first article of impeachment against the disgraced Richard M. Nixon, which alleged obstruction of justice. The second and third articles of impeachment were also approved on the 29th and 30th of that month. A trial would involve a very lengthy national disgrace and would act as a prolonged divagation against any forward progress the nation needed to make to regain its political and economic footing. When presidential aide Phil Buchen asked Special Prosecutor Leon Jaworski what the possible course of action against Nixon would entail, he was told that in all likelihood there would be several felony charges and that it could take one to two years to bring the Watergate investigation and trial to its conclusion. Upon hearing this himself, President Gerald R. Ford resolved to pardon the former President before Richard Nixon was charged with committing any crimes. Therefore, on Sunday morning, September 8, 1974, Gerald Ford addressed the nation to inform them that he had resolved to spare the nation the indignity of what was about to occur, as he "was certain in my own mind and in my conscience that it is the right thing to do."[178] Although time was to prove him right in his convictions, public outcry at the time, along with editorial indignation against the act, was great. It seems that the human mind often tends to gravitate toward lower, and not higher standards.

For Jimmy Carter the events that were to transpire during the latter years of the Nixon presidency and early years of the Ford presidency could have been interpreted as nothing more than an opportunity.

When the Watergate scandal started to gain momentum in early 1973, Jimmy Carter initially advised the Democratic Party against any attempt at exploiting the scandal, as it would prove to be "a mistake to manipulate Watergate in an overly partisan manner."[179] In Addition, at a Democratic Governor's conference he introduced a resolution for national prayer, to include prayers for the embattled President Nixon as well. However, as with many positions he had taken during his political career, he was to modify his position at a later date.

It is occasionally written that fortune has her favorites. According to Georgia law at the time, Governor of Georgia Jimmy Carter was forbidden from succeeding himself in office. Since political polls at the time indicated that his job performance was not good enough to expect re-election, this may have afforded him the opportunity to avoid a potential political setback. In addition, as he had already begun to formulate ideas in regard to national political office in the form of the presidency, he would need some degree of assistance from lady luck. Because he was a political unknown on the national stage, Jimmy Carter would be forced to overcome other individuals who were known to entertain aspirations toward the nation's highest office. He would receive this luck when, on September 23, 1974, Senator Ted Kennedy of Massachusetts removed himself from presidential consideration, an act which would be followed by the announcement of Minnesota Senator Walter F. Mondale to do the same. Although there were numerous other aspirants to the office such as Senator Birch Bayh of Indiana and Representative Morris K. Udall of Arizona, with the removal of Kennedy and Mondale from the race it seemed as though James Earl Carter Jr. might actually stand a chance.

When Richard M. Nixon had won re-election as President in 1972, he had beaten his Democratic opponent by one of the largest majorities in presidential election history. During his initial run for the office in 1966, he was successful for the most part because of his ability to establish a grass-roots organization that was able to energize republican voters and get them to turn out in sufficient numbers at the polls. While perhaps not original or innovatory enough to initiate this kind of political campaign himself, Carter was educated enough to emulate this policy. So, before his term as governor had even expired he began traveling extensively with aide Jody Powell and began constructing just such a grass-roots organization. Although at this time he would be evasive about his future intentions, stating that Democrats should concentrate on the 1974 mid-term elections, it must have been evident to those in close proximity to him that there was little likelihood that he would follow his term as governor with a simple return to peanut farming.

By the autumn of 1974, Jimmy Carter's intentions would begin to become more clear. In the October 28, 1974 issue of the

Los Angeles Times, reporter Kenneth Reich had written that a relatively unknown governor from one of the Southern states had announced, "I'm running for President of the United States. I do not intend to lose." Less than two months later, on December 12, 1974, James Earl Carter Jr. would formally announce his candidacy in front of the National Press Club in Washington, D.C. His decision to seek the nation's highest political office would be a fateful decision, both for himself and for the nation. His announcement that day set the tone for the 1976 presidential election. He stated that in the aftermath of all the troubles that had recently confronted the nation, such as the energy crisis, the Vietnam War, and Watergate, that "it is time for us to reaffirm and to strengthen our ethical and political beliefs."[180] He also referenced his past as a naval officer serving under Admiral Hyman Rickover by posing the question, "Why not the best?"

As for the presidential campaign of 1976 itself, because James Earl Carter Jr. had declared for the office early, he and his team were able to get out early and to outwork his opponents. In 1975, as an indication of his willingness to outwork his opponents, he spent 250 days on the road speaking to groups both large and small and shaking a lot of hands. He and his team were also able to recognize that a victory in the Iowa Caucus would gain solid national attention for his campaign, while a victory in the Florida Primary over George Wallace would show his ability to unify the South in his favor.

To his advantage during the campaign was the fact that in the aftermath of the Watergate scandal he was able to portray himself as being a Washington outsider, a claim many politicians have attempted to use in presidential campaigns since that time. Also to his advantage, was the fact that because he had worn so many different hats in his career, he had the ability to appeal to a large cross section of the American electorate. He was educated, a U.S. military veteran, a farmer, a nuclear engineer, as well as a former governor and legislator. He was also a Christian and a Southerner, and with his views and Kennedy-like looks he had the ability to connect with many of the nation's younger voters. In fact, in the early stages of his campaign when there was a dire need of cash to finance his efforts, a benefit concert featuring the Allman Brothers and Grinderswitch held in Providence, Rhode Island, netted nearly $100,000 when combined with federal matching funds. It was all an innovative approach, featuring interviews with publications ranging from Time Magazine to Playboy. But, it worked. As he and his team had predicted the importance of the Iowa Caucus, when the votes of that contest were tallied he would win 27.6 percent of the vote, far less than the 37 percent who remained uncommitted, but also twice as many as his nearest rival, Senator Birch Bayh of Indiana. Carter would follow his victory in Iowa with another in New Hampshire, which at that time allowed him to become somewhat of a media darling. Carter would also win the Florida Primary, but only by three points, 34 percent to George Wallace's 31 percent.

Jimmy Carter's quest for the nomination as the Democratic candidate for U.S. President did, however, run into some snags. He would suffer a stinging defeat in Massachusetts, and the late entries of Senator Frank Church of Idaho and Governor Edmund "Jerry" Brown of California caused Jimmy Carter to loose primaries in several states such as Oregon, California and New Jersey. What proved definitive in the search for the Democratic nomination was Carter's victory in Ohio, where he received 52.2 percent of the vote with Mo Udall finishing a distant second with 21 percent. The victory in Ohio would be enough to ultimately secure for Carter the Democratic nomination. His running mate Walter F. Mondale of Minnesota would become the candidate for Vice-President.

As for the presidential campaign of 1976, it was generally viewed that due to Watergate and Vietnam that the incumbent Republican President Gerald R. Ford would be fighting an uphill battle, which is surprising given that he had throughout his career shown himself to be a very good and decent man. He most definitely had the advantage of experience over Jimmy Carter. The race would be a close one, with Jimmy Carter receiving 297 electoral votes to 241 for Gerald R. Ford. The popular vote would be much closer, 40.8 million votes for Carter to 39.1 million for Ford. Some time after the election Democrat John Roche would write, "what baffled me all fall was how, in a year when, seemingly, Benedict Arnold running on the Democratic ticket could walk away from Jerry Ford, Carter almost managed to lose the presidency."[181] The difference in the election proved to be a sectional loyalty, as when the Old South was removed from the equation Gerald Ford would most likely have won re-election. If anything can truly be said of the 1976 presidential election, it is that, much the same as Britain had dismissed Winston Churchill in 1945 after he had done so much to save his nation, that the United States would show the same ingratitude to Gerald R. Ford after his act of political courage had done so much to spare the nation from the destructive turmoil of a lengthy Watergate trial and impeachment of Richard M. Nixon.

When James Earl Carter Jr. was sworn in as President in January 1977, it was intended that his presidency would usher in a new age in American presidential politics. At his inauguration he wore a business suit, instead of the traditional morning coat and top hat. Likewise, he would walk down Pennsylvania Avenue to the White House, an act which must have caused much consternation among the Secret Service agents assigned to protect him but was intended to show that he considered himself as nothing more than a servant of the people.

Other things would not change. Just as he had declared for reduction in the size of government in Georgia while just the opposite happened, a similar phenomenon would transpire when he became President. As a candidate for the office of President, he had often claimed that the Executive Branch of government under Richard Nixon had become excessive, and remained so under Gerald Ford. Yet within two months of his taking office, the President's staff would increase from the 550 members of Gerald Ford to a new high of 665. While claiming the need for fiscal conservatism as well, the salaries of his senior advisors would increase twenty-five percent.

When assuming his new office in January 1977, he found himself in a position unlike his predecessor Gerald R. Ford. He was not confronted with the Vietnam War, or Watergate. On the whole, the country was in good shape. The situation was not perfect, but he was afforded the luxury of time before there existed any need toward immediate action on any given issue. Foreign policy was to become an important matter with the new President. For his national security team, Jimmy Carter would resurrect several of the men who had served under Robert McNamara during the administrations of John Kennedy and Lyndon Johnson. Cyrus R. Vance was to serve as Secretary of State, with Zbigniew Brzezinski as National Security Advisor. For Secretary of Defense, Jimmy Carter would choose former Air Force Secretary Harold Brown. As many of these men had served in junior positions during the Vietnam era, they may have thought the worst was behind them. Events in time would prove them wrong.

Even before Jimmy Carter had become President, he began to formulate ideas about seeking peace in a very unsettled world. He would himself write, "Seeking peace between Israel and its neighbor had become a major interest of mine long before I became president. Beginning in 1973 with an extended visit to the Holy Lane as a personal guest of General Yitzak Rabin and Prime Minister Golda Meir, I made an intensive and ongoing study of the area."[182] In February of 1977, less than a month into his presidency, Carter sent Cyrus Vance on a tour of the Middle East to see if he could discover any common ground upon which to build the foundation of peace in the region.

And then there was the ongoing Cold War. In the wake of the Cuban Missile Crisis of October 1962, President John F. Kennedy had recognized the peril to the human race of the ongoing proliferation of nuclear weapons. In May of 1972 President Richard Nixon made measurable progress in his attempts to prevent nuclear war when the first of the Strategic Arms Reduction Talks resulted in the signing of an anti-ballistic missile ban during summit talks held in Moscow. A little over a year later, in June of 1973, two additional SALT agreements would be reached in Washington, D.C., establishing basic principles of negotiations on the further limitation of strategic nuclear weapons, as well as the Agreement on the Prevention of Nuclear War. President Jimmy Carter would continue with these earlier efforts at peace during his administration, canceling the proposed B-1 bomber program with its 100 million dollar per aircraft cost, as well as the MX mobile missile system. Also on the chopping block were the proposed Minuteman III missiles, as well as a 2.75 billion dollar cut in the defense budget during his first year in office. Although many at the time may have regarded this as a sign of the weakening of U.S. resolve, many of these actions simply fell into line with the ongoing SALT talks.

There were to be attempts toward peace with the other Communist power as well. During World War II, the United States and China had been allies. With the Communist takeover of that country on September 21, 1949, there would occur a break in relations with country after years of U.S. attempts to mediate a settlement between the Chinese Communists of Mao Tse-tung and the Chinese Nationalist of Chiang Kai-shek. After years of civil war, the Chinese Nationalists were forced to seek refuge on Formosa, which would eventually become the Republic of Taiwan. In December of 1954 the newly created Republic of Taiwan would sign a mutual defense treaty with the United States, thereby ending the threat of Communist invasion of that island. Chinese involvement during the Korean War of 1950 to 1953 had placed a further strain on the relationship between the two global powers. Richard Nixon had made inroads with China on the eve of his 1972 bid for re-election, and it had done wonders for his credibility as a global statesman. Therefore, in the late autumn of 1978, Jimmy Carter attempted his own foreign policy breakthrough when he announced to the nation in an eight-minute speech that the United States was normalizing relations with the most populous nation on earth. But there was a downside to this event, for by recognizing a new era in American-Chinese relations, he at the same time ended the twenty-three year old mutual defense agreement that had been signed with Taiwan. By this act, numerous other U.S. allies became concerned as to the legitimacy of past agreements with the United States in view of this significant policy shift.

Other tremors were to follow, especially in the Middle East. Whereas Jimmy Carter had concentrated his efforts in that region on establishing peace between Egypt and Israel, events beyond his control would push this effort into the background. For years the oil rich nation of Iran had been the most important ally of the United States in the Mid East. Its ruler, Shah Mohammed Reza Pahlevi, had long been a staunch support of U.S. interest in the region. When visiting the Shah in Iran on New Year's Eve in 1979, Carter was to say of Iran, "We have no other nation on earth who is closer to us in planning for our mutual military security. We have no other with whom we have close consultation on regional problems that concern us both. And there is no leader with whom I have a deeper sense of personal gratitude and personal friendship."[183] Because of this relationship between the two countries, Iran was to receive access to the latest U.S. military hardware, including the lethal F-14 Tomcat fighter plane.

Whereas the Shah at that time seemed to be at the height of his power and popularity, events were to find him fighting for political survival and for his throne within a year. Part of his dilemma may have been brought about by U.S. demands that the Shah institute more liberal policies in regard to how he governed the Iranian people. Much the same as Mikhail Gorbachev had seen a backlash from his policies of parestroika in the late 1980s, the liberal policies of the Shah had allowed Muslim fundamentalists seeking an Islamic Republic and another group of left wing militants who were seeking to establish a People's Republic, to use their newfound freedoms to act in opposition to the regime of the Shah. In writing a column for the Baltimore Sun, diplomatic correspondent Henry Trewhitt was to write, "Iran above all is the test of the moment... For if Iran slips from the influence of the West, the world will hold Carter responsible, rightly or wrongly, for a geopolitical disaster of the first magnitude and treat him accordingly."[184] It was a prescient forecast that would hold as true as the predictions of Ralph Wigram in regard to Nazi Germany.

Iran was not to be the only troublesome spot in the Middle East. On February 14, 1979, the U.S. Ambassador to Afghanistan was killed during a shootout after he had been kidnapped by three terrorists. It was the belief of President Carter that the death of Ambassador Dubs may have been the result of overzealous Afghan officials being too peremptory in their use of force to recover the American diplomat. All of this was to portend future problems for President Carter in that far off land.

And then there was Iran. By the beginning of January 1979, it was becoming obvious that the regime of Shah Mohammed Reza Pahlavi had no chance of remaining in power. To that end, and no doubt fearing the establishment of a revolutionary government, it was hoped that Iranian Prime Minister Shapour Bakhtiar could establish a new cabinet, which might ultimately lead to a regency council. For a short time this council was to exist, though in order for it to survive it would require the Shah to abdicate his throne and leave Iran. Initially the Iranian military proposed to remain loyal to the Shah. Some within the Iranian military even proposed a coup to assume control of the government. But events were to prove beyond the control of the

Shah Bakhtiar, and the Iranian military.

It is perhaps an interesting historical note that just prior to the Cuban Missile Crisis in 1962, John F. Kennedy had read Barbara Tuchman's *The Guns of August*. During that turbulent month of January 1979, President Jimmy Carter found himself reading Barbara Tuchman's *A Distant Mirror*, about the events of the fourteenth century. Hopefully, the historical examples portrayed in both books provided two presidents with a requisite knowledge and wisdom to assist them in very troubling times.

As events were to unfold, the greatest threat to Iran existed in France in the form of Ayatolla Ruholla Khomeini, a religious man who, even though in exile, was influencing events in the now troubled Middle Eastern land. In December of 1978, Khomeini had announced that he was in favor of massive bloodshed during the holy season which preceded the new year. It was the initial hope of Jimmy Carter, as well as the other Western democracies that the Ayatolla Ruholla Khomeini be kept in exile until a new civilian government could replace the Shah. Events were not to prove so. On January 16, 1979, President Carter was to announce during breakfast with several congressional leaders that the Shah had vacated his throne and departed for Aswan, from which he would leave with an eventual destination of California in the United States. By January 21, the Shah had decided against California. Then again, when the Shah was diagnosed with terminal cancer he would eventually find his way to New York for treatment. This would occur in October of 1979, with very serious repercussions.

The Shah was not to be alone in his exile. With his departure from Iran several senior military officials sought sanctuary as well. Bakhtiar would only serve as Prime Minister for five weeks, as the Ayatollah Khomeini eventually branded him as a traitor to the Iranian people. He would reverse places with Khomeini, as the Ayatollah would return to Iran and Bakhtiar would eventually go into exile in France. In 1991, the long arm of the Iranian militants would find him and he would be assassinated. He was neither the first nor the last to be a victim of Iran's revolutionary government. In another of those often ignored events which presage the future, on February 14, 1979, Iranian militants would attempt to seize the U.S. Embassy in Tehran. Two U.S. Marines were wounded during the event, though strangely no one at the time considered it as being an event that would cause the evacuation of the ambassador and his staff. As Iran and the United States had been on friendly terms until the return of Khomeini, there were approximately eight thousand other U.S. citizens within the country. By February 26, all of those citizens in Iran who wished to depart were removed from harm's way. They were fortunate.

Throughout the troubled year of 1979, relations between the United States and Iran would continue to degenerate. Then, on November 4, Iranian students of their own volition seized control of the U.S. Embassy in Tehran, taking as hostages more than sixty embassy staff and marine guards. Though perhaps initially not responsible for the actions of the students, eventually the Ayatollah Khomeini would endorse their actions and use the event to both discredit the United States and use the hostages as leverage in his dealing with the administration of Jimmy Carter. Of the hostage incident, Jimmy Carter was to write, "I spent hours on the phone talking to political leaders around the nation, but early in the morning was quite disturbed to learn that students with the subsequent encourage of

Khomeini had taken over our embassy and captured fifty or sixty of our people. Without the protection provided by the host government, its almost impossible to do anything if one's people are taken."[185]

The decision of the Iranian students very well may have been guided by the October decision to allow the terminally ill Shah to enter the United States for treatment. It may be very ironic, but the next day, November 5, President Carter signed into law the Gas Rationing Act. He would also write in his diary, "The students are still holding our people with the public approval of the idiot Khomeini."[186] On November 6, matters would take a turn for the worse in the hostage crisis, when the more moderate Prime Minister Bazargan and Foreign Minister Yazdi resigned when it became apparent that the Ayatollah would not permit the release of the American hostages. November 7th would see further disappointment when it was learned that the Ayatollah had refused to meet with negotiators William Miller and Ramsey Clark. At the time, Carter would also write, "Its almost impossible to deal with a crazy man, except that he does have religious beliefs and the world of Islam will be damaged if a fanatic like him should commit murder in the name of religion against sixty innocent people. I believe that's our ultimate hope for a successful resolution of this problem. We will not release the Shah, of course, as they demand."[187]

By November 20 it was becoming apparent that there would be no immediate resolution of the issue. As a military man, President Carter decided to take precautions while showing a sign of force. He ordered a second aircraft carrier to the Arabian Sea, increased the refueling capability at the military base on Diego Garcia, and ordered that large helicopters be deployed on the two carriers to be stationed in the area. His actions were perhaps predictable, as it had long been a U.S. policy to use its carrier fleet in a form of "gunboat diplomacy." On the diplomatic front, Carter was to write on November 28, "In the press conference my purposes were to show firmness and resolve, encourage Americans to have patience, let the Islamic world know we have respect and reverence for their religious beliefs, and isolate Khomeini as one who believed in kidnapping, extortion, blackmail, and abuse of innocent people."[188] In his views he was probably correct. However, the need for retribution is usually one of mankind's strongest passions, and the viewpoint of Jimmy Carter was to put him at odds not only with the more hawkish elements of the Congress, but the more hawkish elements of society as well.

As if the events unfolding in Iran were not contentious enough, on November 21, the U.S. Embassy in Islamabad, Pakistan was invaded as well. The incident may have been incited by Khomeini as he had earlier announced, "It is not inconceivable that the United States and Zionist are to blame for the occupation of the mosque in Mecca."[189] This was in reference to the November 20 attack that resulted in the death of an Imam. Although the United States in no way was to blame for the attack, it served as another way for the Ayatollah to incite regional hatred against the United States and its policies in the region.

Although public perception at the time may have been that the President was thus far weak in his response to the hostage crisis, many firm actions were being taken. On November 23, Jimmy Carter informed the Ayatollah through diplomatic channels that if the threatened trials of American hostages took place there would be severe restrictions placed on Iranian commerce and that if any harm came to any of the hostages it would be considered as reason enough to launch direct retaliatory action against the new revolutionary republic. Though this may have seemed to some as a weak response, never again did the Ayatollah engage in threats against the hostages.

On December 27, 1979, the Soviet Union decided to invade Iran's neighbor Afghanistan. As a pretext for this overt act of aggression, the Soviets claimed that their forces had been invited in to assist the Afghan government in suppressing anti-Communist elements within that country. As President Carter had for some time been engaged in further SALT talks so as to limit the proliferation of nuclear weapons, this Soviet invasion of a neighboring country was a fatal blow to any hopes of the reduction of nuclear forces for the foreseeable future, although the Carter administration refused to concede this fact at the time of the invasion.

Of greater importance, the Soviet action was to require a response from Jimmy Carter, who as president was often viewed as being soft in his reaction to international threats by our allies. In fact, former British Prime Minister Harold MacMillan was to say of the Carter administration, "Things are as bad for the West as they could possibly be, and they are getting worse. The Europeans have to deal with the weakest American administration in my lifetime."[190] Publicly, the response of Jimmy Carter to the Soviet invasion of Afghanistan must have appeared weak, though much of that may have been due to the fact that not all of his response could be revealed to the public. There was of course the decision to terminate all grain sales to the Soviet Union, instead of just the eight million tons guaranteed by international agreement. There was also the decision to boycott the 1980 Olympic games that were to be held in Moscow. The first decision in regard to grain sales was perhaps the most difficult, as having been involved in farming himself he knew that such an act could have dire consequences for the grain farmers of the American Midwest. It had been his victory in the Iowa Caucus that had helped launch his campaign for the presidency in 1976. Yet surprisingly, perhaps miraculously, on January 11, 1980, it was announced that somehow grain sales and prices survived the announcement of the decision to cease grain sales to the Soviets. Market reports that day indicated that corn prices were up twenty-three cents, wheat thirteen cents, and soybeans eight cents.

What could not be revealed at the time was that the President had decided to render military assistance to the Afghan rebels who were fighting against the Soviets. So as to remain secretive, most of the weapons supplied to the rebels were manufactured by the Soviets themselves, acquired by the United States from countries such as Pakistan, Saudi Arabia and Egypt, who had all made significant arms purchases from the Soviets in the past.

While the Soviet invasion of Afghanistan was a serious threat at the time, the Iran hostage crisis was to remain at center stage after a failed attempt to negotiate the release of the hostages by Kurt Waldheim. Jimmy Carter was to write in his diary, "Kurt felt that his life was in danger on three different occasions while he was in Tehran. He's convinced there is no government there, the terrorists are making the decisions, Khomeini is unapproachable, the Revolutionary Council is ineffective and timid, and Ayatollah Beheshti is the strongest man on the council."[191] This view may have convinced President Carter that the likelihood of a negotiated release of the hostages was unlikely.

There were further responses to the crisis. Ten days after the seizure of the embassy and hostages, President Carter had ordered negotiator Bill Miller to impound all Iranian assets until such time as it could be determined what if any amount the government of Iran owed to the United States. Then, on January 11, 1980, the President ordered the curtailment of all high-tech sales to the Soviet Union. In regard to the continued Soviet occupation of Afghanistan, during his State of the Union address on January 23, 1980, Carter was to declare a policy which was to become known as the "Carter Doctrine." This declaration simply stated that any foreign attempt to gain control of the Persian Gulf area and its oil resources would be regarded as a direct attack against vital U.S. interest and would be met with a full military response, if necessary. By mid-March of 1980 it was becoming increasingly clear that the chances of securing the release of the hostages in Iran by means of diplomatic negotiations or U.N. intervention were becoming ever more remote. Therefore, President Carter and his advisors began to formulate a plan to extract the hostages from the embassy compound by force. The plan was to involve the use of C-130 transport planes, eight RH-53D Sea Stallion helicopters as well as contingents of U.S. Army Special Forces and Rangers, plus various other personnel from the Air Force, Navy and Marine Corps.

Given the code name "Operation Eagle Claw," the proposed mission was very intricate in that it involved the refueling of the eight helicopters in the Iranian desert at night. It also involved the extraction of the fifty-three hostages from two different sites without detection from a city of nearly three million inhabitants. Therefore, this very complicated mission required not only a tremendous amount of skill but an abundance of luck as well. Included into these variables was the fact that, due to weather conditions in the Iranian desert which affected the ability of helicopters to fly, the mission would have to be attempted by the end of April 1980, or be postponed until the autumn.

Therefore, at about 1905 hours on April 24, 1980, Operation Eagle Claw swung into action on the deck of the aircraft carrier USS Nimitz. Within twenty-five minutes, all eight of the Sea Stallions were airborne and headed for Iran. At a location known as Desert One they were to meet up with four C-130 aircraft where they were to be refueled before flying on to a second location where they would off-load their cargoes of Rangers and Special Forces troops who would move to Tehran to extricate the hostages.

Unfortunately, even though the operation was thoroughly planned and the assigned units trained in the limited time available, adverse circumstances well beyond the control of President Carter would force the mission to be aborted. Though quite capable aircraft, the Sea Stallions would run into trouble during their flight over the desert, as dust storms known as haboobs, lengthened the chopper's flight times and may have contributed to mechanical failures that eventually crippled two aircraft. Furthermore, at Desert One the refueling contingent encountered not only a bus full of Iranian passengers that had to be detained, but a tanker truck full of fuel which was disabled and set on fire. Even worse, as the mission required the use of at least six helicopters, one of those helicopters had been disabled. It was discovered that the secondary hydraulic pump of the sixth remaining Sea Stallion failed after the desert crossing, leaving only five in service. The mission commander Colonel Beckwith was forced to order cancellation of the mission. Up until this point, although three helicopters suffered mechanical problems, there had been no casualties, either military or civilian.

As if the mission had not experienced enough misfortune, at approximately 2:30 in the morning of April 25, 1980 during the refueling process, the blades from one of the helicopters made contact with the forward section of one of the C-130 transports, setting off a conflagration which destroyed both aircraft and killed eight men. With no hope of continuing the mission, all of the Rangers, Special Forces units and remaining aircrew were loaded onto the three remaining C-130 transports and by 0255 on the morning of April 25, departed from Iran.

As a result of the failed mission, eight American servicemen were dead, and seven Navy helicopters and one Air Force transport plane destroyed or left behind. Iran would not learn of the attempted rescue mission until President Carter announced its failure to the American people. There could be no second attempt to rescue the hostages from the embassy since their captors decided to disperse them to a number of locations separated by hundreds of miles. The Iran hostage crisis would resume, not being concluded until January 20, 1981, a total of 444 days of captivity for those who had been so unfortunate as to be captured during the November 4th seizure of the embassy. Although thirteen of the original sixty-six captives that had been taken had been released within two weeks of the embassy takeover, it was to be a lengthy ordeal for those who remained.

As holds true for any failed task undertaken by mankind, there would be an immediate need to find a scapegoat. No doubt in an attempt to assume full responsibility for the failed mission, President Carter would announce that, "The mission on which they embarked was a humanitarian mission. It was not directed against Iran; it was not directed against the people of Iran. It was not undertaken with any feeling of hostility toward Iran or its people. It has caused no Iranian casualties."[192] There was to be some political fallout, as Secretary of State Cyrus Vance resigned over the affair. And of course as 1980 was a presidential election year, the failure of the rescue mission and the prolongation of the hostage crisis would have a negative impact on Jimmy Carter's chance at re-election.

On January 22, 1981, Jimmy Carter flew to Wiesbaden, West Germany to meet with the newly freed American hostages. Advised that there might be some resentment towards him personally he simply responded that if the hostages "could think of any new criticisms that I hadn't faced already in the United States, I would be very surprised."[193] Fortunately, as the former President greeted each former hostage individually there were to be no incidents of hostility. In his diary, Jimmy Carter was to write, "As I went around the room, I spoke to each one, tried to say something about their background or their family, and then put my arms around them. Some of them kissed me on the cheek. I was relieved and pleased."

At the time, the hostage crisis and Jimmy Carter's reaction to it was highly unpopular. The results of the 1980 election were dismal for the then President, as he carried only six states and lost the popular vote to Ronald Reagan by a margin of 50.7 percent to 40.0 percent. It must have been a humiliating defeat, but as history sometimes reflects, his efforts and decisions regarding the hostage crisis, the Soviet invasion of Afghanistan, defense policy, and many other issues may have been entirely correct for the time.

In reference to the hostage crisis, much can be learned about the decision-making process of Jimmy Carter from other incidents of that nature in the years prior to his having taken office. During the closing phases of the Vietnam War, when Richard Nixon was confronted with the issue of American prisoners of war being held by North Vietnam and by the representatives of that nation being intransigent at the Paris peace talks, he initiated an intense bombing campaign on North Vietnamese targets, to include the capital city of Hanoi. It was enough to convince the North Vietnamese to come back to the bargaining table and secure the release of the POWs. But in the long run the act failed, as the North Vietnamese eventually abrogated the terms of the Paris treaty and launched a successful invasion of South Vietnam.

During the tenure in office of Gerald R. Ford, there was the three-day rescue mission of May 12-15, 1975 to liberate the crew of the SS Mayaquez, a container ship operated by Sea Land Services which had been seized by Khmer Rouge gunboats off the coast of Cambodia. The reaction by President Ford to this act of piracy was immediate and decisive. However, in this case the recovery of the vessel and its crew was achieved at remote Koh Tank Island in the Gulf of Siam, and not in a city of three million people in the middle of a hostile nation. Even then, eighteen American servicemen died during the operation, with another fifty wounded. Three U.S.A.F. helicopters were destroyed, with ten others receiving varying amounts of damage. Although the mission achieved its objectives, there was a significant cost associated with this success.

Then also, there was the assassination of U.S. Ambassador to Afghanistan Adolph Dubs in February of 1979. When force was used in an attempt to secure his release, he was killed by his captors, an incident and a lesson that may have been well remembered by our thirty-ninth president. When the hostage crisis began November 1979, President Carter had emphatically stated what his policy would be during that lengthy affair, and that his only concern was the release of all of the hostages. After the failed rescue attempt of April 1980, which may well have broken the spirits of many, he persevered on until, as was his desire, all of the hostages were released alive and largely unharmed. Because of this, his actions must be regarded as being successful.

It is both ironic and unfortunate that during his presidency James Earl Carter Jr. may have been regarded as weak or indecisive. Yet in the long term many of his decisions show an incredible amount of foresight. For instance, In July of 1977 President Carter decided to cancel procurement of the B-1 Bomber, which was intended to serve as the eventual replacement of the long serving B-52 Stratofortress. In his decision, Jimmy Carter believed that the ultra-reliable B-52, which had been purchased for six million dollars each, could perform the same mission as the B-1 when armed with cruise missiles, at much less expenditure than the 100 million dollar price tag per B-1 Bomber. He also knew, though he could not disclose that fact, that the B-2 Spirit Stealth Bomber was already on the drawing boards. Therefore, he regarded the B-1 as unnecessary. As of this writing, the B-52H Bombers armed with cruise missiles are still part of the U.S. nuclear arsenal, whereas the B-1 is relegated to conventional bombing due to the complexities of the Strategic Arms Reduction Talks. In addition, as Jimmy Carter had himself served as a naval officer during the initial years of the U.S. atomic submarine program, it was during his term of office when the newest ballistic missile submarines of the Ohio class began to enter service. Armed with the third generation Trident SLBM, these ships would become the most potent part of the U.S. nuclear arsenal, or Triad.

President Carter must also receive credit for another innovation within the U.S. military establishment. With the May 1975 Mayaquez incident still within memory, beginning in 1978 there would be a string of twenty terrorist attacks on U.S. embassies and diplomatic personnel within one year, the most obvious of these being the November 4, 1979 seizure of the U.S. Embassy in Tehran. Recognizing that the future would see an increase in the use of terrorist attacks that would allow the few to attack the many, President Carter authorized the establishment of a Rapid Deployment Force consisting of 200,000 soldiers, sailors, marines and airmen. Given the nature of the violent world in which we live, the concept of a rapid deployment force must be considered as an integral part of any credible military establishment today.

President Carter may well have been very vatic in his response to the Soviet invasion of Afghanistan as well. Perceived as possibly a weak response at the time, his decision to refrain from direct military intervention would also prove to be historically valid. Afghanistan had long since been the graveyard of armies. The British would discover this during the First and Second Afghan Wars. Although the Soviets, and later our own military, would find it easy to invade Afghanistan, both would find the region difficult to control and nearly impossible to extricate themselves from while leaving behind any semblance of order. The soviets were to remain in Afghanistan until Mikhail Gorbachev removed the Soviet Army from that nation in 1989. Perhaps this was the Soviet Vietnam War, as many lives and much military equipment were lost for no long-term gain.

As we live in a world that is far from perfect, there are always instances where events may conspire to impart to those who may not deserve it severe instances of injustice. Some of the events which occurred during the presidency of James Earl Carter Jr. may in fact prove this, as the Iran hostage crisis and the Soviet invasion of Afghanistan were both well beyond his control. They were major detractors to his hopes of both Middle East peace and the reduction of strategic nuclear weapons. Fortunately, the years after his presidency were more kind to the former president. After years of trying to reduce the risk of global nuclear war and of trying to establish peace between Israel and Egypt, Jimmy Carter would finally be rewarded for his efforts when he received the Nobel Peace Prize in 2002. This honor was to place him in very select company, as only two presidents of the U.S. had won that honor before him; Theodore Roosevelt, and Woodrow Wilson.

In the years since he has left the White House, Jimmy Carter has proven to be one of the most active, and one of the most outspoken of the former presidents. As president he was against the B-1 Bomber, while at the same time he authorized the deployment of the Pershing II Intermediate Range Ballistic Missiles to Western Europe. As former president he is always in favor of making peace, but sometimes against peacemakers, as he has been opposed to every instance of military intervention since his presidency, to include Lebanon, Grenada, Panama, and the Persian Gulf. All to often criticized for his actions as president, there can be little if any doubt or criticism for his motives as former president. In 1998 an NBC/Wall Street Journal poll ranked Jimmy Carter as having the highest moral character of any recent president, with 67 percent of those surveyed affording him "very high" marks. It is fortunate that in recent years his countrymen have begun to appreciate his efforts as a faithful public servant. But that is the nature of Jimmy Carter. As with the Scipios of Rome or Henry Plantagenet, John Jay, Andrew Johnson, Charles Lanrezac, Woodrow Wilson, and Ralph Wigram, he has always been willing to stand alone. And that, makes all the difference.

Bibliography

Bolger, Daniel P., *Americans at War, 1975-1986: An Era of Violent Peace*, Ca 1988

McCain, John, with Mark Salter, *Hard Call*, New York, 2007

Laskey, Victor, *Jimmy Carter the Man and the Myth*, New York, 1979

Carter, Jimmy, *White House Diary*, New York, 2010

Jordan, Hamilton, Crisis, *The Last Year of the Carter Presidency*, New York, 1982

White, R.J., *The Horizon Concise History of England*, New York, 1971

Waller, Douglas, *A Question of Loyalty: General Billy Mitchell and the Court Martial that Gripped the Nation*, New York, 2004

Les Benedict, Michael, *The Impeachment and Trial of Andrew Johnson*, New York, 1973

McKitrick, Eric L., *Andrew Johnson, A Profile*, New York, 1969

Langguth, A.J., *Patriots: The Men Who Started the American Revolution*, New York, 1988

O'Flynn, John Michael, *Generalissimos of the Western Roman Empire*, Edmonton, Alberta, Canada, 1983

Cooper, John Milton Jr., *Woodrow Wilson*, New York, 2009

Prange, Gordon W., *At Dawn We Slept: The Untold Story of Pearl Harbor*, New York, 1981

Rostovtzeff, M., *Rome*, New York, 1975

Matyszak, *Chronicle of the Roman Republic*, New York, 2008

Willmott, H.P., *World War I*, New York, 2003

Schroeder-Lein, Glenna R. and Richard Zuczek, *Andrew Johnson, A Biographical Companion*, SantaBarbara, California, 2001

Jenkins, Simon, *A Short History of England*, New York, 2011

Ashley, Mike, *The Mammoth Book of British Kings and Queens*, New York, 1998

Barber, Richard, *Henry Plantagenet 1133-1189*, New York, 1993

Morris, Richard B., *John Jay, the Making of a Revolutionary*, New York, 1975

Morison, Samuel Eliot, *The Oxford History of the American People*, New York, 1965

Canfield, Leon H., *The Presidency of Woodrow Wilson: Prelude to a World in Crisis*, New Jersey, 1966

Heffner, Richard D., *A Documentary History of the United States*, New York, 2002

Rodgers, Nigel, *Ancient Rome*, London, 2006

Nicolson, Harold, *Peacemaking,1919*, New York, 1965

Manchester, William, *The Last Lion, Alone 1932-1940*, New York, 1988

Ellis, Joseph J. *American Creation*, New York, 2007

Churchill, Winston, *A History of the English Speaking Peoples*, New York, 2011

Bowen, Catherine Drinker, *Miracle at Philadelphia*, New York, 1966

MacMillan, Margaret, *The War That Ended Peace:The Road to 1914*, New York, 2014

Ketcham, Ralph, *James Madison*, New York, 1971

Delderfield, Eric R., *Kings and Queens of England and Great*

Britain, Devon, England, 1971

Berg, A. Scott, *Wilson*, New York, 2013

Ellis, Joseph J., *Founding Brothers, The Revolutionary Generation*, New York, 2002

Cabanes, Bruno, *August 1914, France, The Great War, and a Month That Changed the World Forever*, New Haven, 2016

Hewig, Holger H., *The Marine, 1914: The Opening of World War I and the Battle That Changed the World*, New York, 2009

Olson, Lynne, *Troublesome Young Men: The Rebels Who Brought Churchill to Power and Helped Save England*, New York, 2007

David, Daniel, *The 1914 Campaign August-October 1914*, New York, 1987

Gibbon, Edward, *The Decline and Fall of the Roman Empire*, New York, 2003

Brinkley, Douglas, *The Unfinished Presidency*, New York, 1998

Hochschild, Adam, *To End All Wars*, New York, 2012

Churchill, Winston S., *Memoirs of the Second World War*, Boston, 1987

Keegan, John and Richard Holmes, *Soldiers, A History of Men in Battle*, London, 1985

Morris, Richard B., *The Peacemakers*, New York, 1965

Canfield, Leon H., *The Presidency of Woodrow Wilson: Prelude to a World Crisis*, New Jersey, 1966

Tuchman, Barbara W., *The Guns of August*, New York, 1967

Hastings, Max, *Catastrophe 1914: Europe Goes to War*, New York, 2013

Tuchman, Barbara, *The March of Folly, From Troy to Vietnam*, New York, 1984

Hearn, Chester G., *An Illustrated History of the United States Navy*, London, 2002

3

Prange, Gordon W., *At Dawn We Slept, The Untold Story of Pearl Harbor*, New York, 1981

George, Margaret, *The Warped Vision*, Pittsburg, 1965

Ludwig, Emil, *Bismarck*, New York, 1927

Bowman, John S., *The Founding Fathers, The Men Behind the Nation*, North Dighton, Massachusetts, 2005

---

[1] Duprey, *Encyclopedia of Military History*, 71
[2] Matyszak, *Chronicle of the Roman Republic*, 111
[3] Duprey, *Encyclopedia of Military History*, 71
[4] Mommson, *History of Rome*, 35
[5] Ibid, 36
[6] Ibid, 43
[7] Matyszak, *Chronicle of the Roman Republic*, 121
[8] Mommson, *History of Rome*, 51
[9] Momson, *History of Rome*, 277
[10] Southern, *The Roman Army*, 261
[11] Gibbon, *Decline and Fall of the Roman Empire*, 541
[12] O'Flynn, **Generalissimos of the Western Roman Empire**, 15
[13] Ibid, 13
[14] Ibid, 29
[15] Gibbon, *Decline and Fall of the Roman Empire*, 550
[16] Ibid, 551
[17] Ibid, 559
[18] Goldsworthy, *How Rome Fell*, 298
[19] O'Flynn, *Generalissimos of the Western Roman Empire*, 89
[20] Ibid, 96
[21] Ibid, 103
[22] Barber, *Henry Plantgenet*, 27
[23] Ibid, 36
[24] Churchill, *History of the English Speaking Peoples*, 167
[25] Ibid, 168
[26] Ibid, 169
[27] Ibid, 169
[28] Ibid, 170
[29] Ashley, *British Kings and Queens*, 12
[30] White, *Concise History of England*, 36
[31] Barber, *Henry Plantagenet*, 85
[32] White, *Concise History of England*, 37
[33] Jenkins, *Short History of England*, 57

34 Churchill, History of the English Speaking Peoples, 134
35 Ibid, 134
36 Ibid, 133
37 Ibid, 135
38 Jenkins, *Short History of England*, 60
39 Ibid, 61
40 Barber, *Henry Plantagenet*, 231
41 Churchill, *History of the English Speaking Peoples*, 139
42 Barber, *Henry Plantagenet*, 232
43 Bowman, *The Founding Fathers*, 151
44 Morris, *John Jay, The Making of a Revolutionary*, 507
45 Ibid, 511
46 Ibid, 512
47 Morris, *The Peacemakers*, 289
48 Ibid, 310
49 Ibid, 310
50 Ketcham, *Madison, A Biography*, 286
51 Ibid, 275
52 Monson, *The Oxford History of the American People*, 321
53 Ketcham, *Madison, A Biography*, 358
54 Ibid, 356
55 Ellis, *Founding Brothers*, 136
56 Kennedy, *Profiles in Courage*, 213
57 Ellis, *Founding Brothers*, 138
58 Ibid, 137
59 Monson, *The Oxford History of the American People*, 344
60 McKitrick, *Andrew Johnson, A Profile*, 23
61 Ibid, 24
62 Ibid , 41
63 Les Benedict, *The Impeachment and Trial of Andrew Johnson*, 5
64 McKitrick, *Andrew Johnson, A Profile*, 41
65 Ibid, 63
66 Schroeder-Lein, *Andrew Johnson a Biographical Companion*, 191
67 Les Benedict, *The Impeachment and Trial of Andrew Johnson*, 5
68 Ibid, 7
69 Ibid, 13
70 Ibid, 13
71 Ibid, 22
72 Ibid, 48
73 McKitrick, *Andrew Johnson, A Profile*, 191
74 Kennedy, *Profiles in Courage*, 136
75 McKitrick, *Andrew Johnson, A Profile*, 203
76 Ibid, 209
77 Ibid, 212

[78] Ibid, 212

[79] Ibid, 215

[80] Ibid, 211

[81] Ludwig, *Bismarck*, 207

[82] Dupuy, *Encyclopedia of Military History*, 831

[83] Ibid, 833

[84] Dupuy, *Military Heritage of America*, 339

[85] Tuchman, *The Guns of August*, 89

[86] Dupuy, *Encyclopedia of Military History*, 931

[87] Tuchman, *The Guns of August*, 225

[88] Hastings, *Catastrophe 1914: Europe Goes to War*, 177

[89] Keegan, *Soldiers*, 94

[90] Hastings, *Catastrophe 1914: Europe Goes to War*, 249

[91] Ibid, 305

[92] Tuchman, *The Guns of August*, 250

[93] Herwig, *The Marne, 1914: The opening of World War I and the Battle that Changed the World*, 140

[94] Ibid, 141

[95] Ibid, 141

[96] Tuchman, *The Guns of August*, 448

[97] Cabanes, *August 1914: France, the Great War and a Month that Changed the World*, 117

[98] Cooper, *Woodrow Wilson*, 8

[99] Ibid, 386

[100] Dupuy, *Military Heritage of America*, 366

[101] Ibid, 367

[102] Scott Berg, *Wilson*, 457

[103] Ibid, 441

[104] Dupuy, *Military Heritage of America*, 360

[105] Scott Berg, *Wilson*, 445

[106] Ibid, 453

[107] Cooper, *Woodrow Wilson*, 390

[108] Ibid, 390

[109] Scott Berg, *Wilson*, 471

[110] Ibid, 471

[111] Ibid, 469

[112] Ibid, 513

[113] Ibid, 515

[114] Cooper, Wilson 460

[115] Ibid, 462

[116] Ibid, 462

[117] Scott Berg, *Wilson*, 521

[118] Nicholson, *Peacemaking 1919*, 55

[119] Canfield, *Presidency of Woodrow Wilson*, 171

[120] Scott Berg, *Wilson*, 535
[121] Ibid, 534
[122] Heffner, *A Documentary History of the United States*, 67
[123] Canfield, *Presidency of Woodrow Wilson*, 181
[124] Ibid, 181
[125] Ibid, 184
[126] Ibid, 188
[127] Manchester, *The Last Lion, Volume I*, 661
[128] Canfield, *Presidency of Woodrow Wilson*, 189
[129] Ibid, 190
[130] Scott Berg, *Wilson*, 572
[131] Canfield, *Presidency of Woodrow Wilson*, 195
[132] Ibid, 201
[133] Cooper, *Woodrow Wilson*, 517
[134] Canfield, *Presidency of Woodrow Wilson*, 211
[135] Ibid, 220
[136] Ibid, 229
[137] Ibid, 210
[138] Cooper, *Woodrow Wilson*, 519
[139] Ibid, 521
[140] Ibid, 521
[141] Canfield, *Presidency of Woodrow Wilson*, 238
[142] Cooper, *Woodrow Wilson*, 533
[143] Tuchman, *The March of Folly*, 4
[144] Canfield, *Presidency of Woodrow Wilson*, 260
[145] Nicholson, *Peacemaking 1919*, 70
[146] Canfield, *Presidency of Woodrow Wilson*, 283
[147] Cooper, *Woodrow Wilson*, 592
[148] Scott Berg, *Wilson*, 736
[149] Manchester, *The Last Lion, Volume I*, 866
[150] Waller, *The Trial of Billy Mitchell*, 20
[151] Hearn, *An Illustrated History of the United States Navy*, 109
[152] Ibid, 110
[153] Waller, *The Trial of Billy Mitchell*, 20
[154] Ibid, 21
[155] Ibid, 50
[156] Prange, *At Dawn We Slept*, 63
[157] Ibid, 39
[158] Ibid, 39
[159] Ibid, 39
[160] Ibid, 40
[161] Ibid, 47
[162] Churchill, *Memoirs of the Second World War*, 40
[163] Manchester, *The Last Lion, Volume II*, 113

[164] Ibid, 115
[165] Ibid, 113
[166] Ibid, 114
[167] Ibid, 180
[168] Ibid, 180
[169] Manchester, *The Last Lion, Volume II*, 91
[170] George, *The Warped Vision*, 32
[171] Manchester, *The Last Lion*, 190

[172] Churchill, *Memoirs of the Second World War*, 93
[173] Laskey, *Jimmy Carter, the Man and the Myth*, 96
[174] Ibid, 101
[175] Ibid, 117
[176] Ibid, 102
[177] McCain, *Hard Call*, 335
[178] McCain, *Hard Call*, 359
[179] Laskey, *Jimmy Carter, the Man and the Myth*, 166
[180] Ibid, 182
[181] Ibid, 311
[182] Carter, *White House Diary*, 21
[183] Laskey, *Jimmy Carter, the Man and the Myth*, 380
[184] Ibid, 381
[185] Carter, *White House Diary*, 367
[186] Ibid, 368
[187] Ibid, 368
[188] Ibid, 374
[189] Ibid, 371
[190] Laskey, *Jimmy Carter, the Man and the Myth*, 382
[191] Carter, *White House Diary*, 389
[192] Bulger, *Americans at War, 1975-1986, An Era of Violent Peace*, 99
[193] Carter, *White House Diary*, 515